Storm in the Jungle

A Memoir

Glen Allen, Jr.

Order this book online at www.trafford.com
or email orders@trafford.com

Most Trafford titles are also available at major online book retailers.

Print information available on the last page.

ISBN: 978-1-4907-6539-6 (sc)
ISBN: 978-1-4907-6540-2 (hc)
ISBN: 978-1-4907-6541-9 (e)

Library of Congress Control Number: 2015915612

Trafford rev. 09/25/2015

 www.trafford.com

North America & international
toll-free: 1 888 232 4444 (USA & Canada)
fax: 812 355 4082

CHAPTER 1

The thirty-one day nightmare was finally over. At last we had reached our destination of Qui Nhon, South Viet Nam. All of my energies of the last month had been concentrated on preparing for this moment. Getting off this ship was the only thing that mattered. Now that the wish was to become a reality, many thoughts began to race through my mind.

Lying on the deck in the quiet darkness, enjoying a forbidden cigarette, I could vaguely make out the coast line and the black shape of the mountains looming threateningly in the background. What was the jungle going to be like? Were the Viet Cong going to be waiting for us? Where in the hell were we going? Was anyone going to be maimed or killed?

Suddenly I became very apprehensive and realized why. Life had always had a semblance of order to it, especially in the Army. One gets up in the morning and follows a set routine. That is what makes life bearable. You can always count on certain events repeating themselves. Now, however, the familiar pattern was becoming one of uncertainty. Uncertainty was evolving as the biggest psychological factor I would have to face in the days and nights to come.

One thing was certain and that was that we were getting off of this goddamn ship. If I had known then what nightmarish events were going to unfold in that unfamiliar terrain, stretching before me like a black void in space, I wouldn't have been so eager to leave its safe confines.

The ship was the U.S.S. Patch. It didn't look so bad when we boarded it in Charleston one long month ago. My experience with ships of any kind had been limited. After this taste of sea life, I vowed to keep my record intact. The Patch was a troop ship making its first trip to Southeast Asia. Prior to this voyage it had been making runs from the New

England area to Germany. The Patch, and the other ships in the convoy, was carrying 16,000 men, 477 aircraft, and 19,000 tons of supplies.

I've often wondered if a non-living thing has feeling. I was now convinced that it does. The ship had been angry because it too had been thrust in the midst of uncertainty. The course it followed was entirely new. The familiar events of its day-to-day existence were no longer a reality, due to us, the troops of the First Cavalry Division. As it held us responsible for its precarious state it had lashed out against us determined to make us pay. Its greatest moment had been when it took on the characteristics of a bucking bronco. Jumping, rolling, pitching and careening in every possible manner, determined to rid itself of this monster on its back. Like a horse in a rodeo with a leather strap squeezing the life out its testicles, it was reacting in the only manner it knew. Instead of the rodeo arena, its show was taking place on the high seas. Like the professional cowboy, it was determined to be a winner. I had been ready to declare it the winner and stop my agonizing existence.

I should have known something was wrong from the very beginning of the ordeal. I learned the Army works in strange ways, understandable only to the powers that make policy. The First Cavalry shipped out of Ft. Benning by bus, headed for Charleston, South Carolina. Leaving Charleston, on the Patch, we headed south. The voyage took us down the southeast coast, through the Panama Canal, up the coast of Mexico and finally anchored at Long Beach, California. I was perplexed trying to figure out why we didn't simply board trains and make the crossing to Long Beach by rail. Much of our equipment had already been sent that way. The trip by boat had proved to be twice as long, twice as expensive and twice as boring. Tennyson certainly knew what he was talking about when he penned those immortal works, "ours is not to reason why, ours is but to do or die."

After taking on fresh supplies in Long Beach we were once again under way. The voyage proved to be uneventful until we were a few miles off of Hawaii. The ship had stopped and we were facing Diamond Head and its exquisite looking beaches. Any piece of land would have looked inviting after looking at nothing but water for so many days. Besides being the first land I had seen in weeks, I knew there was something special about the view that was transfixed on my mind. It was the type of feeling one has when he enters a seemingly new environment for the first time. Then, suddenly, because of the apparent familiarity of it, one realizes he has been there before.

Just as suddenly, my thoughts were interrupted by the sound of a small vessel approaching this ship. I was now concerned with mail. Could the mysterious vessel be bringing mail? It had been about three weeks since we received our last mail. Soldiers standing around me were buzzing with excitement. Could it really be true? Adrenaline seemed to enter our bloodstreams as excitement mounted in everyone.

The miracle was not to be. There was no mail. A soldier was being transferred off the Patch and onto the smaller vessel. We later learned he was suffering from appendicitis. What a lucky bastard, getting off this dilapidated ship and onto dry land. All the good feelings we had quickly disappeared. Everyone's disappointment at getting no mail was soon apparent. We found ourselves cursing the soldier who was taken off the ship as if it was his doing that caused the appendicitis. His life may have been in danger but no one seemed to care. He was the symbol for our frustrations and our jealousy was apparent.

Watching the vessel make its way back toward Hawaii my eyes became transfixed on the raw and natural beauty of Diamond Head. Some strange thoughts were building inside my mind. The idea or feeling that I would someday, in the near future, set foot on the beaches of Diamond Head was gaining form. At that moment I could see myself walking along the hot, sandy beach. Cool water swirling around my ankles as the sun beat warmly on my body. My entire being was focused on the thought of returning to that island which was before my eyes. In that instant, I knew I would return.

The following days passed in the same boring, methodical manner as they must certainly pass for a prisoner on death row. Empty, lonely days with nothing to occupy the mind except ones own thoughts. The lines, which formed for everything, were endless, as were the redundant classes. How many times were we going to strip down our rifles? It would have been more relevant to fire them. The M-16 was a new rifle and we had fired them only once or twice prior to leaving Ft. Benning. There had been ample opportunity to fire them into the sea in an effort to familiarize ourselves with them. However, the powers that be had decided our time was to be spent in other ways.

The boring days were intensified by the blazing sun beating down on us relentlessly. When the weather did change, it changed for the worse. I had read about the fury of the sea but was totally unprepared for the agonizing events which were to follow.

3

We were a few days off of the coast of Japan when we encountered a typhoon. The torrential rains came intermittently. When it did rain, it seemed as if it would never stop. Sheets of pounding rain would drive even the bravest of us below deck. In a short while the stench from hundreds of sweating bodies, laced with stale cigarette smoke, would drive all but those too sick to move back on the main deck.

Being on deck was worse than being below, if such a thing can be imagined. The constant swaying of the ship was unbearable. In time, like so many others, I developed a classic case of seasickness. I had suffered from motion sickness since my early childhood but nothing was to prepare me for the excruciating events which were to follow.

I had visions of traveling with my family through the mountains of Virginia on one of our infamous summer vacations. My getting carsick was as certain as stopping for gas. At this time I thought being sick was God's way of punishing me for some wrongdoing. Being a typical boy (always in trouble) He probably had reason for afflicting me with his wrath. The present was a different situation. What in the hell did I do to deserve the punishment which was now being bestowed upon me? The constant vomiting I was undergoing was tearing my insides to pieces. I no longer took to leaning over the railing to vomit as it was becoming increasingly dangerous. The ship seemed to dip farther and closer to the ocean with each successive sway of the relentless waves. Each sway and dip of the ship seemed to increase the intensity of the vomiting.

The Jeckel and Hyde nature of the ocean can be a most potent force. In my past the ocean and its unpredictable beauty had always been a source of pleasure. There were many fond memories of lying on various beaches being hypnotized by the beauty of the water. The magnificent uncontrolled whitecaps, venting their fury on anything in their path on their race to the sands, had always been a most thrilling sight. Poets have generally portrayed the ocean and its relentless rolling waves as a means for one to gain an inner sense of tranquility. Obviously, those particular poets had never ridden on a troop ship.

Any wonderful memories were now washed out of my mind. The taking away of such beautiful experiences seemed a cruel trick to play on someone. Never again would I visit a beach or see a painting of nature's vast oceans and have thoughts of wonder and awe. Rather than beauty, memories of disgust and relentless vomiting would be etched in my mind.

A dog, suffering from the scorching eyes of the sun, often finds refuge in a dark corner. I too found a corner where I could hide from the eyes of my unstricken friends.

On top of a metal generator, covered by a tarp, I found a place where it was possible to stretch out, hang my head over its side and be sick to my hearts content. By grasping the tarp I could prevent myself from falling off while my body underwent its violent contortions. It was necessary to share the generator with another sinner, but it didn't seem to matter. By watching someone suffer along with me the pain seemed easier to take.

By lying there it was possible to watch the antics of a group of carefree individuals who apparently had their sea legs. As the ship swayed to one particular side they would run with the sway, heading for the railings. Just as they neared the railing and certain misfortune, they would turn and try to outrace the onrushing mammoth waves. The waves would crash against the side of the ship with a thunderous roar. With the roar came torrents of water, which would cascade down upon them and send them sprawling like bowling pins. The wetter and closer they came to injury, the more they seemed to enjoy their game. It didn't seem fair that some of us felt as if we were dying and others were having the time of their lives. For many of them it was to be their last chance at fun of any sort.

As the agonizing hours dragged by, chow time would inevitably arrive. The mere thought of food would cause my stomach to react violently. Instead of eating, which required more courage than I cared to muster, I would somehow drag myself below deck and find relief in my bunk. I tried to put my thoughts elsewhere and take my mind off the present. Try as I might, I couldn't escape the extreme feeling of nausea which had overtaken my entire existence.

At one point I opened up by tear filled eyes and say a huge tattooed forearm. A brightly covered peacock with its tail spread wide greeted my eyes. Immediately I knew it was Bordeaux, the huge Cajun. His forearm was the only one I had ever seen big enough to hold the peacock's wide plumage.

"Come on, Allen," he was saying. "I found a spot that isn't quite so bad." Before I could utter a word of protest he was lifting me with his massive arms. He took me off of my throne and moved me near the center of the ship on a lower deck. I immediately felt a little relief, because the pitching of the ship was much less noticeable. By wedging myself into a doorway and thereby gaining stability, I was able to sit in an upright position for the first time in days.

"In your condition no one will bother you," said Bordeaux, leaving me as abruptly as he found me.

I found myself among the non-commissioned officers. Sprinkled about were a few other lower ranking souls who had found this utopia. The situation seemed to be another example of sergeants having it made. With a nice location in the middle of the ship, two-man staterooms and catered meals in a dining room, they probably couldn't have done better on the Queen Mary. The only time they came down to our hole was when they selected one of us for some shit detail. I suppose everyone is a nice guy once you get to know them. Sergeants, however, never give you the chance. They always seem to be playing some predetermined role, us against them. It isn't hard to figure out who won the majority of the time.

Looking through my glazed, and I suppose, jealous, eyes, I noticed of few of them had not escaped the scourge of the sea. Too bad all of them weren't sick. Maybe then they would get off their superior asses and come down to a human level. Smug bastards, it wasn't so long ago that they were Privates. One would think they would show a little compassion once in a while. In a perverse way, seeing a few of them retching made me feel a little better.

Being in a relatively calm area for a couple of hours had a soothing effect on my insides. Maybe it was seeing some of our fearless leaders sick, or perhaps a miracle had happened and I was getting sea worthy. I remember looking over the railing and watching the waves leap higher and higher as if they were competing for some prize. I could envision the ship being tossed around much the same way a child haphazardly plays with a toy boat in his bath. Considering the small size of the ship in comparison to the vastness of the ocean, it seemed incredible we were not sent to the bottom of its black depths.

Amazingly, I found myself wishing to remain alive. Only a few hours earlier I was wishing for death to soothe my agonizing existence. I came to the conclusion that life under the cruelest of circumstances had to be better than death. The sweet breath of life; God, how one doesn't realize the beauty of it until one is about to lose it.

Reflecting on those past days had done me some good. I was able to avoid thinking of tomorrow and our departure. A mosquito buzzing about my ear brought me back to reality. I soon found myself staring into the distance at the dark jungle which was soon to welcome us. Dark and forbidding now, but soon to be agonizingly alive and dealing death as if it resented our arrival.

Tomorrow we would begin setting up our base camp. Somewhere out there in the unknown a new way of life was going to evolve for us. My eyes searched the coastline and the dark void beyond for a clue to tomorrow. I could see nothing. Nothing in my past experiences could possibly have prepared me for the horrors which were to develop. What did a twenty year old, white, middle class guy like me know about war? I had never even shot a rifle prior to entering the Army. War was just a word I had been conditioned to use. All the training, all the stories, and all the movies were not enough to comprehend the true misery which was to follow.

CHAPTER 2

The long awaited day of departure had finally arrived. I was happy to be getting off the ship that had caused me so much misery. At the same time I was extremely apprehensive. Not having any idea of what was about to take place certainly didn't make the situation any more bearable. Standing below decks with the rest of my Company, listening to some final remarks from the First Sergeant, I glanced at some of the faces of the other men to see if I could detect any other signs of anxiety in addition to my own.

Many of the guys were trying to look nonchalant about the situation. Some were whispering amongst themselves while others were listening with forced attention to what "top" was saying. Most had a look of apprehension that was classical. Sort of similar to when a group of guys go to a whorehouse for the first time. One tries to remain aloof and maintain a degree of coolness, but, at the same time, you are scared shitless. A window in which, if one looks closely, he can, in a haphazard way, imagine what secret thoughts are being experienced. Suddenly I felt relaxed and more at ease; everyone was scared.

My eyes stopped for a moment on Brave Eagle, the Indian from Nebraska. Just yesterday, in a moment of intellectual inquiry, I asked him what it felt like to be fighting in the 7th Cavalry Regiment, the same regiment that General Custer commanded in his western campaign. He said, "I'm glad to be getting up in the world., I only hope we don't meet the same fate as he did at the Little Big Horn." Little did we realize at the time the slaughter bestowed on Custer was again and again going to be what we were to experience as men of this 20th Century Cavalry. Instead of horses and guns, we were playing with helicopters and high powered rifles. The name of the game was still the same, WAR. Kill or be killed, only the equipment for killing had changed.

Continuing my survey of men, my eyes next focused on Harold Reed, son of the famous news commentator, Edwin L. Reed. How in the hell Harold ever ended up in an infantry company, I'll never know. With his pull it was hard to understand how he even made it in the Army. I thought it would be interesting to take a survey and see how many eligible sons of fat cats such as senators, congressmen, company presidents and other assorted "important men" made it into the service, let alone the infantry. I would venture to guess the number would be quite small.

Harold had nobody to blame but himself for his present predicament. Like myself, Harold and flunked out of college after a couple of semesters, and decided to enlist for lack of something better to do. Harold also felt he had to prove himself to his father. Since he evidently couldn't do it in the field of academics, he would try to do it on the battlefield. I wondered how many other guys were here to prove themselves. It seemed to me that an individual should have another option besides war to prove himself a man. For if one lost in his attempt to prove himself, where would he be? Most likely, six feet under and no one to care except his family and a few friends.

As I continued to watch the men, I was brought back to reality by Sergeant Cannon's voice ricocheting off the steel walls. "Saddle up," he was yelling. "Get your gear together and quite farting around."

Getting our gear together proved to be quite a painstaking task. We were loaded down with enough equipment to make Hercules struggle. We had on battle-packs, which consisted of a pack filled with a fresh change of clothes, shaving utensils, extra ammunition and anything else one cared to bring., The pack was attached to straps and a belt. The belt encircled our waist. One strap went over each shoulder and attached to the belt in front of the waist. The outfit resembled a harness of sorts. That, however, was only a miniscule portion of the total picture. Attached to the belt, from left to right, but in reality any damn way you could get them on, was an entrenching tool (shovel), bayonet, two or more ammunition pouches (5 or 6 magazines were in each pouch), two plastic canteens and a first aid kit. If there was any more available room, I'm sure the Army would have found something else to take up the void. Unfortunately, there was more to carry in addition to what was around our waist.

9

On the top and sides of the pack, in an inverted "U" shape, went our portable "home." Comprising the "U" shaped roll was a shelter half (half of a pup tent) which was interchangeable with any other to form one whole pup tent. Inside of this shelter half was placed an air mattress, one lightweight blanket, rubberized poncho and more ammo magazines. The whole affair was then rolled up and attached to the back by a length of rope. One would have thought that would be sufficient to send anyone into battle, however, since our arms were free of gear, there were additional supplies to be carried.

Our duffle bags had to be carried off the ship and to the site of our base camp. These bags contained the remainder of our clothes, which consisted of fatigues, field jacket, extra boots, socks and underwear, all of which had been dyed varying shades of green. Personal items were also included in the duffle bags.

I might add that all of our clothes and boots were standard issue. We had not yet been issued jungle fatigues and boots. These were to come much later (if one remained alive long enough to collect them.) We were still not ready to disembark the ship. Each man in an infantry platoon is assigned to some sort of weapon in addition to his personal M-16 or 45 pistols. The additional weapons consisted of M60 machine guns, grenade launchers, or a 90 millimeter recoilless rifle (bazooka.) These had to be carried off also, plus the additional ammunition each weapon required.

After hours of getting organized and loaded up we were assembled on the top deck in readiness for our descent into the landing craft. Fortunately we didn't have to climb down cargo nets to enter the landing craft. To do so would have been suicide. Walking any distance with all that equipment required one to have the balance and grace of a tightrope walker. One can only imagine the potential mishaps if we had tried to go over the side. Rather than a net, we went down on a ladder. It ran from the top deck down the side of the ship onto the landing craft, a distance of 25 to 30 feet. Attached to the bottom of the ladder was a set of wheels. The wheels helped the ladder maintain its position in the boat. When the ship pitched one way and the landing craft another, the ladder would roll along the bottom of the landing craft.

Looking around, I could see everyone was loaded with some sort of equipment. Everyone was bitching about the amount of gear they had to carry. Those that had any room to carry anything else were promptly loaded down with cases of C rations or additional cans of ammunition for the machine gun.

Baker, a black trooper from Alabama, was adamant about the fact that he was a short timer; due to be discharged in less than 90 days. He didn't feel it was place to be doing "nigger work," his own words. It didn't seem right that he should be here with less than 3 months of active duty left to serve. As a matter of fact, the majority of the guys in our company was to be discharged on December 8th; here it was September 15th, 1965. Only a few months to go and they would be free of all this bullshit. I, however, was the platoon lifer due to the fact that I had two more years to go. God, how I envied those guys who were short timers. Tragically, many of those who were to be discharged in December would never live to see the day.

As I was helping Baker adjust his harness straps, the order came to descend. My body immediately broke out in a cold sweat of anticipation. No one knew what the coming hours were going to bring. I was certain we were not going immediately into combat with all of that damn gear. A pack of boy scouts could have wiped us out the way we were loaded down. If only we had some idea of what to expect. But, true to the Army practice, we were kept in the dark.

Sweat began rolling down my forehead and into my eyes as it was my turn to descend the ladder. It was useless to try and wipe them; to do so would mean shifting approximately 100 pounds of weight while climbing down a rolling ladder. Adding to my misery was the fact that my steel helmet was sliding around on my newly shaved head, similar to the way a ball bounces around a roulette wheel. After a few precarious steps, I felt the landing craft beneath my feet. Looking up at the soldiers trying to balance that gear and maintain balance was a comical sight, especially after making it down safely myself.

I had a strange feeling come over me while waiting for everyone else to descent. I impulsively reached out and touched the side of the ship. In a bizarre sort of way I felt I was saying goodbye. I was leaving some bad experiences behind but at the same time I was leaving the safety of the ship. We were facing many unknowns.

On the landing craft were some high ranking individuals, including Generals. I knew we were going to have a safe landing. With the big wheels on board, hostile fire was the last thing we would experience, because they were the last to go into any potential trouble spot. For the first time in my Army career, I was happy to be around brass. Soon, the landing craft was ashore.

My eyes began to survey the first dry land I had seen in weeks. Simultaneously, I was overcome by disbelief. There, not 50 feet away, was an Army band. I thought I was having some kind of delusion. I didn't know whether to laugh or cry. In my imagination, I had envisioned the type of landing one associates with World War II. Bullets and mortar rounds flying overhead, ships in the background with their canons spewing forth smoke and flame, airplanes coming in over the horizon ready to unleash their bombs as thousands of enemy soldiers are ready to charge with fixed bayonets. Here, we were being greeting by a lousy band playing a welcome song. A couple of guys behind me began laughing in a relieved manner.

Picking up my gear I followed the wave of men ashore. Photographers began taking pictures and the Generals were being welcomed by members of our advance party. Sergeant Cannon's voice soon broke up the joyous atmosphere. "Pick up your shit and get on the trucks, and make it snappy."

"Trucks?" I said to myself. I didn't even see any as I looked over the area. Just then, the band stopped playing and broke ranks. Directly behind them stood a convoy of trucks.

Getting to them proved to be quite a feat. They were lined up about 50 yeards away, which sounds like a reasonable distance to walk while carrying all that gear, but in order to get there, it was necessary to walk through soft sand. As I would take a step forward, I would find myself sinking into the sand, stumbling, dropping some of my gear, stopping, picking up the gear, rebalancing it and going through the whole procedure again. Upon reaching the trucks, we were out of breath and sweating profusely.

After being packed into the trucks like the proverbial sardines in a can, we moved out. In a matter of minutes we passed in front of a small hamlet. The first Vietnamese individual of my entire war experience was standing a few yards away. The trucks had slowed to a crawl and various Vietnamese were coming closer. The first person I saw was a female of about middle age. In one had she was holding a small child, and both wore clothes of filthy rags. In her other had she was holding a coconut. She was repeating a word, "adeeo." While saying the word she kept pointing with the coconut, alternating between her and us.

"What the hell does she want?" I asked of no one in particular. Barry, sitting next to me, said "She wants to trade that fucking coconut for a radio, can you believe that, a coconut for a radio? What the hell does she think we are, rich Americans or something?" Needless to say, the radio men could not be persuaded to trade. It seemed like all the villagers were offering to trade coconuts for any kind of merchandise.

Kirkwood was busy passing out little American flags to every villager. I remembered him going into town outside of Ft. Benning and buying all the flags he could find. At the time I thought he was crazy. He must have known what he was doing because he was the hit of the platoon. You would have thought he was passing out dollar bills, the way the people were flocking around our truck.

One feature that the majority of the people seemed to possess was the color of their teeth. I couldn't help but notice as it was so unusual. Their teeth appeared to be stained by something resembling blueberry juice; dark purple, almost black. The younger ones looked more unusual because their teeth were light purple. Occasionally I would detect a gold tooth standing out bright and shiny like a star in the night. Later I learned that the Vietnamese chew beetle nuts as avidly as many Americans chew bubble gum. It is the juice of the beetle nut that gave their teeth their unusual coloring.

The villagers crowding around our truck were composed of women, old men and children. Occasionally I could see a younger male, but they appeared to be crippled in some manner. It didn't take a genius to realize the draft age men were in the Army, either South Vietnamese or Viet Cong.

Most of the guys in the truck were yelling and pointing, much as if they were in their hometown zoo. "Look over there, look at that," became a well used phrase during the truck ride.

Each villager seemed more filthy and tattered than the next. It was similar to being driven through the worst slum in the world. It was a very depressing sight.

We came upon a gate of barbed wire outside of the village. We realized that the whole village was enclosed by the barbed wire. Outside of the barbed wire was a small, old house, currently being used as a guard house. As we passed it, I got my first glimpse of a Vietnamese home, which I was to see time and time again. Weather beaten and ready to collapse, the walls of this house appeared to be made of a muddy material. In places, the walls had weathered away. Replacing the walls were flattened out metal containers ranging from what appeared to be Vietnamese beer cans to American ammunition containers. Later, time and time again, I was to see people urinating, defecating, and generally disposing of all types of waste in villages right outside their huts.

My mind was suddenly focused on that last day at Ft. Benning prior to being shipped out. I was standing at attention with the rest of my company. A Captain was asking me a question I shall never forget. "Private All," he asked, already sure of some standard answer. "Why do you want to go to Viet Nam?" I felt like saying because I don't have any fucking choice, but instead I answered in a proud voice, "My father and uncles fought in World War II, so I guess it's my turn now."

AS we began to travel farther fro the village, the trucks began to pick up speed, swirling billowing clouds of dust around us. With the heat, dust, and sweat, I felt as if I were encased in a huge hot ball of cotton candy. Then and there I learned a very important lesson which was to take me through some of the roughest times imaginable. No matter how unbearable a situation seemed, I merely had to look around me and I was sure to see someone else holding up under the strain. If that person happened to be smaller than me, it age me all the more courage to go on.

We came upon a makeshift airfield, with rows and rows of helicopters. There were two man "bubbles" as well as the biggies able to carry a whole platoon. The trucks rolled to a stop and turned off their engines. Before we had time to take another breath, Sgt. Rockford, one of Cannon's henchmen, appeared at the tail end of a truck as if by magic. He was yelling "saddle up!" as only a sergeant can. The phrase "saddle up" was becoming a very distinct attribute of the First Cavalry Division. I guess with its history of the wild west, it was inevitable. Also the division insignia was very large and featured a black horse's head on a field of yellow.

Getting our equipment together again proved to be a formidable task. However, with a lot of cussing and bitching we were soon lined up in a half-ass platoon formation.

Lieutenant Cline, nicknamed Lurch because of his 6'5" frame, called us to attention and told us that in a minute we would be boarding helicopters and heading for our base camp. That was the first time in days we had been told by anyone with some degree of authority what in the hell was going on. Having an idea of what was forthcoming made it easier to cope with the situation.

After a quick cigarette break we began boarding one of the platoon sized helicopters for our journey to base camp. A month before our departure from Ft. Benning, an advance party had left to reconnoiter the area where we were now heading.

CHAPTER 3

Flying at about two hundred feet or so it was possible to peer out of one of the windows immediately to my right. Staring down I could see the vast expanse of jungle. Even from high in the air it was possible to detect the thick green forbidding scene below. Again I started to wonder what it was going to be like living and perhaps even killing in such a foreign place. Never having been in such a similar environment it was useless to contemplate the situation any longer. Luckily, I had no notion of what it was going to be like. If I had I probably would have shot myself in the foot long ago. My eyes left the window and I began glancing at the men surrounding me. The looks of apprehension was blatant. Clearly everyone was scared shitless.

After approximately one-half hour of flying I was able to detect the descent of the helicopter. Quickly glancing out of the window, I hoped to get a better view of the surroundings. Immediately coming into view was a pagoda type building. The first thing that struck my eye were the colors. It was painted blue and yellow. At one time the colors must have been quite vivid, however, after many years of rain and the relentless burning of the sun, they had become quite faded. I suppose I was impressed by the colors simply because it was the first time in over a month I had seen any color but grey or green. I was equally impressed by the chunks of the pagoda which apparently had been chipped away by forces of nature. Chipped away by nature, my ass; those were bullet and mortar markings! It was like a kick in the groin; the sudden realization that this was it was overwhelming. I wanted desperately to be away from this place. Eventually, we would be in combat doing the things man has done to man since the beginning of time. Being in a helicopter made it even more ridiculous. If man can go from a stone ax to riding about the countryside in a helicopter surely he can come up with a way to solve his differences besides killing each other. All this thinking wasn't going to improve my immediate situation. I was here with one hundred and eighty-nine other men in my Company. It was up to me to make the most of it and try to come out of it alive. Dreaming, wondering, and pondering about the way things could be wasn't going to make things any better. A sudden whooshing sound snapped my mind back to reality. Outside the helicopter was kicking up a small dust storm as it began to land. After a few seconds a slight thump indicated that we had touched ground. Turning to my left I could see the rear door slowly lowering itself much like the jaws of a huge dragon would look as it disgorges some half-eaten prey.

The first individual out of the door was Sergeant Rockford. He appeared to be playing the role of some goddamn know-it-all. What made him appear especially obnoxious was that he obviously was enjoying playing that know-it-all role. As soon as his feet touched ground he began shouting his fucking orders. "Fall in, fuck sticks," he was shouting, his voice resplendent with glee. My God, I thought, the dust from the helicopter hasn't even settled and here this idiot is giving orders.

"Fuck you," I heard someone say in a voice too soft for Rockford to hear. Looking around I could see that it was Tom Kirkwood. "You'd think that son-of-a-bitch would have learned his lesson by now," he continued in a most irritated manner. My mind flashed back to a night in the swamps of Savannah, Georgia. We were on a night training mission, being transported by armored personnel carriers. This particular Sergeant had been riding Tom's back about some trivial matter regarding the cleanliness of Tom's carrier. Tom took the criticism in a congenial manner. However the next morning it was discovered that Sergeant Rockford's duffel bag was missing. Everything he owned for a one month training exercise including personal as well as government issued articles were bobbing around in an unknown swamp. Knowing Tom, and the desire he possessed to get even in such matters, it was remarkable that it wasn't Rockford floating in those stagnant waters. At that particular moment I was kind of sad it wasn't. The incident with the missing duffel bag re-enforced the point that there were certain guys you just didn't fuck with. They always found a way to get even with you. Obviously Tom was one of those guys.

Getting even Stateside usually involved getting even by a non-violent means. However, in a Stateside situation ones life usually isn't at stake hence the retribution is small. Here in Viet Nam the stakes are slightly higher. Here you are fighting for your life. I couldn't help but wonder what the process of getting even would involve.

The sound of Sergeant Rockford yelling, now joined by Sergeant Cannon, soon drowned out my ability to think about anything else except lining up in squads and with all that damned equipment it was no easy task. Soon our platoon was lined up in some semblance to the way it was supposed to be.

Sergeant Cannon, our platoon Sergeant, soon called us to attention. Standing there in that hot sun loaded down like pack mules and for no apparent reason, I and I'm sure everyone else, began to wonder just what in the hell was going on. Very shortly two officers approached Sergeant Cannon. After a brief conversation the officers and Cannon saluted. The officers departed and Cannon began to address us.

"At ease," he shouted. The order to relax was met with a sigh of relief from the platoon. The order came none too soon as the weight of the packs and the heat of the sun was rapidly becoming unbearable. It wasn't that we had become soft on the voyage, for there was daily physical training. It was because we were not used to the weight and digging into our neck and shoulders by those goddamn heavy packs.

"Take a smoke break and shake it out," Cannon continued. "Henderson and Mira are on their way to guide us to our base camp. We are going to walk so try and get some rest." Walk, I thought, how in the hell are we going to walk with all of this crap. Just thinking about the ordeal drained my body of all its strength. How I was actually going to do it seemed an impossibility. I soon learned that doing the seemingly impossible was going to become a common occurance.

In what seemed to be only a few seconds but in reality was ten or so minutes we were on our feet. Sergeant Henderson had made his appearance. Henderson and elements from each Company of the Division had flown from Ft. Benning to Viet Nam about a month prior to our arrival. As an advance party it was their job to scout the area where the base camp was to be located. In addition it was their responsibility to lay out exactly where each Battalion and Company was to be located. The idea behind the advance party was to facilitate our setting up. In a short time we would see what kind of job they had done.

After struggling with our equipment trying to arrange it so it could be carried in somewhat of a comfortable manner, we found ourselves moving out in single file. All of my energies both physical and mental were put to use trying to cope with the unbelievable weight digging into my neck. Looking around me I could see that everyone else was having an equally hard time carrying their load. Clark, who was the gunner of the recoilless rifle of which I was assistant, was directly in front of me. Clark was very much overweight and had the reputation of being the laziest soldier in the platoon. He was the first guy I would have expected to fall out yet there he was, plodding along and with a degree of determination I didn't know he possessed. Sweat was running off of him and soaking his shirt much more than anyone else. For some unexplainable reason I knew he was going to make it. I thought if that ass can make it, dammit, so could I. Upon deciding that I could do it I seemed to gain some sort of inner strength. Walking, even with all that weight, suddenly seemed easier. After about a half hour of walking without a break I heard Sergeant Rockford bellow, "hang on men, about a hundred yards more and we're home." The hundred or so yards passed relatively quickly. Magically the order to halt and break ranks floated into our minds.

Without having to be told by anyone I and the rest of my compatriots immediately sank to the ground grateful for the relief, much as a drowning sailor must feel when he is graciously washed ashore and feels the life saving land under his fingers.

Laying on my back with my head propped on my steel helmet I was able to look back over the area which we had just traversed. While actually walking one was too concerned with wiping the sweat out of ones eyes and keeping the heavy load adjusted and merely walking to notice the immediate surroundings. Now, however, I could see that we had walked across a large expanse of open terrain. Looking to my left I could see a stand of trees, thin near us but increasing in density the farther they extended into the distance. Concentrating more carefully and following the line of thick shrubs and trees I could determine that the outline of growth was following the pattern of a circle. As my eyes moved from my left to almost straight ahead the pattern of the circle was broken by more trees angling sharply inward. Looking far off into the distance to my right I could vaguely make out the outline of more trees. We seemed to be sitting on the edge of a rough circle which was composed of dense growth. The center, which we had just crossed, seemed to have been cleared away. The cleared center was to become the helipad for the vast numbers of helicopters which the First Cavalry possessed. The infantry Companies were stationed around the circle offering protection for those within. The number of men in the Division was probably near eighteen thousand. To spread that many men and that much equipment geographically in and around a circle required it to be many miles in circumference. Thus our base camp probably covered an area larger than many cities.

The tranquility of just laying there on the ground and feeling strength returning to our tired bodies was soon broken by Sergeant Cannon announcing the increasingly familiar words of "saddle up."

Slowly our platoon began to methodically pick up all of our equipment. After a few minutes of cussing and struggling to arrange the equipment so that it could again be carried to some unknown point, we were ready to move out.

"Just a few more minutes, troops, and we will be setting up," said Sergeant Rockford. "Right over there is your new home," he continued. Looking straight ahead from where we had been sitting I could see him pointing to an area of relatively clear ground. Immediately to the left of where we were to pitch our tents I could see dark and forbidding looking trees. The growth was thin as it reached inward toward our area. Looking farther to the left it was possible to see that the trees and brush became increasingly thick. The farther it spread to the left and the thicker it became the darker in color it appeared. This was due to the fact that because the growth was so thick no sunlight could filter through the branches. Naturally, without any light, it would appear dark. I suddenly became conscious of the fact that I could hear no jungle sounds. There were none of the various bird or insect sounds one associates with the jungle. Perhaps the noise of us, the interlopers, frightened whatever was out there in the jungle into temporary submission. One sound I did hear was Rockford telling us to get the lead out and start moving.

Very shortly we were at our presubscribed location. Equipment went falling haphazardly to the ground; we soldiers soon followed. Laying across my duffel bag, squeezing out some lumps in order to make myself more comfortable, I glanced in front of me at the terrifying jungle. Again the awful apprehension of not knowing what was out there began to disturb me. If only I could conjure up some inkling of what in the hell was out there I would have felt a little better.

Before I could think about it any more, Clark was asking me when I thought we would be getting mail. Mail! My God, I hadn't thought about it seriously for weeks. Not having mail and knowing that we weren't going to get any for the length of the cruise, the thought of it had been erased from my mind. Now, however, we were off of that goddamned ship and we should be getting some very soon. Knowing that I would soon be reading words from Mom and Brenda made my spirits soar. I knew that reading and thinking about home would take my mind off of this uncomfortable place. Before I could wallow in anymore leisurely thoughts I heard Sergeant Rockford babbling.

Looking to my left I could see him approaching our squad. As he came closer I could hear him giving orders to start setting up our tents. Moving like drugged animals we began the laborious task of disassemblying our packs and removing the necessary gear. Shelter halves, tent poles, weapons, ammunition, clothes, and seemingly a thousand other articles soon lay at my feet. Looking to my left and stretching for fifty yards I could see that everyone else in the platoon was as disorganized as I. The platoon was stretched out in a straight line of sorts. Our squad was the farthest up the line. To my immediate right there was an area of perhaps fifty to seventy-five yards. The area was covered with trees, however, it was nothing compared to the thicker growth only a few yards away. Beyond this relatively open area I was able to tell that another Company was making preparations to establish some sort of headquarters. Facing the thick jungle I was able to determine some sort of organization developing. To my left my Company, A Company, 2nd Battalion, 7th Regiment of the 1st Cavalry Division, was forming. Directly behind me other Companies of our Battalion were also in the process. I couldn't make out the designation of the men to my right, however, just knowing they were there gave me a sense of security. Directly ahead, facing me, was nothing but goddamned trees and that didn't make me feel very secure. We knew that the 101 Airborne Division had supposedly cleared out any enemy in the immediate area a few weeks ago. But, glancing out into the unknown jungle before me, I knew it was an impossibility. An army of Viet Cong could have been hiding right before my very eyes! Nobody, not even that pseudo bad-ass outfit of paratroopers, could have swept through, let alone cleared out, that impregnable appearing jungle. Fuck it, I thought to myself. Take your mind off of it. If I let it get to me now what kind of shape would I be in six months from now? I didn't want to answer the question. I decided to put my energies on the matters at hand.

Working together with Clark, we managed to assemble our shelter halves and poles. Soon we had our pup tent assembled. Just as we were about to celebrate with a drink of water Cannon came running toward us carrying a large dirty gray bag. I knew immediately we were about to have mail call. A feeling of well being flowed over my body. I could see that Cannon even had a smile on his face. He began calling out names and passing out letters with such obvious glee that he would have rivaled a Santa Claus on Christmas Eve. So the son-of-a-bitch was capable of a little humanness after all. Ah, what wonders a little mail will do for a man, even a Sergeant in the Army.

Soon everyone was sitting, ripping open the dozens of letters that had accumulated over the past month. My thoughts, as were the thoughts of all about me, were for the moment with our loved ones. As everyone was reading or thinking, an eerie silence had fallen over the entire platoon. All of our minds seemed to be intertwined on one common goal, home, which at that particular moment in time had to be the strongest bond between men. I suddenly had an impulse to stand up and shout 'let's go home'. I'm positive many would have followed.

The tranquil moment was shattered by Rockford yelling at us to put the letters away and get those goddamn tents lined up right. Lining them up right meant tearing them down and reassembling them so that the front tent pole on each tent was lined up exactly with the first tent. Since the first tent was a long distance to my left I decided to wait until they lined up in order, moving toward me. To do otherwise would have meant tearing my tent down repeatedly. Many of the others were doing just that.

In the hot sun I could think of better ways to spend my time. One of the squadleaders saw the futility of each individual person trying to line up his tent with one that wasn't lined up with its immediate counterpart. He went to the first tent, lined it up straight, then went to the one next to it and lined it up with the first. Following this procedure he was able to line up the entire row of tents in a short time. Now there is a Sergeant who is capable of using his head, I thought. Too bad there aren't more of them around.

Within a short period of time the sun began to descend. With the dusk came the realization that we hadn't eaten since we left the ship.

With the excitement of arriving at base camp no one really had time to think of eating. I asked Clark when in the hell we were going to eat. He didn't seem too concerned about it, however, he did notice that there was no attempt by anyone to set up any type of a field kitchen. That meant that we were going to eat those damn C rations. Suddenly I realized that the food some of the guys carried off of the ship was going to be our immediate meal.

"Hey, Sarge," I yelled in the direction of Rockford. "Where's chow?"

"Come over here and pick it up, Private," he yelled back.

Private, your ass, I thought. Why in the hell can't you call me by my name. Begrudgingly I walked over to where the chow was stacked and returned with a case. At least I would have first choice at the various meals.

Returning to our squad with the food, I began randomly throwing a prepackaged meal in the direction of various men. No matter what each received they would bitch about it not being what they liked. That's not too hard to understand as one meal was as bad as the next. I kept the fried ham and fruit which was the most popular. After eating there was the standard police call. With no specific orders there was nothing to do but try and rearrange our equipment into some sort of liveable order. Most of our gear went into the two men pup tents which didn't leave a lot of space for us to get comfortable in.

Soon Clark and I had things stored so that we could crawl into, and with a minimum of movement, stretch out on our air mattresses. Standing back a few feet from our tent Clark and I could take a temporary pride in our achievement. The tent looked like it would stand as well as offer some sort of temporary cover in case it should rain.

By now it had begun to grow dark very quickly. Clark decided to light a candle and locate his missing cigarettes. No sooner had the candle been lighted than Sergeant Rockford came running and asked us what in the hell we thought we were doing. Before we could answer he told us to collect the canteens from the rest of the squad and fill them up down at the water truck. The truck was parked about a hundred yards away in front of where our Company headquarters was to be located. Almost everyone had two canteens to be filled. We were not yet wise to the ways of the jungle and everyone had drained them nearly dry during the course of the hot, physically exhausting day.

"How in the hell are we going to carry thirty canteens," mumbled Clark to no one in particular. Thinking the easiest way would be to find a large, narrow, but sturdy stick which we could slide through the handles of the plastic canteens and carry them slung across our shoulders. I moved out to find one. Finding one the right size proved to be no problem in the wealth of growth a few yards beyond our tent.

Soon we found ourselves at the water truck. There must have been twenty or so other men with as many canteens as Clark and I had. The truck had only eight faucets and the others were fighting over them as if gold were flowing from inside. I wanted to wait for them to finish before we attempted to fill ours. Clark said no as he could hear others approaching and it would only be a matter of time until it would be dry. Fearing returning and facing Rockford with empty canteens we decided to plunge into the chaotic scene. Clark was fat but he was also big. Through a process of cussing and shoving it was but a short time and Clark had a faucet from which we could draw water. We began immediately our laborious task of filling the canteens. As one was filled it was placed on the branch we had brought. Soon the branch was loaded and we began our walk back to our squad.

Stumbling through the dark and unfamiliar terrain we at last reached our tents. After passing out the canteens we sat down by our tent and proceeded to take a long delicious drink of well earned cool water. No sooner had the water started its journey down our parched throats than we both began to simultaneously gag and spit as if we were swallowing gasoline.

"Jesus Christ," Clark managed to say through repeated coughing spells. The water was like none I had ever tasted. Brackish and tinged with what I thought was chlorine. The thought or anticipation of drinking normal tasting water only compounded the obnoxiousness of the moment.

Later we would be issued water tablets to purify our drinking water. The engineers who had arrived with the advance party had erected a sort of primitive water purifying station at the nearby river. Months later they would perfect their system and the tablets would not be necessary. However, in the field they would always be a necessity. The only problem was that the tablets always made the water taste like an indoor swimming pool. Since they were composed mainly of concentrated chlorine that wasn't too surprising. It was only after months of drinking the vile tasting liquid that someone decided to write home for Kool Aid. The purpose of which was merely to disguise the taste of the water. It was a strange sight seeing grown men, often in the lull of battle, exchanging packs of Kool Aid with each other. A letter from home wasn't complete unless it contained a pack or two of the sweet tasting additive.

Rockford soon arrived with news that added to our discomfort. We could turn in immediately, however, there was to be guard duty right outside of our tents. Each man was to pull two hours on and two hours off. Another Company had moved out about fifty yards behind us to form a perimeter of defense. However, with the thick jungle only a short distance away it was possible for someone to slip through and create a problem. I decided to pull first watch and Clark immediately withdrew to the inside of the tent.

I had been sitting outside of our tent on the verge of falling asleep when suddenly I heard shooting. It was coming from the men who had taken up positions on our outside perimeter. I grabbed my rifle and in a split second was fully awake. The firing continued unabated and I was fully expecting a full scale attack. My eyes searched the blackness before me but I could see nothing moving. Suddenly the firing stopped and the tenseness within my body eased. What in the hell did they see out there; what were they shooting at? I remembered stories I had heard of G.I.'s in the Korean War being killed in their sleeping bags. Was this about to happen to us? I decided in my naiveness to spend the night fully awake.

My mind was taken away from my thoughts by movement from the tent next to mine. Tom was changing guard duty with Barry Knight, his tent partner. I decided to awaken Clark and change places also. It was almost as though I expected to find security behind the confines of that flimsy canvas of my tent. I had vowed to stay awake but no sooner had my head touched the air mattress and I was in sweet, safe sleep. The two hours I slept passed unbelieveably quickly. Clark was shaking me telling me it was time to change. He said there had been sporadic firing from the outside perimeter, however he had seen nothing but the blackness behind us. Again I found myself all alone. Of course there were thousands of green troops all around me but undoubtedly they were thinking similar things. Because the situation was so unique it made the experience all the more frightening.

The sporadic firing continued all through the night. After a few shifts of guard duty and seeing nothing but hearing much I deduced that the troops on the perimeter were firing at anything they thought was moving. The sounds of the gunfire were all the same, sharp and crackling. After listening to it for hours it was easy to tell there were no incoming rounds of a different source. Knowing this I was able to relax a little. However I wasn't completely sure of the nature of the shooting. Thinking on one's own was not a common practice in the Army. Some Sergeant was always telling you what was happening. Thus I was in the unusual predicament of thinking I knew what was going on but not being entirely positive. Again the thought of not knowing was beginning to affect my reasoning.

Daybreak soon began to melt the darkness of the night as well as the darkness of my clogged mind. Daylight seemed to bring a degree of safety. Man obviously has an aversion to the night. What he can't see he can't understand; not understanding he can't react in a rational manner. Suddenly, the thought occurred to me that I was going to have to spend three hundred and sixty-four nights in the darkness. A darkness made all the more terrifying by more unknowns than I had ever known in my short life. The idea of spending that much time in this foreign place was incomprehendable. I was overwhelmed by the feeling of helplessness. Thinking about it only made the situation worse. I decided to make myself focus on something else. Clark's boot was sticking out of the tent. Why should he be sleeping, oblivious to the situation, when I was in such a state of displeasure. Without thinking I gave his foot a quick kick and told him to get his ass up. Besides the sun was up and it was only a matter of time before Sergeant Rockford would be coming to wake our squad up to start the day's activities. What they would encompass I could not imagine.

Feeling a terrible urge to urinate, I glanced around to locate a spot which would serve my purposes. The trees directly behind my tent offered the most likely spot. Rifle in hand I walked quickly toward them. Moving deep into the brush I was soon hidden from view of the tents. I noticed for the first time how incredibly thick the growth was. Not only were the countless trees reaching into the sky, there were other plants of every type filling in the void between the thin trees. Added to this was the network of vines which encircled everything in their search for sunlight. Watching my urine splash and scatter a group of ants I realized that I was an intruder. I wondered again what in the hell I was doing in this unknown place pissing where I didn't belong. The whole idea just didn't make any sense. Hearing footsteps I forced the remaining urine out of my bladder with a forceful grunt.

Glancing through the trees I could see other men about to join me in their morning ritual. Rejoining my squad I had learned that Rockford had just left and had given orders to line up for chow. Walking to where the Company field kitchen had been set up with the rest of my squad we soon heard a phrase which we were to hear over and over again. "Spread out and keep fifteen meters between you." This advice was to keep an incoming mortar round from taking out more than one or two men at a time. Thus, we were soon strung out in a long line awaiting our morning meal.

I had, as most of the men, eaten only the barest minimum of our C rations from the night before. This meant eating the meat and fruit and throwing the bread, cookies, peanut butter, or chocolate away. One didn't receive each of the items but one or the other, depending on which meal was selected. For example, peanut butter and bread went with the ham and the chocolate and cookies went with the boned chicken. Each packaged meal also contained a small amount of toilet paper and a small package containing four cigarettes. The cigarettes were usually the best part of the meal.

Soon I found myself standing before a cook who was ladeling out hot coffee. Next to him was another handing out small boxes of corn flakes. A third was handing every fourth man a large can of cold precooked sausage. Walking past Rockford I heard him say something to the effect of don't eat too much, you might get sick. He said it with a not too subtle laugh. I felt like shoving it down his fucking throat. Continuing to file past other Sergeants, surveying the situation while walking, I was expecting someone to hand out milk for the cereal. Much to my dismay there was none.

We walked back to our tents, breakfast in hand. I was really hungry after eating practically nothing the previous day. Staring at the unappetizing food in my hands I knew I wasn't going to be able to eat it. I soon found myself trying to eat some of the dry flakes. Even pretending they were pieces of crisp bacon did no good. I just couldn't force them down. Tom had received one of the cans of sausages. He had the can opened and was passing them out to anyone interested. I passed them up and watched the others attempt to eat them. After a nibble or two one and all began to throw them into the neighboring trees. Each heave into the trees was accompanied by a string of swear words, each soldier trying to outdo the other. It was almost as if a better description would atone for the meat being so rotten tasting.

A shouting commotion coming from the area of the outer perimeter allowed us to take our minds off the miserable food in front of us. We could see that the troops who had been on the perimeter last night were returning to their Company area. They were greeted by sarcastic shouts from the rest of the men. Most of the returning men, judging from their haggared looks, were in no mood for jokes. By this time everyone was aware of their haphazard shooting during the night. Most of the insults were directed at these men for keeping us awake at night as well as scaring the shit out of everybody. Most of the returning men merely smiled and I heard one guy say, "Laugh now, mother fucker, because tonight some of you smart asses are going to be out there". Laughing and shouting insults at each other seemed to take some of the hostility out of us. The diminishing hostility was soon replaced by the appearance of Sergeant Rockford. It seemed everytime he showed up bad news was right behind.

He gave the order to "saddle up". In this particular case we were to load up with just our rifles, entrenching tools, canteens, and extra ammunition. Lined up in a platoon formation we discovered we were going to spend the day cutting down trees. The purpose, I assumed, was to clear a field of fire. This meant clearing out an area so that if one had to fire at something in front of him he would be able to see what he was shooting at. I soon discovered, after marching a short distance, that we were going to clear out the whole goddamned jungle. We stopped marching when the growth became too thick to walk any further. Behind us was a sparse growth of trees and smaller bushes. In front, however, was an almost inpregnable wall of trees. No wonder those guys last night had fired so often. One could only imagine what each man had thought he had seen emerging from the jungle.

We were told to ignore the small stuff behind us and concentrate on the thicker growth directly to our front. Someone asked Sergeant Cannon what we were supposed to use to cut the shit down with. "Your entrenching tools, stupid," he replied. I couldn't believe my ears. Entrenching tools, I thought, what a crock. Here we were, representatives of the richest nation on earth, supposedly the best trained and equipped army in the entire world, and we were supposed to cut down trees with a blunt-edged shovel no bigger than a childs' toy. Why hadn't anyone thought to bring saws, hatchets, or any goddamned thing. Jesus Christ, if this was the type of planning we were going to be accustomed to, it was going to be a disastrous stay. Little did I realize the truth in my sarcastic observation.

On order from Sergeant Cannon, like so many dancers on cue from their choreographer, we began swinging our shovels at the monsterous growth. The shovels, being rather blunt (unwise to jungle warfare we hadn't as yet learned to sharpen the edges of the tools), merely bounced off of the trees as if they were made of rubber. After repeatedly swinging at the same spot on one tree one could begin to make a little progress and see a crack develop. By concentrating on that one spot, the tree, after much expanded energy on behalf of each soldier, would topple to one side. One then had to reach down and strip the green bark from the stump and the tree itself. Everyone has surely had a similar experience trying to split a green twig.

After working a short while our fatigue shirts were soaked with sweat. Stripping the hot uncomfortable shirts off and working in our undershirts made the situation temporarily bearable. The sun rising higher and higher overhead was making the work increasingly difficult. The humidity that enveloped us made breathing difficult. The fact that we hadn't had a decent meal in days soon began to take its affect. We began slowing down. Swinging the shovels with any degree of authority became an impossibility. Sergeant Rockford became aware of the situation and ordered a five minute break. We dropped our shovels as if they had become poisonous and raced to where our canteens were. The water inside the plastic containers had become tepid, the taste of plastic was also evident, along with the chlorine. I could imagine the dirty brackish water from which it originated. Drinking it was a most disgusting experience. However, when one is in a certain predicament, one will do anything and I emphasize anything, when there are no other alternatives. Drinking the vile tasting liquid, I remembered reading about individuals who had resorted to cannibalism when the situation had demanded it. I recalled my revulsion at the thought of eating another's flesh. My situation wasn't at the present anywhere near what theirs must have been. However I could at that moment understand how an individual could make himself do anything no matter how uncomprehendable to another it may seem.

Looking around at the other men I noticed the various green colored undershirts we all were wearing. Every shade of green from the lightest chartreuse to almost black was represented. Prior to leaving Ft. Benning we had been ordered to dye all of our white clothing green. A simple enough request. However the Army didn't figure on all of these shades of green. I suddenly could see my mother, and I'm sure everyone elses, taking pains to insure that everything was tinted a pretty green. I wondered what they would say if they could see their precious sons chopping trees in the middle of a jungle. I'm sure it's what none of them had in mind.

The five minutes went by all too quickly and we were soon back swinging at the rubberlike trees. By lunch time our hands were torn and ripped by the thorns which seemed to adorn every limb of every tree. Blisters were developing on every part of our hands. It was almost as if we were being punished for cutting them down. We were slowly knocking them down but they in turn were inflicting a punishment upon us.

Lunch, even though it was C rations, offered a welcome relief from the punishing work. While eating we were informed it was a court martial offense to get a sunburn. Many of the men had stripped down naked to the waist. Evidently someone was worried about a serious situation developing. Glancing at the sun and feeling the burning rays one could well imagine the havoc it might play with ones skin. As uncomfortable as it seemed we soon found ourselves back to wearing our fatigues minus the green undershirts. We had heard rumors that we were to receive new lightweight jungle fatigues, however, it was to be many months before we saw them.

The day continued on relentlessly. The sun became increasingly hotter with each passing minute. Lifting ones arms to swing the seemingly ineffective shovels was developing into a superhuman effort. We had considered ourselves in superior physical shape, however, running and doing hours of exercises in Georgia was vastly different from chopping trees in the unbelievably hot sun of Viet Nam. The jungle, just by standing there, was proving to be superior. What was it going to be like when we had to wade through it, cutting its tentacle-like branches every step of the way? Clearly it was proving to be more of a problem than I had anticipated.

The order to stop cutting came none too soon. Our work was becoming increasingly ineffective. Our movements resembled those of robots, slow and methodical. Monotony, heat, and a feeling of helplessness against the giant task before us contributed to the situation. We loaded up our gear and marched to our Company area.

The thought of eating a leisurely meal, even if they were C rations, helped to make the situation seem bearable. After forcing down a small can of boned chicken followed by the vile tasting water, any thoughts of relaxing were disspelled by Sergeant Rockford. It seemed that Lieutenant Cline, nicknamed "Lurch" from the Adams Family, had given orders for us to dig trenches immediately behind our tents. The trenches were to be our protection in case of a mortar attack.

Thus, we again found ourselves digging and chopping the cursed ground. Instead of trees we were now engaged in a struggle with the soil. The soil was relatively soft, facilitating the digging aspect. However, after digging down a few inches we discovered that the earth was laced with a network of roots. The roots were only an inch or so in diameter. The fact that there were so many thousands of them made the work extremely hard and slow. The trenches had to be three feet in depth and run in a zigzag pattern. The farther down we dug and chopped, the more roots we unearthed. The whole task became increasingly difficult. The longer we worked at it, the more frustrated we became.

In all of my past experience I had never known such frustration and hopelessness. No matter how tedious or difficult a situation had seemed there was always the realization that it would soon be over and something better would follow. Stateside, even after a twelve-hour day of the most physically exhausting work, there had always been the knowledge that it would be followed by a few beers and a bed. Sweet uninterrupted sleep had a way of righting the wrongs of the previous day.

But what the hell did we have here? Hour after hour of hard physical labor in the hot unrelenting sun. When that was over we could count on more hours of the same grueling labor. Plus it was being done with tools that men of the bronze age would probably have laughed at. Sleep would not help because we were being awakened every two hours for goddamn guard duty. Although it had not happened as yet there was the uneasy realization that at any second a mortar round could come raining down on us and tear us to pieces.

To ease the tension, I found myself caught up in the bitching and complaining that was engulfing everyone. I soon found myself talking back to Sergeant Rockford in a tone that he could hear.

"Dig a little deeper, Allen," he said.

"Fuck it, Sarge," I responded. To my amazement he said nothing. To talk back to a non-commissioned officer in such a defiant tone back in the States usually meant some sort of disciplinary action would be taken. However, at this particular moment he chose to let it pass. He seemed to be getting backtalk from everyone he approached. Of course he usually had some smart ass comment which invited some sort of reply. The backtalk had always been present, however, it had been subtle and usually muttered under ones breath. Now everything seemed to be coming out into the open. What could they do to us now that we were in Viet Nam? We were at the end of the road and everyone knew it.

The fun and games at Ft. Benning was replaced with a deadly seriousness. The atmosphere of soldiering, as I had known it, was changing before my eyes. Of course it didn't happen in one magical moment. The seeds of change were, however, being planted. Sergeants would no longer play their games of being holier than thou. Indiscriminate harassment would soon slack off to a semi-tolerable condition, although it would not totally disappear. It was almost as if the Sergeants realized that you can only push a man so far then he is going to respond. Previously for an enlisted man lower in rank than a Sergeant to respond meant to lose and everyone knew it. As a result one found himself taking a great deal of physical and mental abuse and not doing a damn thing about it. Now there was something one could do about it.

Men began responding to harrassment by telling the various Sergeants if they came around their foxholes at night they would very possibly get mistaken for a Viet Cong and get their damn head blown off. This defiant attitude was by no means directed at every Sergeant in every situation. It was only directed at the ones who constantly engaged in the overt harrassment. Most of the men realized it was the Sergeant's job to give orders and theirs to take and carry them out. The day to day routine of Army life was still being carried out. Now, however, it was being done with a small degree of humanness involved. The rank of Sergeant was still being respected in most situations. They merely had to demonstrate that the privileges were not being taken advantage of at the expense of the men. The idea of tell me what to do but do it with a degree of decency' seemed to be the general feeling of the men. In time we realized that at any moment we may be killed. In the meantime we didn't need any

Sergeant fucking up any precious remaining moments with their Mickey Mouse routines.

As darkness slipped upon us we were told to quit digging and turn in. We stopped working but without the happy anticipation that tomorrow would be better. If anything it would probably be worse. Clark and I returned to our tent only to find that our air mattresses had become deflated. Too exhausted to care we flipped a coin and Clark found himself pulling the first two hours of guard duty. With the exception of sporadic gunfire and broken sleep the night passed safely.

The next day started the same way as had the previous. Hot coffee and dry cereal was the extent of our breakfast. We were again lined up by platoons and marched off to the jungle and the tedious job of cutting the thick growth was at hand. The area we were working had quickly become known as the Green Line. Everything has a name, especially that which is unpleasant. Thus our daily activities for the next couple of weeks would be confined to working on the Green Line. However something greeted our eyes that was to make the arduous task seem more endurable.

Moving toward us was a column of Vietnamese civilians. There were probably a hundred or so in their group. They were marching in single file. Walking beside them were individuals who were serving in the capacity of leaders. These leaders appeared to be keeping some sort of order. I could see by their arm movements and head gestures that they were giving them orders. The scene matched exactly that of a group of soldiers marching with their Sergeants walking beside and keeping order. The column of civilians passed in front of us and appeared to be moving in the direction of the Green Line. We soon found ourselves marched off to the same general location.

Arriving at the same spot we had abandoned the previous day we could see that the Vietnamese were already engaged in the process of clearing away the thick growth. They appeared to be enjoying their work as there was an atmosphere of gayiety among them. Many of them were singing, others were joking and laughing amongst themselves. Seeing them in good spirits seemed to affect my general outlook. I no longer felt so overwhelmed by the task of clearing the jungle. Seeing that we had help and the fact that the Vietnamese obviously enjoyed what they were doing were probably the major factors that changed my mental outlook.

Watching them work for a few minutes I became aware they were using some sort of hatchet-like device to cut the trees. Using my entrenching tool in place of an ax I felt like an ass. Again the idea that we Americans were supposedly superior to these people came into my mind. The idea was soon cast aside for the absurdity that it was. I was witnessing the fact that a people will adapt and become proficient in what they have to do. These people had probably been clearing jungle for as long as they could remember. On the other hand there wasn't an American in the whole Company who had seen a jungle of this magnitude, let alone attempt to clear one. As a result the Vietnamese were the superior ones. If they were so at ease and natural at fighting in the jungle as they appeared to be in working it, we were in for extremely rough going.

The morning passed slowly under the hot sun. If only we could have taken off those damn steel helmets we had to wear every second we were awake. As every second wore on the helmets, or steel pots, as we called them, became agonizingly heavy. They seemed to squeeze the sweat from our heads. As one moved, the helmet would slide back and forth on our semi-bald heads. Upon leaving the ship many of us had our hair cut to basic training length which meant there was almost no hair at all to act as a buffer between our heads and the helmet liners. As the helmets slide back and forth, the effect was the same one gets when a wet cloth is wrung out by hand. In this case our heads were the cloths and the helmets had the same wringing or twisting effect as that of hands. It was soon time to break for lunch. We gratefully stopped and collapsed in a heap around our gear. Lunch again was cold C rations.

During the break a few of the men from our platoon had ventured over to where the Vietnamese civilians were working. Through some sort of barter they returned with some of the cutting tools the Vietnamese were using. The tool was about a foot in length. A wooden handle accounted for about four inches of the total length. The remaining eight inches was comprised of a heavy steel blade. The blade was sharpened to a razor sharpness on both edges. The last two inches of the blade near the tip was curved. Thus one could cut and slash and pull at the same time. This idea of cutting and then pulling proved to be very helpful. When cutting into thick growth one must be able to pull the fully and semi-cut growth out of ones way. Cutting the growth would be similar to cutting down a large, thick, full elm tree. Instead of attacking the trunk, start cutting in the middle of the thick branches and you have an idea of how you must pull the cut material out of your way before proceeding.

The tools were shared by the men as we continued our job into and throughout the increasingly hot afternoon. The tools made the job much easier but it was by no means a pleasant task. Our hands were still being continually scratched and ripped by the abundant thorns. Blisters were also a constant problem. Progress was, however, being made. Large piles of brush began to dot the area. The wall of the jungle was slowly being pushed back.

The afternoon passed in the same slow methodical manner as had the day before and many more to come. Glancing over to where the civilians were working I again felt relieved to know that we had help. Watching them work I noticed something peculiar. Every now and then one of the women would leave her group, walk a few feet and squat down for a minute or two. I didn't know what to make of the situation. At first I thought perhaps they were merely taking a break from the monotonous job of cutting the dense jungle. But why would they only take a break for such a short while? Why would they squat in the manner of those who are about to relieve themselves of their feces. The more of the ritual I witnessed the more curious I became.

As the afternoon was about over the order to take a ten minute break greeted our ears. I moved off to my left to where one of our squads was working. They were closer to the Vietnamese than where I had previously been. I wanted to get closer to them and hopefully get an unobstructed view of what these women were doing in their moment of solitude.

Walking over to Vera, the lone Mexican in our platoon, I bummed a cigarette and proceeded to engage in small talk. As we were talking about how hot it was one of the women nonchalantly left her work and moved a few yards in back of her co-workers.

"What in the hell is that broad doing?" I asked in an inquiring voice.

"If I didn't know any better," said Vera, "I'd swear she was taking a piss."

"What?" I answered incredulously. "They aren't even taking down their pants!" Standing there dumbfounded I watched the woman move closer to our position. When she had apparently found a spot to her liking she stopped and squatted. I couldn't understand why she had stopped where she did. She was out in the open. Certainly if she had intended to relieve herself she would have picked a more private spot. Obviously there were plenty of bushes around so finding one certainly wasn't one of her prime objectives.

Being this close I noticed something that I hadn't before. While in the process of squatting, she grasped one of her pant legs near the ankle and pulled it outward. The pants were quite baggy and she was able to pull them a few inches from her leg.

The woman looked quite funny to my naive eyes. Squatting, pulling her pants outward with one hand while the other rested on her knee. I had never seen such a sight yet there it was, happening before my unbelieving eyes. To her it was probably the most natural thing in the world. It was then I noticed her black pants turning an even darker black near the bottom. A small rivlet of water trickled onto the ground beneath her outstretched pant leg. When she finished urinating she casually stood up and proceeded to walk back to where she had been working.

I stood there mesmerized; the whole thing was uncomprehendable. How could anyone be so crude. Pissing on a tree is vulgar enough but to urinate purposely down ones leg and onto ones clothes was unthinkable. At least to my Western ways it was unthinkable. But to these people it obviously wasn't. If I had not witnessed it I wouldn't have thought it possible. Mumbling to myself, I left Vera and walked back to where my squad was proceeding to leave for our Company area.

Arriving back at our tent, I told Clark what I had seen. He too had noticed the women doing the same thing and figured that they were probably taking a piss. But he was as astounded as was I. Soon the method of urinating amongst the Vietnamese women was the talk of the Company. No one could quite believe it. However, all hoped that they were a little cleaner when they fucked.

After another appalling meal of cold C rations Sergeant Rockford informed us that our platoon was pulling guard duty on the Green Line that night.

"Son of a bitch," said Clark, reflecting the feelings of everyone.

Darkness found Clark and me sitting on the edge of a shallow but adequate foxhole. We were staring into the darkness of the night made darker by the surrounding jungle. Seeing more than ten yards in front of us was an impossibility. All around us were trees and vines entwining each other to form every type of diabolical figure imaginable. Sergeant Cannon came around and gave us the password for the night, 'Jiminey Cricket'.

"Don't fall asleep," he warned before he faded off to the next position to our right.

"Don't be too sneaky," I replied in a voice he couldn't help but hear.

Due to a flip of a coin Clark got first watch. With my M16 beside me I tried to relax in a reclining position. Due to the abundance of trees and stumps it was impossible. Thus I found myself falling to sleep in a half prone, half sitting position.

When Clark awoke me two hours later my neck and back felt as though I had been sleeping in a shoe box. Not knowing what was in the blackness before me or who may be watching me, getting up and stretching was an impossibility. Thus I sat there amongst the eerie surroundings imagining the whole Viet Cong Army was going to attack me at any moment. Adding to my misery was the fact that a heavy rain began to fall. I thought the canopy of trees overhead would act as sort of a shield. To my dismay the rain had a way of finding its way downward. Putting on my rubber poncho and steel pot afforded me some protection. Putting on that goddamn steel pot was the last thing I wanted to do. It seemed like there was no escaping its oppressive weight. Sitting in the rain I realized my rifle would have to be protected from the rain. I stuck it under my poncho so that the barrel opening rested under my armpit.

The M16 was a new rifle, lightweight, with a minimum of rust inducing parts. However, as with any metal in the humid jungle, it could and would rust. It was then that I realized again how unfamiliar I was with the damn thing. We had been shown pictures of the damage it could do to any living thing. The high velocity of the rounds fired made for its high degree of destructiveness. I suddenly had a strong urge to fire it on full automatic into the darkness before me. By merely flicking a small lever one could fire automatic or semi-automatic. The M16 could put out fire power almost equal to an M60 machine gun. With a whole Army equipped with these rifles one can only imagine the tremendous fire power it would possess. This Army of powerful new weapons, helicopters, and an awesome Air Force, I felt, would enable us to be out of Viet Nam in six months. How could it be any other way? Maybe we didn't have axes and saws at the moment but in the long run how much could it matter? When the shooting started there could only be quick and complete victory. But then as I have stated before, I was one very naive young soldier.

Thinking about fighting the enemy was just a flitting dream. I had no real concept of what it would involve. The ideas and thoughts so innocent at the present would turn into a nightmare of reality later.

My thoughts were suddenly broken by movement behind me. Something or someone was moving noisily upon my position. Reaching under my bulky poncho in a panic induced uncoordinated moves. I fumbled and dropped the damn rifle in the mud at the bottom of the foxhole. Realizing I wouldn't have time to pick it up in time to be of any use, I turned and shouted "halt" in the direction of the noise.

"Jiminey Cricket" came the reply. It was Sergeant Cannon responding with the password.

"Just checking to make sure someone was awake," he replied. "Lieutenant Cline was around," he continued. "He made it absolutely clear he didn't want any unnecessary firing going on, not like last night."

"Don't worry about a thing," I said, in a voice resplendent with a sudden cockiness. "I won't fire until I see the whites of their eyes."

"All right then," I heard him say as he moved off to pass the words of our noble leader.

Those were the first words I had heard directly or indirectly from any of the officers. Since our arrival none of them had dealt directly with the platoon. They slept and ate apart from us and generally kept their distance. But then we had only been on work details so their absence wasn't hard to understand. They were probably being briefed on information about enemy activity in the area. Suddenly I thought of our immediate officers. Lieutenant Cline was new to our platoon, arriving about a week before we moved out of Benning. The word was that he had only been in the Army less than six months and was fresh out of jump school. In addition, this was his first line platoon. He appeared to be very 'gung ho'. Being a greenhorn and airborne we would be in for some rough and foolish undertakings. Foolish would probably be the more adequate of the terms.

Captain Black was the Company Commander. If anyone didn't fit the stereotype of a Captain in the United States Army Infantry, it was Captain Black. Essentially skinny, but with a midsection larger than his shoulders, he resembled an egg. The word was that he was just as tough. Cline on the other hand was a powerful physical specimen. The addage of 'you can't tell a book by its cover' didn't hold true here. In time, like the egg he resembled, Black would crack. Cline on the other hand would come through time and time again. Most guys, myself included, bitched and complained about his unrelenting pushing and aggressiveness. However, that is exactly what we needed to see. Someone with authority showing lots of guts. In a perverse sort of way everyone under him hated, but respected, him at the same time. General Custer himself would have been proud to have him carrying on the tradition of the 7th Cavalry Regiment.

The eerie sounds of the night snapped my mind back to the immediate present. I glanced at the luminous dial of the watch hands and realized it was time to awaken Clark for his guard duty. After wiping the mud off my rifle as best I could, I fell asleep in the dry spot Clark's body had preserved from the rain. The next sound I heard was Clark's panic stricken voice telling me to get up. It was just turning light and he had fallen asleep on guard duty.

"Be quiet about this," he warned. "I just closed my eyes for a second and the next thing I knew it was light."

"Don't worry about it," I said, trying to sound reassuring. "You're just lucky Cannon or one of the other hatchet men didn't come nosing around while you were asleep." Realistically I knew I would have to watch Clark. I didn't want to be out in the bush and have him fall asleep on me. Before I could say any more about the incident the call to "saddle up" came filtering through the trees. We packed up our drenched and mud splattered equipment and moved back to camp.

Breakfast was soon in the making and again it was hot coffee and canned sausages. The meat was heated this time. Washed down with the hot coffee, it was at least filling. After the morning police call we again found ourselves moving out toward the Green Line to resume our chopping activities. After a short time of hacking and chopping we saw the Vietnamese approaching us.

Working all day, stopping for only an occasional smoke break and lunch, the day was mercifully drawing to a close. It seemed that with each passing day the heat was becoming more and more unbearable. The rain of the night before only added more oppressive humidity to the already sauna-like atmosphere. There was an exposed portion of our necks between our helmets and shirt collars that were being seriously burned by the white hot rays of the sun. Since no salve was being supplied by the medics, we began wearing handkerchiefs under our helmets and allowing them to hang down much like the style of the French Legionaires. Once again I was amazed at the stupidity of the Army for not providing for the situation. True, it was only a minor thing, but it gave everyone another thing to bitch about, adding to an unending list of gripes.

Suddenly the sound of "V.C." rang out loud and clear. I dropped my entrenching tool and dove behind the nearest log. Peering over the top I could see two Pfc's moving straight ahead into the jungle.

"Everyone keep your fucking heads down," boomed Sergeant Rockford. In a few moments the two troopers returned empty handed. Evidently they had seen someone spying on them. When they spotted him they yelled out loud. The mysterious figure took off with the Pfc's in pursuit. V.C. or not the incident made everyone aware that we were indeed in a War Zone.

The Green Line had taken on the aspects of mere work details. Since we had expected to land at Qui Nhon in a blaze of bullets and had not done so, our minds had become unaccustomed to the thought of fighting. Working like slaves in a cotton field we were being forced into our old roles of hard laborers. A most dangerous frame of mind to be in. This one incident, for me at least, had changed all of that, if only for a brief moment. As the days passed with no real action we were to find ourselves slipping more and more into a lackidazical attitude.

After more exhaustive cutting and chopping the order to "saddle up" rang out. We moved out and soon found ourselves back at base camp. The prospect of more work in the form of digging those damn trenches lay before us. Needless to say our morale was as low as the trenches were going to be.

Digging with despair at the unyielding roots I suddenly felt very lonely. I thought to myself that I must be undergoing some sort of punishment for some wrongdoing I had committed in my past. Try as I might I couldn't imagine what in the hell I had done to deserve this. It would soon be dark. Then we would have to stop. We couldn't be expected to go on working forever. Sleeping, even if it was on the ground, began to look good. Most of the air mattresses we had been issued had gone flat after the first night. Thus another small but important comfort had been taken away, intentional or not.

Just prior to darkness we stopped digging at the miserable ground. The platoon moved toward the tents in a languid manner befitting zombies. I couldn't think of anything but sleep. Clark and I again found ourselves rearranging our equipment in order to make room for our tired bodies. No sooner had we succeeded in shuffling our gear into a position that would accommodate us, we heard the dreadful sound of "saddle up".

It was Sergeant Cannon. I couldn't believe my ears. "Where in the hell were we going at this hour?" I thought to myself.

"You've got two minutes to be ready to move out," he continued. No word of where we were going, just be ready in two damn minutes. Clark and I looked at each other in disbelief. We had already stripped our combat packs to make the harness fit the items we needed for working on the Green Line. Now, in two minutes, in the dark, we were to rearrange them. Actually, it was just a matter of rearranging a few items on the pistol belt and attaching the combat pack and sleeping roll. The problem was finding the shit. All we needed, as far as I was concerned, was our rifle, ammunition, water, and a few other necessities. However we had to have all of the other paraphernalia green troops take into a combat situation. No one around me knew any better, thus everyone was in a turmoil trying to locate their equipment. The usual cussing and bitching was especially rampant during our ordeal.

Lieutenant Cline soon arrived at our squad area and proceeded to chew our asses out for not being ready in the prescribed time. There was no mumbling this time, merely silence. Though we were starting to dispute and, on occasion, question the wisdom of our non-commissioned officers we had not reached that point with the regular officers. They were still feared by the majority of men. Since we never associated with them except in a subservient manner, we had but no other choice to make. They were individuals who called all the shots. Their unique power enabled them to maintain this aura of omnipotence. They received our obedience. However, it was out of fear and not respect. Later individual officers would receive our respect and undying loyalty from actions they showed on the battlefield. On the other hand some would gain our hatred for the identical reasons.

After much hurried gathering of various articles I and the rest of my squad were moving double time toward the center of base camp, a quarter mile away. This was where the helicopters were stationed and serviced. The area was later called the 'Golf Course'. It got the name because of the nature of the short grass which dominated the entire area. It was the only terrain in the whole base encampment which didn't need thinning out.

Upon arriving we were told to take a break while our specific helicopters, or choppers, were located. Collapsing in our tracks after our tiring trek we started to talk about where we might be going. Since no one had any real idea about our sudden mission, I paid no real attention to the hearsay. Cannon soon appeared in the darkness and told us to follow him to the choppers.

"Where are we going?" I asked more out of habit than actually thinking I would get an answer.

To my surprise I actually remember him telling us that an engineering unit on top of a nearby mountain, later called Hong Kong mountain, was receiving sniper fire. They had requested support from an infantry unit and Lt. Cline had volunteered our services. This was the first of countless missions 'Lurch' would volunteer our platoon for.

Hearing his words I was filled with fear and simultaneous gladness. We were finally going to see some action. How would we react? Or more specifically, how would I react? Would I actually have to shoot someone? Would I be able to do it, was becoming an agonizing question. I had no real doubts as to my ability. However, subconsciously I had seen and read of many well intentioned individuals who couldn't do it. Would I fall into the same category? God, I hoped not. Again the thought of wanting to prove myself a man came looming into my mind. I would do it, goddamn it, I would. I ran my hand over my M16 the way one caresses a lover. How I wished we had more time to become better acquainted with the weapon.

Shortly we boarded the choppers, four men on each side of the ship. To my right was a helicopter machine gunner inspecting his weapon in a most prodigious manner. It was for him the first time he would have to fire his weapon in a real combat situation. For a moment I wondered what thoughts were going through his mind.

Sergeant Rockford soon broke the quiet atmosphere by saying he didn't want anyone fucking up our first mission. No one knew what was going to take place, but nevertheless there were to be no mistakes. Suddenly I hoped he had made a mistake so that he would incur the wrath of Lt. Cline.

Soon the whirring of the helicopter blades drowned out any further conversation. In a matter of seconds we were in the air. The movement upward was quite quick and I felt myself pushed forward and I almost went sailing out through the door opening. At Benning we had mastered entering and exiting various types of helicopters. There, the choppers had sliding doors. It was the responsibility of the last man aboard to shut the door. Now, however, there were no doors. Plus being on the Patch for over a month many of us had lost the sense of balance that was needed to keep from being pitched forward. The day was soon approaching when we would be able to lean out of the chopper, no matter what the altitude or angle the chopper was flying with no danger of falling.

After about fifteen minutes of high altitude flying I felt the chopper descending. Peering cautiously over the edge of the floor boards I could see lights below. As we got closer to ground level I could see a figure going through all kinds of configurations with a flashlight. He looked about as experienced as we. At one point I could feel the chopper veer left then suddenly we would veer sharply to the right, all the while we were steadily descending. My immediate thought was only that we land safely. With a heavy thud which caused us to bounce in all directions we landed. The machine gunner and crew chief were yelling to us to get our asses off the chopper.

Stumbling out of the helicopter, I and the man next to me went crashing to the ground. In the darkness it was impossible to tell that we had landed on a pile of huge boulders. In our haste and prodding by the men on the chopper we fell off the large rock the ship had landed on and fell to another level about two feet below. Gathering myself to a standing position I could hear Cline calling to form up over near him. Moving as if I was walking on eggs I moved toward his voice.

Before taking too many steps the helicopter started upward. The downdraft from the whirling blades forced me to stand still. The pressure of the downdraft was like an invisible hand pushing me down. In an instant it was gone and I crept forward. Slipping and falling on the jagged boulders like a toddler I soon found myself with the rest of the squad.

We were distributed in two man teams in the usual circle, about twenty meters apart. The engineering platoon we had come to protect was in the center. We were spread out along the side of the mountain, approximately thirty meters from the top. The engineers occupied the very top.

Rockford told us we were to fire only if we saw the individual who did the firing. Now that made a hell of a lot of sense. In the blackness of the night I could barely see Kirkwood who was assigned to me. And he was standing right next to me. How in the hell was I going to see anyone off in the distance. "Dig in," were his parting remarks as he moved off to the next position.

"Fuck" said Kirkwood. "How in the shit are we going to dig in amongst these rocks?" Seeing that he was right, we started to grope in the darkness for large rocks in which to build a small but adequate wall in front and around us. Soon we had somewhat of an enclosure around us. We were also told that there was a hundred percent alert. That meant that no one could sleep the entire night. That didn't make any sense at all. If we couldn't see, how in the hell were we supposed to fire. I couldn't imagine anyone walking up to my position and identifying himself as a Viet Cong. Thus Tom and I decided to gamble and sleep, one on duty and one off. If we had decided that both of us were to stay awake we both would have surely fallen asleep. This way both of us would get some much needed sleep.

The engineers had received much sniper fire during the late evening. Thus we knew that out there in the darkness of the night lurked the enemy. The night passed very slowly. Every second I expected a bullet to come ripping its way toward me. I then realized that if I couldn't see them they couldn't see me. I realized that if we made a minimum of noise we would be relatively safe. The night was spent with the barest of movement on the part of Kirkwood and myself. Without moving he would sleep for two hours and I would stay awake. When it came time to switch I would jab him and again, without making a move, he would announce that he was awake and ready to take over. The night passed uneventfully. There were no rounds fired in our direction. We, in return, fired none. That in itself, I felt, was a real accomplishment. Looking out into the darkness one imagines every movement and sound to be that of the enemy. The temptation to fire ones weapon is constant. Keeping your finger from squeezing the trigger requires the utmost personal discipline.

During the night a light rain had fallen. It wasn't heavy enough to drench, merely enough to make us very uncomfortable. As it became progressively lighter I could make out the outline of the jungle coming into focus. As the sun began to rise one could make out a light fog covering the base of the trees. The rays of the sun became more intense, the haze was being burned away enabling me to make out our surroundings.

We were indeed on the side of a mountain. The jungle was threateningly close. The outcropping of rock that we were perched on was no more than twenty feet away from the massive growth of jungle. I could determine that it would have been relatively easy for someone to fire at us from the safe confines of the jungle and we would never see them. Worse yet, they could still pull off such an accomplishment.

Immediately I was overwhelmed with a sense of thankfullness that we had made it through the night.

I was suddenly conscious of something protruding into my side. Reaching behind me I grasped a piece of wood on which there was attached a piece of paper. On the paper was written the words: Latrine, and the date Sept. 16, 1965. Kirkwood and I had been sleeping on a pile of shit. It had been buried only a few days. Outraged, I told him to get up and take a look at where we had been sleeping. His only comment was something to the effect that it was a good thing that we hadn't dug down very far or we would have been up to our ears in shit. I merely offered agreement.

It is customary in the Army that when a site that has been used for a latrine has been filled, it is then covered and the date staked into the ground. This prevents another group from coming along later and setting up a kitchen or other related activities. In our case it had been too dark to see where we were camping. Even though I was outraged at spending the night on a pile of shit, the hilarity of the situation seemed to break some of the tension that had been building up in me.

The sound of an incoming helicopter indicated we were about to move back to the Company area. Looking up in the direction of the powerful bird, I could distinguish the large yellow insignia of the First Cavalry Division painted proudly on its nose. Knowing that these powerful machines and the tremendous firepower they possessed were on our side I was overcome with the feeling of invincibility. I wondered if Custer felt the same feeling when comparing his rifles to the Indians bows and arrows.

"Sure am glad we have those choppers," said Kirkwood, breaking my train of thought. "It's really going to save on the walking."

"Yeah," I replied sarcastically. "But just think that if we ride we can cover ten times the area than if we walked. Shit man, that also means that our chances are probably ten times greater to meet the V.C." As time evolved that was to be one of my most astute observations.

Years later I would see in print that one of the faults of the Army was that it had too many support troops for its infantry. Only one out of ten men assigned to Viet Nam could be counted on being in the field. Because of the excess baggage, ones chances of getting killed or wounded in Viet Nam were quite minimal. That particular observation is true for any group except the infantry. For the men of an infantry unit just the reverse is true. Flying into village after village you are eventually going to find the enemy. 'If at first you don't succeed, try, try again' certainly paid off in these particular situations. The more times you come into contact with the enemy the greater your chances of getting hit become. Clearly then, the infantry was, or was not, the place to be, depending on ones outlook. After my first encounter I decided it wasn't the place to be.

It was decided our services were no longer needed by the men on the mountain. It was not the last time we would be called to the top of Hong Kong mountain. We were herded onto the choppers and in an instant were airborne, leaving the mountain in a cloud of dust from the whirring rotor blades.

Flying high, the cool air felt refreshingly clean blowing on my fatigued face. Looking down I could see the rich green foliage below. The jungle below was spread out like a green quilt, the unbroken expanse interrupted by an occasional square of another color, indicating a rice paddy. Meandering through was a small river. Its silver cast offered a strange contrast to the green which seemed ready to snuff it out.

All too soon our journey was over. We landed at the helipad and started our walk back. Being in the middle of the morning the entire Division was busy in the construction of base camp. The engineers seemed to be everywhere, heavy construction equipment was in use wherever we looked. Roads were slowly being carved out of the landscape. Bridges would soon appear and creeks and pagodas would disappear just as quickly. I began to wonder why we couldn't borrow one of those bulldozers to help us clear away the jungle on the Green Line. The newly cut roads were quite muddy but this didn't appear to hamper the eagerness of the engineers. The wet season in Viet Nam is between April and October. As this was late September, we were nearing the tailing off period. Winter, November to February, is dry and relatively cool. From February to April the temperature and humidity start to rise and in April another monsoon season begins.

We soon found ourselves at the Company area, haggard and exhausted. Anticipating some sort of rest, if only for a few hours, we were astounded to hear that we must report immediately to the Green Line for further chopping and clearing duties. Powerless to do anything about the situation we sauntered off and spent the rest of the day whacking away at the jungle. The only break we got from the monotony was watching the

Vietnamese women urinate in their peculiar manner. As often as I was to see that incredible sight, I never could quite accept it.

After another evening meal of C rations Tom and I decided to ask permission to take a shower. We learned that the nearest shower point was over a mile away. The only way to get there was to hitchhike or walk. After the days of hard physical labor in the unrelenting sun a shower would have done us much good, both physically and mentally. We were soon standing on a recently formed road, rifles acting as thumbs in the standard hitchhiking pose. We were soon picked up by a Sergeant driving a jeep. He too was headed for the showers.

Arriving at the shower point, I thought half the Division was also there. The lines to use the showers were immense. Realizing we only had to look forward to digging more trenches back at the Company area we decided to wait our turn. The 'showers' were located in a large tent. The water was pumped from a nearby river into four standing pipes about six feet tall. Protruding from these pipes at various angles were some type of nozzle. Thus a large group of men could stand around these spraying devices, lather, and rinse off in a minimum of time.

At long last we reached the showers. Soon we had striped and were under the spraying water. The warm water spraying like needles on our aching bodies was pure ecstacy. Much too soon we concluded our brief showers with a feeling of regret. It had been well over a week since we last showered. I wondered how long it would be before we would get the chance again. As a matter of fact that was the first time I had had the opportunity to wash my hands with soap and water in over a week. The many cuts on my hands had become infected. I felt them immediately tighten from the medicinal effect of the soap. Keeping myself clean was to become a monumental but necessary aspect of living in the jungle.

CHAPTER 4

The next couple of days passed in the same fatiguing and monotonous manner as had all the others preceeding them. The days were spent in the hot, strength consuming sun, chopping at the loathsome jungle. The evenings were spent digging the trenches behind our tents. The only deviation from the ordeal was when someone broke their entrenching tool. The Sergeants, however, always managed to find another new one to replace it, thus ones relief was only temporary.

One particular day I and a few others were chosen to work on a special detail. The thought of not having to work on the damn Green Line made me temporarily ecstatic. My joyful feeling was soon shortlived when I found out the nature of our detail. We were assigned to construct a field urinal. The Company needed a place where the men could urinate in one central semi hygenic location.

The first step in the process involved digging a pit approximately ten feet wide and five feet in length. The depth of the pit was six feet. After the pit was dug it had to be filled in with stones. The stones at the base of the pit were large in size. As one neared the top the stones were to become progressively smaller until the last foot was covered in with a fine sand. The size of the stones acted as a filtering device for the urine as it filtered downward. Protruding out of the pit were five cylindrical tubes which previously had held some sort of rocket. They were approximately a yard in length. One foot of the tube was stuck into the sandy part of the pit. One merely had to urinate into the tube and the problem of sanitation was temporarily solved. The tubes worked quite well the first couple of hours. After that they started to fill and overflow. The net affect after a couple of days was the same as having no pit at all. The urine merely collected in pools and gave off a most obnoxious smell. After a long period of time it did filter downward but not in the manner intended. A few months later the whole affair was bulldozed under and a larger, but similar affair, was constructed away from the Company area.

We soon received word that a Company-sized operation was going to take place shortly. We would be gone for approximately two weeks. Everything we needed was to be carried on our backs. We were to be resupplied after one week with food and ammunition. The operation was one of merely search and detain. The infamous search and destroy missions would come later. We spent a whole day in preparation. Rifles were cleaned endlessly, equipment of every description was checked and double checked. The activities offered an escape from the drudgery of the past weeks. Something different was about to take place. No one, including the officers and sergeants, knew what was coming, thus we were uninformed as to what to expect. We were all relieved to be getting off the Green Line but at the same time hesitant to embark on such an adventure with no real idea of what to expect. "Hang loose and keep your eyes open" was the general reply we received in response to our many questions.

As all inexperienced troops are prone to do I was carrying much unnecessary equipment, including clothes for two weeks and other equipment that would never escape the confines of my backpack. The weight of the individual backpacks weighed at least fifty pounds apiece. Yet we would be expected to walk and run day and night in search of the elusive enemy. All the while our smiling faces were expected to be seen. Later I would look back and marvel at our stupidity. However, with inadequate leadership, one has to learn by trial and error. In this case an error usually meant ones life.

Nightfall found everyone packed and ready to go early the next morning. We expected a night of uninterrupted sleep but had to stand guard duty at our tents. We began to look on this as a form of harrassment. There were troops on the Green Line less than fifty yards away performing the identical guard duty we were forced to do. If any possible danger did materialize, their warning would have afforded us an ample opportunity to set up a defense. Thus we had more fuel to fan the already smoldering fires of disrespect for our leaders.

Pulling my turn at guard duty I was seriously considering going to sleep. What the hell could they do to me that they hadn't already done. I was being worked day and night to the breaking point. Jail couldn't have been much worse. The feeling of complete exhaustion had a powerful influence on my thoughts. I knew I couldn't go on like this much longer, then, out of necessity, I would fall asleep. I suppose I was merely trying to rationalize the inevitable.

Just as I was about to crawl into my tent and fall into a beautiful sleep I heard laughter off in the distance. As I strained my ears to concentrate on the noise I realized it was moving in my direction. It couldn't be V.C. I reasoned; they wouldn't be laughing in such an obvious manner. Who in the hell could it be? A few minutes later the laughter was only a few yards in front of me. Releasing the safety switch on my rifle to automatic I raised the weapon to my eye and was ready to scream 'halt'. Before I could utter a word the drunken voices of Tom Kirkwood and Barry Knight pleaded for whoever was on guard duty not to shoot.

"Don't shoot!. I ought to blow your mother fucking heads off," I responded in a voice filled more with anger than with fear. "Where in the hell have you been?" I asked.

"In town," responded Kirkwood. "Since we are so short we thought we might not get a chance to see it so we took off after chow." In the atmosphere of preparing for tomorrow no one had missed them.

"And look what we brought back," said Barry, simultaneously dropping a pile of goods. "Aren't they beautiful?" he said, pointing to some Oriental blouses and China dolls.

Before I could answer they began telling me how it felt to screw a Vietnamese woman. "Oh man, it must be like screwing a young girl," responded Kirkwood. "So small and tight."

"Beats those broads in Columbus," answered Barry.

Not wanting to appear ungrateful for their news I reminded them we were moving out early in the morning and they had better get their shit packed.

"Guess you're right," said Tom. "Catch you later." Picking up their trophys of the night they moved off toward their tent laughing all the way.

My eyes followed them with envy as they walked off. I was worrying my ass off and they go into town and probably had the time of their life. How they could remain so aloof of the present situation was beyond me. They weren't even worried one iota. Was that a blessing or was it a curse, I wondered.

Soon my turn at guard duty was over and I gratefully awakened Clark. The next thing I remember was the loud voice of Sergeant Rockwood telling us to "saddle up". No breakfast, no nothing, just "saddle up".

We moved out for the helicopter pad in Company strength. During the walk we passed Company after Company of non-combat personnel. As we walked by them they watched us with a curiosity I didn't fully understand. I felt immensely proud to be part of a real combat outfit. I suppose it was part of the manhood idea; the more dangerous the situation the more of a man one becomes. It was also possible they were wondering how anyone could be so stupid or unlucky to be in the infantry.

Soon the Company was loaded onto many choppers. After flying for what seemed hours, I suddenly saw a village below me. As we descended I could make out a large group of people pointing up into the sky at us. It was probably the first time in their lives they had seen a helicopter, yet twenty-five of them would soon descend into their backyard. What a rude awakening. The sight, judging from the look on their uncomprehending faces, must have been overwhelming.

A Company command post was immediately set up on the outskirts of the village. Our platoon, led by Lt. Cline, was soon humping it through the village toward the open terrain. As we walked through the village I could feel the eyes of the villagers following us every second. We were the first Americans these people had seen. I couldn't help but wonder how they felt about our presence. Would they accept us as conquering heros or would they turn on us during the night? Unfortunately many of them would choose the latter. Distinguishing the real enemy was to become the hardest factor in fighting in Viet Nam. Because many of the people did become Viet Cong when the mood struck them, we soon learned not to trust any of the Vietnamese. That was probably the most unfortunate aspect of the situation. Not trusting them it became increasingly hard to think of them as anything besides gooks. Gooks to be killed the instant we suspected them of any wrongdoing.

In a matter of minutes we had passed through the village. Stretching before us was open terrain consisting of dried-up rice paddies. Someone had seen male figures running toward the mountainous area miles beyond. We were going to go and look for them. The pace began at a fast walk but soon developed into a trot. The weight of the packs on our backs became unbearable. Why in the hell didn't we leave them at the command post and proceed with the bare essentials?

It was only late morning and already the sun seemed as though it was only a foot over our head. My neck was terribly sunburned. The pack, rubbing and digging on the tender flesh with each successive step, added to my misery. I had a burning desire to drain my canteen with one large gulp. To do so would have meant a case of the cramps. I settled for a short taste on my lips. As I did I was aware of the obnoxious taste of the water. However it was wet and those precious drops of water cleared my head for a few minutes.

After a couple of hours it became increasingly hard to concentrate on the simple matter of merely walking. Sweat was pouring down my face blurring my vision. Gnats, attracted by the sweat, were buzzing around my entire body. I felt like Atlas carrying the weight of the world. Just as I felt I could go no farther I heard the order to fall out and take ten. Grateful for the pause I searched for some shade in which to rest. I spotted Kirkwood walking over a small hill and disappearing from my view. I walked over to where he had gone. He and some others had found a footbridge and were collapsed underneath it in its refreshing shade. I immediately joined them. No one said a word. We all tried to catch our breath and allow strength to return to our bodies.

In what seemed like seconds we were ordered back on our feet. Lying on my back without the oppressive weight of the pack digging into me I was oblivious to what was happening to me. Reaching behind me for my harness straps I could feel the terrible weight on my shoulders before I actually put it on. Thinking about it made it worse. Thus I learned not to think about a task before doing it; merely follow through and do it. It seemed to help some.

Walking at an accelerated pace I found myself hoping someone would take a shot at us so we could stop and get rid of these miserable packs for a few seconds. We soon stopped but for a reason none of us had expected. Sergeant Woods, one of the other platoon sergeants, collapsed from the strain of the walking. It was just a matter of time before someone passed out so I wasn't really surprised. Instead I was grateful that someone had done something to stop our insane pace. We seemed to be running toward nowhere with no real idea of what the hell we were doing.

Twenty yards ahead of me I could see the crumpled body of Sergeant Woods lying on the scorched earth. The medic had his head cradled in his arms offering him water. The picture was reminiscent of a mother offering her breast to a newborn baby. Suddenly the imposing body of Lurch broke the tranquility of the moment. He was screaming and ranting at Sergeant Woods like a man possessed by the devil. I wondered if the sun hadn't gotten to him. When he finished screaming at Woods he began kicking him like a spoiled child kicking a toy. I couldn't believe what I was seeing. An officer kicking a sergeant. The fact that he was doing it in front of everybody made it seem worse. He soon spent his anger and moved off to where Sergeant Cannon was sitting. The order to break for lunch soon echoed out.

Searching for some shade my thoughts were taken away from the scene I had just witnessed. I spied some bushes and decided they would offer the best chance of finding some shade. Reaching them I was aware that there was but very little shade available. The sun was directly overhead offering but the barest amount. But there was some and I was determined to make the most of it. Removing my steel pot I laid down, pushed my head along the sandy ground under the thorny bushes searching for any protection from the burning rays of the sun. With the rays finally blocked I closed my eyes hoping for a few seconds to let my mind escape the present. Large black ants began crawling around and over my head. I was too weary to fight them. I had discovered the precious little bit of shade and was determined to keep it. Their bites soon became more than I could stand. I felt myself brushing them aside frantically and in a matter of seconds I was sitting up, again with no shade. I snapped off a large bushy branch and stuck it behind the elastic band which encircled my steel pot. Rearranging it with the finesse of a florist I succeeded in at least keeping the sun off of my face. Dirt encrusted, soaking wet and wishing I was dead, and all the while sitting there like a displaced Indian, I realized how ridiculous I must have looked. I began laughing at the thought of myself. Kirkwood sprawled a few feet away from me told me to shut up and quit acting so fucking stupid. His words brought me back to the present.

I opened a can of C rations and washed them down with the vile tasting water. If one can believe such a thing, the water, being in the plastic canteen, had actually tasted worse than before. It had become almost hot. This seemed to make all the chemicals react more strongly.

Oh God, how I wished for a cold glass of clear water. A lousy glass of water, something we all take for granted. Yet, at that particular moment in my life, I would have sold my soul to the devil for a few precious drops.

The food seemed to give me much needed energy. My head was clear and I reflected on Cline and his treatment of Sergeant Woods. I certainly didn't think he was right in kicking him the way he did. The one positive thing it did was give me and I'm sure everyone else, an inner strength. I would never give the son of a bitch the satisfaction of treating me like that. I would pass out before I would consciously fall out. By being a bad ass and showing he would not take failure of any kind, Cline would bring out the best or worst in all of us. The sound of "saddle up" brought us scrambling to our feet.

We moved off to our right for a couple of hundred yards then turned and began a fast pace back toward the way we had originally come. Buildings off in the distance but directly in our path would offer us some shade and a place to rest if only Lurch would stop.

He must have gotten the word over the radio that there were V.C. in the buildings as we slowed down and approached them cautiously. Having checked the various buildings, which were mud huts, in the most haphazard of methods we discovered no V.C. Lucky for us we didn't. The sergeants were busy trying to impress Lurch with their searching techniques and Lurch was busy impressing the sergeants with his. Each would issue orders more contradictory than affirmative. If there had been any enemy in the vicinity they could easily have killed many of us and made a successful escape. That is how disorganized we were. We departed from the area and for the first time, many of us were glad we hadn't confronted any danger.

We marched back to the Company headquarters and located our specific platoon area. All I could think of was resting under the branches of a large shade tree. I thought of the past days we had spent on the Green Line clearing those damn trees. Remembering how exhausted I was, I had thought my body couldn't possibly take any more. Yet here I was a few days later and had just withstood much more. I was suddenly very angry at my plight. I felt like I was being picked on by everyone around me. I hadn't done anything wrong; why in the hell was I being asked to go through so much hell? I had no answer.

While walking along a path toward our camp area, some members of the mortar platoon came into view. They were the men who handled various heavy weapons. As a result they did not go out on patrols and engage in combat in the same manner as did the infantry. When I saw them they were sitting under a large tree playing cards! Playing cards, I thought to myself. How dare they enjoy themselves when we are out running around in a hundred plus degree heat like a bunch of ignorant asses. I wanted to choke them for being so fucking lucky. Possessing more self control than that I merely walked on mumbling to myself about the injustice of it all. Suddenly I could control myself no longer. I screamed out the words 'mother fucker' with all the strength I could gather. I immediately began to curse everyone in sight. My actions surprised those around me as much as I surprised myself. How often is it when one is in an unpleasant predicament and wishes he could say these very words? But, out of upbringing and the dictates of society, one dares not. Ones feelings are pent up inside seeking release in another form. Here, however, no one gave a shit so I blurted out what was inside. I remember feeling much more calm and less hostile after the outburst.

After an hour's rest and a leisurely meal of C rations we found ourselves being marched off a short distance for guard duty around the Company perimeter. We set our trip flares and claymore mines in front of our positions to give us warning of approaching danger. After that was completed we had to dig two-man foxholes. After the strenuous activities of the past day I don't know where the energy originated from but it somehow found its way into my various extremities and allowed me to go on. After another night of interrupted sleep I found myself watching the sun rise. The sun, preparing for another days savage tricks with its unrelenting burning rays.

The sound of "second platoon, saddle up" didn't leave much doubt that we wouldn't be playing cards. Lurch had volunteered us again for some goddamn mission. We were going to pull security for an artillery outfit miles away in the boondocks. With a minimum of fanfare we were soon airborne in the ever present choppers.

We flew for miles over dense jungle spreading below us looking more ominous than ever. Landing in a naturally cleared area, contact was soon made with the artillery company for whom we were to provide security. Lurch evidently couldn't stand the thought of us sitting around doing nothing, for in a matter of minutes after landing he had the majority of us out on patrols, the purpose of which was never made clear.

The jungle in this particular area wasn't extremely thick as was the Green Line. Rather it resembled a thick forest. It was almost refreshing to walk under the green canopy. The air was clean and most importantly it was cool. If this had been another time we could have been mistaken for a nature group out on a Sunday excursion. However this was Viet Nam and the thought of the enemy presence was always in the back of ones mind. We covered many miles through the thick forest. It had been the first time since arriving in Viet Nam that I hadn't worked my ass off. As dusk was fast approaching we received word over the radio to report back to where the platoon was now located.

Arriving back at the point from which we left a curious sight greeted us. There, parked in the clearing, was a huge Chinook helicopter. The artillery company was loading the large weapons into it. They were obviously being moved to another location. The ability to move so rapidly with the maximum amount of firepower would soon become the trademark of the 1st Cavalry Division, its infantry, unfortunately, serving as its vanguard. I was fully expecting the order to come for us to board. The order that came was not to board but to dig in! The order fell on my uncomprehending ears. Of all the absurd things we had been asked to do, this was by far the most asinine. Dig in! The whole idea was simply uncomprehendable. There was nothing to do but follow through with the order. Laughing at the ridiculous nature of things, I began digging with Clark. At least the ground was sandy and afforded us the opportunity to dig a nice deep hole with relative ease. The hole reminded me of a grave. With night approaching, the feeling had a morbid flavor to it.

Our foxhole was ahead and to the left of a machine gun emplacement. Sergeant Cannon and two other men were on the machine gun. Having Cannon on the M60 and only a few feet away I felt relatively safe. As big a prick as he was, at least he wouldn't be shooting at nothing. To open fire usually meant everyone else in the immediate vicinity would follow. With all the firing by panicky individuals one wasn't always sure they would be shooting in the right direction.

Just as we were beginning to feel at ease, swarms of large horsefly-like insects descended upon us. Their bites were most painful. The only relief we had was to cover ourselves with our heavy plastic ponchos. Almost suffocating beneath the pastic cover I could hear and feel the insects bouncing off the plastic in their frantic search for our bodies. As fast as they appeared they mysteriously disappeared. Their presence was soon taken over by mosquitoes. Another unwelcome guest in the form of Lieutenant Cline also visited before the blackness of night engulfed us. He said something to the effect that there were no friendly troops in the area. If we heard anything we were to open fire immediately. This was a direct rebuttal of what we had been told previously. Prior to then we were told not to fire on anyone unless they fired first. All troops at that time were under the same standing order. He further stated that if there was any firing and no bodies to show for it our asses were grass. Judging from his actions involving Sergeant Woods I knew he meant every word he was saying. He left to pass the word on to the other men.

During the night a rain fell drenching everyone regardless of any precautions we took. Our foxhole was deep but not very wide. Soon we were ankle deep in water and mud. Lying down was an impossibility. Thus the few hours sleep we managed to get was attained by stretching the upper parts of our bodies out onto the wet ground and literally passing out. The foxholes represented safety and we were not going to jeopardize that safety by venturing out of them very far.

Just as I was about to fall asleep in this awkward position I heard the unmistakeable sound of voices. Slipping back into the hole with lightning speed I was suddenly wide awake. The adrenaline was gushing through my veins with an utmost urgency. I punched Clark and asked him if he heard the noise.

"Shit, ya," he said, his voice trembling with fear. "What are we going to do?" he whispered.

"Don't fire. Wait until Cannon opens up," I responded. "Besides," I continued, "it might only be a patrol. They may pass us right by."

"Yeah, especially if they are as organized as we are," Clark said, with a tone of cynicism.

The next ten minutes we sat in total silence. Only our breathing and the falling rain broke the silence. By now I was crouched on my knees, finger wrapped tightly on the trigger of my rifle, starring into the darkness. It was impossible to see more than a few feet in front of us. My imagination was running rampant. One thing was certain, the sound of voices was growing increasingly nearer and nearer. The sounds seemed to be of troops moving. Canteens, rifles, and other types of equipment banging against each other could now be plainly heard. Beyond any doubt troops were moving toward us. The voices were too far away to distinguish the language. Remembering what Lurch had said about no friendly troops being in the area caused me to imagine the most irrational things.

Slowly time passed, the voices became unmistakeable, those were Vietnamese voices. Since there were no friendly troops in the area they could only be those of the North Vietnamese. That realization almost brought me to the point of hysteria.

"Clark," I said, almost pleading for an answer. "What are we going to do?"

"Wait for Cannon," was his reply.

Shit, I thought to myself. He must have fallen asleep. Why wasn't he firing? They could only be fifty meters away, he had a clear field of fire, yet he wasn't doing anything. I was not thinking rationally and could only think of opening fire in the firection of the voices. My finger was steadily increasing its pressure on the trigger. I felt that by firing, the problem would go away. The voices by now were only twenty yards away. I had never known such panic as I experienced then. I suddenly envisioned myself crawling over to Cannon and asking what in the hell he was waiting for. Realizing the futility of such an idea, I broke my thoughts by telling Clark I was going to fire. I hoped the noise would awaken Cannon and prod him into action.

I crouched lower into the hole, my eyes barely able to see over the top. By now the voices were directly in front of me, a few yards away. I squeezed the trigger with all of my might. I was expecting the loud explosion of the round being fired. To my amazement nothing happened. I looked at my rifle, and discovered I left the goddamn safety on. Releasing it and preparing to squeeze off the round I heard the unmistakeable voice of an American saying "Halt." My first reaction was to associate the voice with Cannon. But it had come from the direction opposite him. I was suddenly overcome with bewilderment. What in the hell was going on? I was about to scream out, who goes there, when those exact words were shouted by Cannon. After a few seconds of silence, which seemed like an eternity, the unidentified American voice identified itself as Special Forces. I heard Cannon bolt from his foxhole and I could hear him approaching the individual. After a brief discussion Cannon approached us and told us they were South Vietnamese troops led by an American advisor. They were going to camp in front of us and there was to be absolutely no shooting of any kind.

My God, I thought, I almost killed an American. If the safety hadn't been on we might have all been killed.

To have fired into such a large group would have meant a chain reaction by everyone on both sides. Thus there would, in all probability, have been a large loss of life. The thing that really irritated me was that it would have been my fault. How in the hell could I live with that? I was disgusted with myself for panicing in the situation. I would have to be extremely careful in the future, or there may not be a future.

The realization of knowing that I held the power in my hands to actually kill someone brought a wave of nausea over me. I had thought about killing someone many times before. Now, however, I had actually faced the situation and had reacted in a manner I wasn't proud of. I couldn't help but think of what could have happened if the safety hadn't been on. At the same time I realized that I had answered the question that had been nagging me for so long. I knew that if faced with another similar situation I could kill another human being with no hesitation.

The fact of knowing that I could kill someone was most important. Feeling quite content I managed to fall into a deep sleep while Clark pulled duty for the few remaining hours of darkness.

The chirpping of birds awakened me just as daylight was beginning to unfold. Immediately the events of last night flashed into my mind for a few seconds. Suddenly I was very anxious to see the individuals whom I had almost killed. Furthermore, I had never seen South Vietnamese Forces and was quite excited to do so. What I saw was in no way what I had expected.

The foreign troops in front of me were starting to awaken. Formless piles of blankets and sheets of plastic evolved into men. The first thing that impressed me was their small size. I hadn't expected them to be tall but their very short stature was most unexpected. Standing 5' 10" and weighing 175 myself, I felt like a giant when compared to them. Their youthful appearance was also surprising. They all looked in their early teens and, in some cases, that was a generous estimate. I could have been looking at what a children's crusade looked like hundreds of years ago.

After gathering their equipment they began to assemble into platoon size formations, ready to move out into the jungle. With the American advisor they began to file past us. As they passed us their eyes met ours and to a man each broke out into a big grin. It was as if they were saying thanks for being here. For the first time since being in Viet Nam I had the feeling that someone was grateful for our presence.

Even though they had the weapons indicative of an Army they certainly didn't look like one. Each man, as he filed past, was wearing a different uniform than the man in front of him. Some had camouflaged fatigues, others merely had green shirts and trousers, obviously civilian in nature. The footgear was also equally rag-tag. Shoes and boots of every description was in evidence. Many of them were wearing shower shoes! Some were wearing steel helmets, others were not. Berets of various colors seemed to be the most popular. I wondered if this was a French influence from another time.

Their organization and behavior did not appear to be indicative of a well-trained Army. Many were carrying pots and pans of every size and making no attempt to keep them from banging against each other. There was no standardization whatsoever in any of their equipment. The most fantastic sight was in seeing the live animals they carried on their backs. Ducks, chickens and other assorted birds were inside bamboo cages. The cages were carried anywhere on the body where there was room. Some individuals were carrying live pigs strapped across their shoulders. The animals, not being muzzled, were making their own peculiar noises. Seeing this, I wondered what kind of upper echelon management the South Vietnamese Army possessed. Obviously it wasn't much.

The one aspect of the troops which was an indication that they were an Army was the weapons they carried. The weapons were almost as large as many of the men who carried them. Thus they looked larger and more impressive than they really were. The weapons looked new and very powerful. I wondered how well these little people could handle such monstrous instruments. But then by the same token none of us were exactly experts with our newly issued M16's.

I had expected perhaps a Company-sized unit to be in front of us; roughly 200 men. What passed before me during the next hour was a Battalion-sized unit; four times the size of a Company. Each succeeding unit appeared to be in rougher shape than the one preceding it. No matter how rag-tag they appeared one couldn't help but be impressed by the amount of equipment they carried. Being much smaller than us they were nevertheless carrying much more than we. From that moment on my own cumbersome pack would always seem lighter.

They also carried their weapons in a most peculiar manner. We had always been taught, and it had been drilled into us, to carry our weapons in a ready position. This meant carrying them with the butt under our arm, barrel outward and finger near the trigger. This facillitated a quick firing position if the need should arise. The troops in front of me were carrying their weapons in a manner which seemed to me quite unorthodox. The style was a standard method of most Vietnamese forces. The men would hold their rifles by the barrel and rest the butt of the weapon on their shoulders. A position exactly the opposite to one which would be appropriate to taking action in a sudden and unexpected situation. The excuse of inexperience could probably be used to justify their slovenly appearance. Nevertheless I felt apprehensive at having them as allies. Ones personal appearance isn't necessarily a good criterion by which to judge their fighting ability, however, I do believe that when an entire Army is in disarray the results can't be very promising.

Shortly after the last of the South Vietnamese passed our location, Lieutenant Cline arrived on the scene. Without asking for an explanation from anyone in regard to what had transpired, he began dressing down Sergeant Cannon in front of everyone. Watching him tower over Cannon and seeing his face become redder and redder with each passing second, I suddenly felt very sorry for Cannon. He had no recourse but to stand there and be subjected to the worst kind of humiliation. Lurch was especially incensed over the fact that he saw no dead bodies lying around. Cannon tried to explain that he had waited until he was sure it was the enemy in front of him before he fired but his explanation was falling upon deaf ears. Cline was in no mood to listen rationally. His orders had been to fire at any movement and, as far as he was concerned, they had been disobeyed. The fact that there were no bodies seemed to especially infuriate him. It was as if seeing dead bodies was the only acceptable answer. The fact that they could have been bodies of our allies didn't seem to matter. I was stunned at hearing this absurd diatribe by Cline. The fact that he was absolutely serious made it all the more horrifying. I suddenly had a queer feeling that Lurch was going to be responsible for many asinine predicaments. I was going to be right.

Our reward for screwing up his orders was most unappreciated. Rather than fly back to where the Company was located, we were going to walk. The march took the best part of the day. There were only a few breaks and they came because Lurch himself had become tired. The journey took us through terrain we had not encountered before.

The jungle, although thick, did not require a machette to chop our way through. Progress was very slow. The vines and entwining plants were like an elastic spider web. The harder one fought against them, the deeper one became enmeshed in its tentacle-like grip. Large areas of very tall grass quickly became known as elephant grass. It got its name because of its height and rough leather-like stalk. It grew so thick and tall in places that before it was possible to pass a man had to hurl himself directly into the grass. Then using his weight he had to press it down until it was possible to walk across it. It should be remembered that this was being done under the blazing sun and carrying those goddamn miserable backpacks added to our misery. Naturally, our progress was very slow and deliberate. We had, as yet, not encountered any booby traps of any kind. The threat of them would come only too soon and would present more fear and worry.

Due to the fact that we became lost we only changed directions two or three times. Getting lost in the jungle was a routine procedure. Evidently map reading was low on the list of priorities for our officers. The word soon spread among the men that we were nearing base camp. I, and everyone else, seemed to acquire a sudden burst of energy at the good news. Shortly, after exiting from a stretch of jungle, we could see the rough outline of "home". We crossed an open area about fifty meters wide. The barbed wire that met us was quickly climbed as our safety waited on the other side. It was as if the wire was a definite line existing to keep all the danger outside.

We were allowed a short break, barely long enough to enjoy a cigarette. Finishing my cigarette and feeling quite pleased that another day was about to pass, I was startled to hear Kirkwood blurt out that we had just crossed a fucking mine field! Standing and looking over to where Tom was standing I could see that he was pointing to a newly painted sign. It was clearly marked in big red letter--Mine field, No trespassing. Quite naturally it had been posted to serve as a warning for anyone leaving base camp, but not for anyone entering. If the sign were true, and I saw no reason to disbelieve it, then it was truly a miracle that no one had stepped on one of the mines. We had walked across the area in a most haphazard fashion. Men were walking abreast rather than in single file. I couldn't understand how at least one mine hadn't been set off.

But if what I had experienced over the last week, and especially the last couple of days, was characteristic of the Army's competency, then indeed it was understandable. Someone had fucked up royally or we had been astronomically lucky. It was probably the former.

We found ourselves back at the Company area shortly after the main body of the Company had arrived. The feeling I had was one of happiness for arriving back safely. The tragic thing was that I hadn't been overly concerned about the Viet Cong but by our own incompetency. I could only hope that in time we would become much more experienced and wise in the ways of fighting in the jungle. It would take tragedy after tragedy but the 7th Cavalry would emerge as one of the best and bravest units in Viet Nam. General Custer himself would have been proud. At least those were the words we were to hear time and time again from our illustrious leaders. It seemed that by making the analagy to Custer, our officers were paying us a compliment. Judging by Custers record and his own rather uninteresting ending, I, for one, didn't care for the comparison.

The next week or so passed slowly and monotonously. Each day was the same as the preceeding one. Chop on the Green Line all day and dig our silly little trenches in the evening. The nights passed even slower, if one can imagine such a possibility. We had guard duty every night and the waking up every two hours made them twice as long as they really were. The only change in the routine was when Lurch volunteered us for any patrol that came along. The one positive aspect that came of the patrols was that we did gain valuable experience.

The food consisted basically of C rations. Occasionally these were supplemented by hot chile. The chile often caused one to develop a case of diarrhea. Even though the food was warm, the majority of the men chose to eat the bland C rations. Harrassment by the NCO's was at an all-time high. I felt it was just a matter of time before someone would get shot. It happened a day before the Company moved out on another mission, which was to last two weeks.

It happened in another Company, but I personally knew the Sergeant involved. He was Sergeant First Class Gonzales. He had been my platoon Sergeant while we had been stationed in Ft. Benning. Through a stroke of good luck he had been assigned to another Company just prior to leaving for Viet Nam. All of the Sergeants engaged in harrassment but no one could top Sergeant Gonzales. He was the best at driving an individual to the point of collapsing. Most Sergeants knew when to quit. Gonzales, however, took a sadistic pleasure in driving the individual even further. He was equally adept at punishing an individual both mentally and physically. He evidently had pursued his favorite pasttime one too many times. I don't know exactly what he did as there were just too many rumors to accept one story over another. Suffice to say he was shot in the legs at very close range by an individual of lower rank brandishing an M60 machine gun. I wasn't especially sad at hearing the news for I had felt the wrath of Gonzales on more than one occasion. I did hope that the incident would cause the other Sergeants to become less stringent in their demands.

After another night of restlessness and too few hours of sleep, the morning arrived. Another order to "saddle up" was issued. As usual we were packed very heavily but not in the manner as before. Gone were the excess clothes, blankets, and undesirable food. In its place were extra rounds of ammunition, hand grenades, claymore mines and other items necessary for killing.

Moving out toward the helicopter pad we again passed through Company after Company of non-combat troops. I noticed a most interesting sight. The majority of individuals in these areas had the opportunity to devote time on their personal living areas. Many of them had constructed living quarters off the wet ground. The men had been quite ingenious in the use of materials and knowledge of construction. All in all they looked quite comfortable. I thought back at the area we were living in. Living in the mud with various insects it was easy to understand why I had felt envious of these other troops. The disparity between the types of living conditions and treatment in general became wider and my envy increased with each passing day. The thing that really pissed me off was that these same individuals were getting combat pay. The closest these guys would get to a VC was screwing a female VC agent in some An Khe whorehouse.

Passing the last non-combat Company we came to the helicopter pad. We boarded and were soon airborne. Stretching below me was the green jungle looking as foreboding as ever. Thoughts of death raced through my mind.

We landed near a village consisting of the usual mud huts. A Company headquarters was set up. The next couple of days were spent chasing or rather searching for VC suspects. We neither found nor saw one bona fide suspect. Walking at an unmerciful pace set by Lieutenant Cline we grew increasingly frustrated. The sun was unbearably hot and seemed to become only more intense with the passage of time. Lieutenant Cline was aware of our frustrations developing from our endless, meaningless chases. In order to break the monotony he volunteered us for a different type of duty.

Our orders were to secure the top of some high, but nameless, mountain. Once on top we were to cut a landing zone and set up a 50 caliber gun for its protection. The thought of being in one place for a couple of days was most pleasant. Walking to the top was anything but pleasant. The mountain was not very high, however, it seemed straight up. The thickest jungle we had as yet encountered covered it completely. In addition to our personal equipment, which was heavy in its own right, we had to share carrying the 50 caliber machine gun which was extremely heavy as well as cumbersome. Progress in climbing was very slow. In order to move upward it was necessary to grab hold of whatever vine or tree was available and pull ourselves upward step by step. After an agonizing couple of hours we finally reached the top. Some of the men were immediately assigned to clear away the trees and brush to form the helicopter landing zone. I and others were assigned to clear a field of fire. After hours of hacking away at the growth we were allowed a break. Relieved to know a break was coming I was particularly shocked when I found out I and two others had been picked to go down the goddamn mountain for water. A creek was at the base and we were to fill up the canteens for the platoon. I had been so excited to reach the top because it meant an end to tiring ordeals. Now I was being asked to go down and then up again. Jesus Christ, I thought, what next?

Going down required more energy than going up. The slope downward was steep and slippery. One had to hold onto a branch and slide downward to a point where ones balance could be maintained. The process was repeated until we reached bottom. Along the way we fell many times. The scratches and bruises were mounting. Our arms had countless scratches, some deeper than others. No wonder the mosquitoes couldn't wait to get to us; they had their blood with a minimum of work.

We had the canteens filled up in record time. The thought of being separated from the rest of the platoon made us uneasy. The water we used was taken from a standing pool. It wasn't especially clear but we figured our purification pills would do the necessary job.

The climb back up the mountain was harder than it had been previously. The weight we carried was less than before but our physical state was near the point of collapse. After much agonizing effort we reached the top. We distributed the canteens and began chopping and digging with the rest of the men.

I was digging my foxhole when I encountered a large rock that was extremely hard to extract. Seeing it as a challenge I was determined to remove it. Digging around it in order to get a grip on it I succeeded in getting both hands around it. With a hard pull I dislodged it. What I saw beneath the rock caused my heart to skip a beat. Only a few inches in front of me was a nest of small scorpions. Because of the sudden flash of light upon them they were scurrying around with their tails arched in the familiar attack pose. I found myself enchanted by their beautiful scarlet red color. How so beautiful a color could be wasted on such a vile insect was beyond my understanding. Realizing they were about to escape from the rockhole I immediately slammed the rock back in its initial resting place. I filled the cracks around the rock with dirt. I hoped they didn't try and dig their way out. We already had enough to worry about.

For the first time the night didn't seem so frightening. In this particular instance we had the upper hand. If anyone tried to approach our positions coming out of thick jungle they would surely be spotted. Our field of fire was cut outward for a distance of about twenty feet; beyond that point it was total blackness. Our claymore mines and flares were put on the edge of the jungle. If they were tripped we would have ample warning in which to retaliate. This was the way I was to spend the majority of my nights in Viet Nam. Lying in a hole starring into blackness, waiting for the enemy to come. Only the flash of a flare to tell me if he had come.

The night passed safely but not pleasantly. A rain had fallen again and succeeded in making the situation unpleasant. Since arriving in Viet Nam there hadn't been too many nights in which I remained dry. While sweating profusely throughout the day and the rain drenching us at night, I began to feel like something aquatic.

The next day we heard news that made us ecstatic. We were to stay on top of that mountain until further notice. The prospect of not walking or running in the oppressive heat was the reason for our jubilation. We began estimating on how long we would remain there. Everyone was hoping it would be for at least a week. Even Sergeant Cannon was expressing a desire that it would be for a long time. The time spent there was a little less than anyone anticipated. We stayed there a total of six hours. To say that we were dejected would be putting it mildly. Broken-hearted would be a more adequate term. The effect on our already low morale was crushing. We felt that we had been cheated. To feel brokenhearted and cheated at being able to spend a few lousy hours on top of a mountain in the middle of a jungle shows the low mental state we were in.

Loading my gear in almost absolute silence I glanced at the rock that protected the scorpions. With one swift kick I dislodged it and watched the red heinous insects swarm out. I hoped some gook used the hole and got bit in the ass.

The trip down the mountain was interrupted by various individuals slipping and falling. Many of them would fall long distances. They would go one way and their equipment another. Trying to be extra careful was usually worse than acting natural in such a situation. It usually caused one to over react. The comical scenes afforded everyone a chance to laugh. The effect of laughing at ourselves did us much good. It was especially funny watching the Sergeants succumb and follow suit. Lurch was so far ahead of everyone it was impossible to tell if he had fallen. I hoped he had.

After many stops to retrieve equipment we finally reached the bottom. Lurch was already there, standing in his usual superior manner hands on hips. His radio man was receiving orders. As a result we moved out immediately, not even resting for a cigarette.

Our objective was a hamlet, miles away. Evidently there were suspected VC in the area and we were to round them up for identification. The mission took us over rolling foothills which we spent the next couple of days traversing. In those couple of days we saw no one.

The vegetation was starting to change as we proceeded onward. The trees became more numerous as did the surrounding vegetation growing around their bases. The trees were not particularly tall, however, they were magnificently full. I had never seen such luxurious growth. Such beauty seemed out of place here in the middle of nowhere. As we walked on, the branches were so thick and low that it became necessary to walk in a stooped position and in single file. It was a perfect place for booby traps to be set. However, being inexperienced, that thought was not even in our minds. We were also walking extremely close to each other, a very dangerous habit.

There was much joking and general grabassing going on between the troops. No one was being especially serious about the game of war. But we had been in Viet Nam for some time and had not even fired a real shot at the enemy. As a result we had lapsed into a most lackidasical attitude. This attitude was especially rampant among the lower enlisted men. All we had accomplished was walking many, many miles and chopping many, many trees. No one was prepared for what immediately followed.

While walking through the thick vegetation I had become entangled in some thorny branches of a low lying tree. I was completely engrossed with removing my harness strap from the vines when a sudden explosion broke my concentration. The sound came from a short distance in front of me. Due to the thick growth it was impossible to see what was actually happening. I had no time to ponder the situation as the scream for "medic" came ripping through the air.

Our platoon medic, Corporal Sweeny, came past me on a dead run, heading for the plea of help. No one knew what was happening; as a result we were standing around as if in a daze. Again not knowing the truth of the moment was the most difficult thing to endure. Was someone shot by a sniper? Were we being attacked? Or had there simply been an accident. Not knowing what had happened we didn't know how to react. Not knowing how to react is a very frustrating experience. It is especially frustrating when one is in a situation where any moment may bring sudden death. Sergeants of various rank were standing around in as much a daze as were the troops. Being inexperienced was, at this point, a most definite disadvantage. Standing there very disorganized made us very vulnerable to any sort of attack.

Lieutenant Cline, who had been up front where the explosion originated, came running back to where most of the men had become bunched up. He had a look of panic on his face and it was the first time I had seen him with such a worried look. It made him seem almost human. He began shouting orders for everyone to begin chopping a landing zone immediately. We found a spot immediately to my left where the trees were not especially thick. With entrenching tools and bayonets and anything else that had a tip or cutting edge we began chopping at the spindly trees with all of the energy we possessed. Cline left our group, returning a few minutes later yelling, "faster, faster, a medivac is on its way. By the time it gets here I expect a place for them to land." He turned his attention to his radio man and began yelling grid coordinates of our location to someone on the other end. In a matter of moments we could hear the whirling blades of a helicopter off in the distance. To facilitate its finding us, he pulled the pin on a couple of yellow smoke grenades and tossed them a few feet from our position. Hopefully the chopper would see the smoke and save a few precious seconds in trying to locate us.

I still didn't know what had happened and was full of curious wonderment. I knew it wasn't good or there would have been no need for the medivac. The medivac located us shortly and was soon on the ground. Two older and more knowledgeable-appearing medics jumped off and ran toward the area of the explosion. In a matter of moments they returned, their arms around Pfc Maddox and Pfc Simpson, aiding them as if they couldn't stand up under their own power. They had bandages on their faces and arms. Their shirts had been ripped off; in their places more bandages of various sizes dotted their backs and stomachs. Blood began to stain the snow white cloth. Blood was seeping out of various holes scattered sporadically over their upper bodies. Maddox also had blood seeping through his trousers. One didn't have to be especially experienced to realize that they had set off a booby trap of some sort.

The look on their faces was one of total shock. They looked like they were a million miles away. Their eyes had a peculiar blank look. It was as if they were not comprehending what was happening to them. The sight of all the blood made me nauseous. I turned away from them to avoid the grisly sight. It was nothing compared to what I was about to see.

As they passed and boarded the medivac, the call for two volunteers to come up front offered me an oppotunity to leave the scene. Moving on the double to the front of the trail we had been following I reached the area where the booby trap had exploded. Lying on the ground in a crumpled heap was Sergeant Wilson. He was lying on his stomach in a fetal position. On any other day it would have appeared as if he was napping. However this was one nap from which he wouldn't awaken.

Two troopers had cut some saplings and were preparing to strip off their shirts. They would push the limbs through the sleeves of their shirts and form a very crude but efficient litter. It took a number of individuals to pick him up as he was a large man. I reached down and grabbed one of his legs while others lifted his arms and trunk. With much struggling we managed to lift him onto the litter. It was then that I saw the damage that had been done to him.

While on the ground the front part of his body had been hidden. Lying face up on the litter one could see what was left of a once recognizable warm and friendly face. Now one half of it was gone as was the upper part of his neck. His jawbone was fully exposed beneath the raw red meat. It had been broken and was dangling downward through the hole in his neck, much like the snapped wishbone of a chicken. His eye on the same side was gone as was much of his lower forehead. Blood was everywhere on his face and upper body. The sight was completely overwhelming to me. Someone threw a poncho over him to cover the terrible sight. We carried him to the helicopter as if we were in a trance. I was carrying the rear part of the litter and noticed one of his arms slipped from its resting place and it dangled freely. Blood was dripping down his fingers and onto the ground. It was if he was making a path toward the helicopter. We put him on the medivac and in another second it was gone, as was the life of Sergeant Wilson. It didn't seem fair. He was one of the best-liked Sergeants in the whole damn Company. He was also near retirement and had a large family to support. Now he was gone and his family would never be the same, nor would I. What was it all for? He died on some unknown hilltop thousands of miles from his loved ones. Try as I might I couldn't justify it. Nothing made sense.

We turned to our left and began descending the hilltop we had been on. The order to watch for booby traps was ringing in my ears. As I was about to descend the hill I heard another explosion. Quickly glancing to my right I saw Sergeant Rockford being hurled into the air. To my amazement I saw him immediately rise and he began laughing, obviously out of nervous relief. He had stepped on a mine but in such a way it did him no harm. I didn't wish him any bodily harm but I couldn't understand how a mother fucker like that could escape injury and a guy like Wilson die. There didn't appear to be any justification for the events in my mind. I suppose it was merely luck.

Continuing out of foothills other booby traps were being spotted. One in particular was located in some branches about eye level, exactly like the one that Wilson tripped. It was composed of three hand grenades grouped together so that a tug on the branches would pull the trip wire. We had to pass underneath it as making a detour would have been too time-consuming. Passing underneath them I felt as though I was passing under a nuclear bomb. I could almost feel it going off the second I was under it. I have never proceeded with more caution in my entire life. I prayed silently for the first time in months all the way down the slopes of the foothills. When we reached the bottom a sense of security overwhelmed my entire body. I was glad I had made it and thanked God for bringing me down safely. I glanced up at the trees from which we had just come and could think of nothing but Sergeant Wilson's blood soaking into the ground. I was still trying to rationalize his death when the yell of "punji sticks" rang out loud and clear. Glancing downward at the ground I could see the vicious sharpened bamboo sticks sticking upward like the teeth of a tiger.

Punji sticks was one aspect of jungle fighting we had been warned about. Although we had been warned about them, this was the first time we had actually seen them. Seeing them for the first time makes them especially ominous. They are simply short lengths of bamboo sharpened to fine points and stuck into the ground like spears. To increase their effectiveness the VC urinate or deficate on them to increase the chances of infection for those that step or sit on them. Since they are usually placed on trails or near landing zones where unsuspecting troops are prone to come in contact with them they can be most effective, especially to the inexperienced. The new combat boots had a steel plate in the sole to protect from such an unfortunate encounter. However we were wearing the standard hot leather boots and they offered no protection whatsoever. It was to be many months before we were issued the new boot. That is unless one was fortunate enough to buy a pair on the black market. Since the combat troops were usually in the field it was the non-combat troops who usually went into town and got them first. The same rule applied to the lightweight jungle fatigues.

We continued walking, the new danger of punji sticks making us all the more cautious. I felt as though I was walking in the fires of Hell. The sun was beating upon us seemingly hotter than ever. In addition to our own heavy packs we had to share carrying the gear of the three casualties which had not been put on the medivacs when they left. The death of Wilson was like an extra weight on everyone's shoulders. It was the first death any of us had ever seen. The effect was numbing. No one knew what to say so we said nothing. The first death, because of its uniqueness, was the one most remembered.

Walking in single file under the hot sun like an unthinking animal I suddenly became aware of myself growing weaker and weaker. The weakness came on all of a sudden. It was a different feeling from that of fatigue. One always gets tired but the feeling I had known was a total submission. My entire body felt like rubber. My legs were losing their coordination and I was sure I was going to collapse at any second. Mercifully a break was called. I slumped, half squatting, by the side of the path, checking the ground quickly for punji sticks. Seeing none, I collapsed in a heap under the weight of my pack.

Smoking a cigarette and taking a few leisurely, long drinks of water, as vile as it was, I suddenly felt better. I hoped it was the emotion of the hour that was making me feel the terrible way that I was. After an extra long break we were back on our feet and moving at a slow pace through the knee-high grass.

Shortly we came to a highway and spotted a large group of Vietnamses civilians who were being detained by another platoon from our Company. The civilians were mainly comprised of the usual women, children and old men. There were a few military age males but they were obviously rejects due to their twisted and misshapen bodies. Our platoon took charge of the group and were to march them to some detention center in order that their identification could be authenticated.

Looking at the individuals I was suddenly filled with the most vile hatred I had ever experienced. Some of them most surely had been responsible for the setting of the booby traps we had encountered a few miles back. I thought of Sergeant Wilson and suddenly wished these peasants would discover a similar fate.

There were large water containers that had to be carried to the detention center. I was glad to see the women and old men being made to carry them. To my amazement, they picked the heavy containers up and began walking without a word of protest. I was particularly impressed with one young male who appeared to be crippled with polio. The container appeared to weigh more than did his own frail body yet he carried that goddamn water can for miles under the blazing sun without once sitting it down. When I had only a few minutes earlier been filled with hate, I was now overcome with a sense of curious respect. As we neared our destination I was again overcome with the feeling of weakness that plagued me a few hours before. In addition to the general feeling of weakness, my eyesight became blurred. Wiping away the sweat which was pouring from beneath my helmet did no good. I was beginning to see double. My legs became increasingly uncontrollable. They seemed to have a will of their own. I felt as though I was experiencing a classic drunk. My pace began to slow down and soon I was falling behind the other men in the platoon.

I was not going to fall out, for to do so I felt, would be to incur the wrath of Lieutenant Cline as did Sergeant Woods a few days back. I had never fallen out of any physically exerting activity and I wasn't about to start. But now it was as if I had no conscious choice. I wanted to continue but my body wouldn't let me. My legs refused to move and my head felt as if it was on fire. Slowly I sank to the sandy ground beside the highway, completely unaware of what was happening to me. The medic approached me and immediately popped a few salt tablets into my dry mouth. He assisted me in stretching out and stuck a thermometer into my mouth. Without saying a word he walked over to Lieutenant Cline and exchanged a few words. In a moment he was back. A smile was on his face when he said I was going for a ride to a rear medical battalion. A jeep pulled up to where I was lying. I was helped into the medical vehicle and in seconds we were bouncing along the dilapidated highway.

Rather than head for the rear area medical facility we headed directly for the Division's base camp. Evidently the rear medical company had a backlog of individuals. Thus it was decided to return me to the main area. I was not aware of what was wrong with me. I had a suspicion it was merely exhaustion and thought no more about it. Riding in the jeep was pure heaven. I was shielded from the burning rays of the sun for the first time in days. Realizing I was actually riding rather than walking brought a rare feeling of comfort over my entire body. I was grateful for the rest which I was sure wouldn't last very long.

Arriving at the main medical battalion I was led into a large tent. I was immediately overtaken by the coolness inside. The effect was overwhelming but in a most pleasurable manner.

An aide approached me and asked for my name and other pertinent information. I was asked to strip to the waist. Barely finishing the task, I was met by an officer who proceeded to give me a brief physical in a most nonchalant manner. I was then quizzed on what I had eaten, where our Company had been located in the last couple of days and finally, had I been taking my malaria pills regularly. Recording the information, he then proceeded to draw a blood sample from my arm. Watching the blood flow from my veins into the large syringe I was reminded of Sergeant Wilson. I could see his blood dripping down his lifeless fingers and onto the ground. The thought made me extremely nauseous and I felt myself fainting. The doctor, upon seeing my sick condition, responded with "I thought you guys were tough. You going to let a little needle get the best of you?" He obviously thought I was getting sick from the drawing of blood. I was in no mood to offer a defensive reply. The sight of Wilson lying on that path, blown apart, drenched in his blood, was etched in my mind. It would never leave.

The officer, finishing his work, pointed to a bed and told me to take a rest. The bed in reality was a simple standard army cot, canvas stretched taut between two wooden poles. There were no blankets or sheets. However, it was dry and away from the sun.

I fell onto the cot and was immediately overcome by a feeling of total well-being. The hard ground I was accustomed to sleeping on made this simple cot seem like the height of luxury. I was immediately overcome with the feeling of peace. The good feeling induced by the cot had the same effect as being engulfed by a cloud. I was simultaneously lulled into a deep sleep.

I awoke from this wonderous sleep many hours later. I was immediately aware of a loud ringing in my head. My pores were perspiring madly and my clothes were stuck to my body from the sweat. The coolness of the tent had suddenly been transformed into a suffocating heat. I struggled to take off my clothes but, due to my continuing weakness, it developed into an exhausting chore. My lips and throat felt as if they were made of sandpaper. Swallowing my saliva was very painful. I began to shout for some water or at least I thought I was shouting. After repeated shouts on which I swear the Devil himself could have heard, an aide appeared with a pitcher of water.

The water had a wonderful soothing effect on my lips and mouth. For a moment the vile taste of the liquid was forgotten. After drinking a couple of cupfuls, the orderly asked if I was hungry. The mere thought of food was sickening. Eating was out of the question. It was to be weeks before I would be able to swallow any solid food, regardless of what it was.

The water I drank had a continuing soothing effect on my condition. I began to feel cooler and cooler with each passing minute. Then a most curious thing happened; the coolness turned into a frigid cold. In seconds my body was covered with goose pimples. My teeth actually began chattering. The rest of my body began shaking uncontrollably. I felt as if I was lying in a snow bank completely nude.

Blankets were magically thrown over my shoulders and legs. Looking up I could see the orderly who had brought me the water staring at me with pity in his eyes. He looked as if he wished there was something he could do to relieve my suffering but he knew he was powerless to do so. I remembered the same helpless look when others had been gathered around Sergeant Wilson.

I knew something was dreadfully wrong but didn't have the faintest idea what it could be. Through my chattering lips I managed to ask the orderly what was wrong. His reply came matter-of-factly, "Malaria."

Malaria, I thought. How in the fuck did I catch that? I had been taking my pills daily, beginning two weeks before we even landed in Viet Nam. I knew the disease was carried by the Anopheles mosquito, but I had thought the anti-malaria pills offered complete protection. Could I have caught it from drinking some stagnant water? It was very possible as I wasn't always fastidious in remembering to use the water purification pills prior to drinking. As my body was covered with many mosquito bites, it was highly likely that I had indeed been bitten by an Anopheles type. I had the disease and there was no use in conjecturing how I got it. I now began to wonder how long I would be away from the rest of my platoon. I wasn't particularly anxious to get back because of the many hardships. At the same time it didn't seem fair having them do all the dirty work. I suppose wanting to carry my fair share was one of my unfortunate middle-class values. As the days progressed the guilt I felt for not being with my friends out in the boondocks weighed heavily on my mind. That is, when I was able to think clearly.

My body was undergoing something strange and completely foreign to me. Not knowing what was actually happening made me all the more miserable. I was constantly experiencing the changes from hot to cold. Overall body weakness was becoming more and more evident. Not eating only made my body more subject to deterioration. Being aware that it was over 100 degrees outside the tent and at the same time cowering under layers of heavy army blankets made the situation hard to cope with mentally. You know that your actions are completely unwarranted but, at the same time, your body is demanding action. Your mind tells you it is wrong, yet you follow through with inappropriate actions.

I don't recall exactly how long I lay in that tent, as the time passed in a blure. I received no medication and began to worry as my condition was growing steadily worse. After what seemed a couple of days I awoke from a frigid sleep to hear voices. I thought I heard the words "move out" and "Japan." The following time interval was quite foggy. I could see figures approaching me as if they were moving through a thick fog. My next rememberance was awakening in a much larger medical facility. Rather than a tent I was in a metal Quonset hut. Men were lying on cots with bandages and casts on various parts of their bodies. An entire head bandaged there, an arm there, an eye over there. Every individual seemed to have a different wound than the man next to him. I began to wonder if 2 people were ever shot in the same spot as another. All the cots had mosquito netting over them. It reminded me of a scene from a foreign movie. In time mosquito nets would be standard issue to all the troops but at this moment it was something new and strange.

An intravenous bottle was hooked up above me. I followed the tube downward to a large needle inserted into my arm. I watched the clear liquid enter my body drop by drop. Again I was watching something new happening to my body. The experience was frightening, but at the same time, fascinating. How many times had I seen this scene in hospitals and wondered what it felt like. I had never thought I would experience it. Actually undergoing the experience added something interesting to a dismal situation. I spent many hours watching the liquid enter my body and imagining I could picture it travelling to the various parts of my inner body. My fantasies made for a fantastic way to pass the time. I could see the fluid as if each drop was a separate entity, complete with its own brain. The trips they took through the arteries and veins were wonderous journeys as they tried to escape being absorbed into my system. When I urinated I imagined their escape was complete. The mind is truely capable of marvelous things.

While in this particular medical unit I began receiving quinine. As I was thinking more clearly than before, I supposed they were having a positive effect. I began to think I would be sent back to my platoon in a matter of days. Again, the feeling of wanting to go and simultaneously not wanting to, plagued my mind.

Just as I was beginning to notice progress in my condition, the hot and cold flashes returned. The time between attacks came more quickly and were more intense. The sweating was also more profuse. Going into this relapse while on medication, made me realize that I was more seriously ill than I had imagined.

While awake in one of my semi-conscious states I saw a face come into view. It was the face of an older man, showing many wrinkles of age. He was surrounded by a field of white, as if in a cloud. His steel gray eyes showed strength and I immediately felt a trust in him. I felt as though I was experiencing a spiritual being. Could this be an agent of God? His words quickly indicated that it wasn't. In a voice resplendent with goodness but indicating authority, he asked me, "How would you like to go to Hawaii?" Before I could answer he indicated I would be leaving on the next flight out.

I was too stunned to comprehend what was happening. I thought I had been talking to a spiritual being and was almost positive I was in Viet Nam. Having just been told I was going to Hawaii I couldn't be sure of anything. Perhaps the malaria was causing me to hallucinate. Was I really leaving or was it just a hidden thought in my subconscious that had been brought to the level of consciousness. When I felt myself being strapped onto a flight stretcher and the attendant call me a lucky son of a bitch, I knew I wasn't dreaming.

CHAPTER 5

On a beautiful day in October our medical air-transport landed in Hawaii. We were greeted by the medical personnel as if we were royalty. Hawaii had not as yet seen the influx of troops as did Japan. As a result the sight of us must have been a curious event. The personnel had been trained to heal and treat the sick in a wartime situation. Now they were getting their first practical experience.

The malaria cases were assigned to a special ward. After processing, we were assigned beds. Being bedridden, it was a real treat having people lift and carry me wherever I had to go.

Prior to being assigned a specific bed I found myself lying on a cart type apparatus in a hallway waiting to be taken to my bed. I was in a position to see many individuals I knew from my own Company as well as others from the Battalion. As I saw no bandages on any of them I assumed the majority of them had malaria. One curious aspect of the situation was that many of them were walking. Being too weak to lift my arms I thought this most unusual. I wondered why I was lying there feeling as if I was going to die at any moment and yet they were walking around as if they were on leave. Later, I learned that there are various strains of malaria. Furthermore, each type affects each individual in a different manner. Because of each individual's chemical makeup, two men could have the exact type of malaria and yet react in totally different ways.

One individual whom I saw pass by me brought a weak smile to my face. It was the huge cajun, Bordeaux. As he was getting out of the Army in less than two months, I felt relieved in knowing he was safe here in Hawaii. After he helped me in my sickly state on the troop ship, I felt a deep respect for him. I only wished those other troops in my platoon could be here with us also. As they were so near getting discharged, it seemed a special injustice they had to spend their last days in Viet Nam.

A voice weakly muttering "hey, man, how's it going?" took my mind off my friends back in Viet Nam. Turning my head I could see the chocolate brown body of Randall Thompson lying on a cart opposite me on the other side of the hallway. I was not mentally prepared to accept what I saw. Only a few weeks ago he had possessed a muscular body. His large chest and arms were particularly impressive. Looking at him now one would have thought him to be a different person. He must have lost at least twenty-five pounds. He was weak and soft looking, this frail appearance was especially noticeable where he had once been so muscular. The skin was drawn tight around his facial bones making his fatigued look appear all the more noticeable. His rich brown skin had an unusual faded appearance to it. I have never seen a black person look so faded; not even a dead one.

I was about to ask him how long he had been sick when he started having a convulsion. He started shaking in an uncontrollable manner. He was trying to draw his blankets up around his chin in an attempt to ward off the cold. I wished I could have helped him, however, I was powerless to help. All I could do was offer sympathy as I knew exactly what he was undergoing.

In a few minutes he stopped shaking and began sweating as if he were an icicle suddenly thrust into a direct heat. Sweat was draining from every pore of his body. I have never seen so much perspiration on an individual at one time in my life. Watching the water drain out of him as if he was punctured by a thousand needles, I realized why he had lost so much weight. I also got a view of what was happening to my body when it underwent one of its attacks. Weeks later I asked him what it felt like when he was having an attack. I was trying to determine what various individuals felt like when having an attack. His simple description was one of the best I heard. He stated, "I felt like a bar of soap that had been left in the water overnight; soft and useless." I could only laugh and realize how right he was.

Soon we were assigned to beds and the sight of clean, crisp white sheets greeted our weary eyes and bodies. After falling into a heavenly sleep I felt myself being gently awakened by an orderly. He was handing out quinine pills. Later he returned and withdrew blood for various tests. This routine of handing out pills and drawing blood samples was to continue for days. I was encouraged to eat but the mere thought of food made my stomach quiver and feel as if it wanted to explode. The only nourishment I received was through an intravenous feeding. I was beginning to feel that the i.v. bottle was an extension of myself.

After a week of this same routine my medication was changed from quinine to chloroquine. My particular strain was diagnosed as falciparum malaria. Evidently chloroquine was not an effective cure thus another type was tried. The daily blood samples must have given some indication that the newer medication was proving effective. My alternate attacks of chills and fever were slowly subsiding. The over-all weakness was to continue for weeks. The new medication was increased and after about three weeks it was determined I was to be taken off of the intravenous bottle. It was like losing a friend when an orderly disassembled the set-up. However, it meant that I was recovering and in that respect I was glad to see it go.

The next morning it was decided that my days of being pampered were over. I was to be issued hospital pajamas and sent down to the main kitchen for something to eat. An orderly brought me blue, two-piece pajamas and assisted me in getting dressed. He left and I suddenly felt very much alone. My whole body was extremely weak. To lift my body up from a prone position required all of my strength. The main kitchen was down two floors and on the other side of the hospital. The thought of going was overwhelming. I would never be able to undergo the actual experience.

A fellow trooper whom I had seen around the ward said he was going to the kitchen and offered his assistance. He looked relatively strong so I decided to at least give it a try. Merely standing resulted in my head swimming in the most light-headed manner. A hot flash came over me and I felt as if I were going to faint. My friend sat me on the bed and got me a glass of cold water. It was cold and so wonderfully fresh tasting. I felt as if I had drunk from the fountain of youth. Mentally it perked me up enough to want to try again. We decided to go halfway in a wheel chair and the rest of the way on foot. It worked.

I soon found myself standing in a line waiting for breakfast. The closer the line moved to the serving area the more conscious I became aware of a most obnoxious odor. The smell of eggs was becoming overwhelming. The longer I stood there the stronger the smell became. Its increasing intensity was causing me to become nauseous. I decided to stay and fight the feeling. Soon it became completely overbearing. I felt the vomit surging up from my empty stomach and into my mouth. The situation was completely out of control. I couldn't stand there but I didn't know what else to do. Being in a strange place I was unsure of where to find a washroom. I suddenly bolted out of line and double timed to the rear. My eyes began frantically searching the doors along the corridor for a men's room. As I passed door after door with no results I began to panic. My mouth was already full of vomit when I felt another upsurge coming. Walking faster I turned a corner and saw a round drum used for disposal. I reached it just in time. The upsurging vomit forced what was in my mouth out and into the drum. I spent the next couple of minutes vomiting and cursing the doctor for sending me down to the kitchen. Luckily I was out of view of any observing eyes. Thus my embarrassment was kept to myself. Surprisingly the vomiting made me feel a little better but I was by no means ready to go to breakfast.

I returned to my bed and reported the incident. For the next couple of days I was served meals in bed and lived a leisurely existence. My appetite was slowly returning and after repeated attempts of forcing solid food into my stomach I could feel a small degree of strength returning to my frail and weakened body. A month earlier I had weighed a solid one hundred and seventy-five pounds. Now, however, I was down to about one hundred and thirty. And that was a generous estimate.

Feeling a little more human I was able to reflect upon the past weeks. The majority of days were but a blank in my memory. Barely being conscious, there wasn't a great deal to remember. The things that stand out in my mind are the days of miserable existence I spent in going from the periods of fever to periods of frigid cold. The daily blood withdrawals stand out like a brand upon my brain.

As soon as I was physically able, taking a slow, cool shower was one luxury I promised myself. I spent so much of my time in the showers that I'm sure various individuals on the ward probably thought I was engaging in daily masturbation. Feeling the water cascading over my body had more than a mere superficial cleansing effect. In a manner, I could visualize the memories of the short but unforgetable month spent in Viet Nam being washed down the drain with the rest of the dirt.

Although the showers offered much comfort, they were also the source of much discomfort. Other individuals who were suffering from high fevers were often forced to sit on benches located under the shower head. Streams of ice cold water would gush down upon them like a river running wild. The thought isn't very heart rendering until one realizes that these men were out of their minds with fever. Screaming and thrashing about as if they were fighting death itself; they struggled incessantly with the orderlies. If the showers didn't produce the desired lowering of body temperature, they were often placed in an over-sized bathtub. A heavy canvas covering would be stretched across the top. A slit would allow only their heads to protrude. The water of course was ice cold. To make sure the water remained at a freezing temperature, trays of ice cubes would be added. To sit in this polar bear atmosphere must surely have been a torturous situation. Screaming and yelling at the top of their lungs usually resulted in more ice being added to the tub. Realizing the men were getting the ice treatment for their own protection should have made the situation understandable and easy to watch but I shall never forget those men imprisoned in their baths of ice.

My physical condition was steadily improving. Except for a few small reoccurrences of chills and fever the major fight was over. The doctor told me that these attacks would probably bother me for many, many years to come. As the years passed by they would become less frequent. That bit of knowledge somehow seemed to be a shallow consolation.

The ward I was assigned to was becoming increasingly crowded with new malaria cases. As they were much more serious than our original group which was responding favorably to medication, we were assigned to a new ward. I began to wonder how much longer we would remain in Hawaii. Having been there almost one month, I was expecting orders any day to return to Viet Nam. The news I received while in the new ward made me absolutely ecstatic. Because there were so many men suffering relapses it was decided to keep us for a one month period of observation. One additional month in this safe haven was almost too good to be true. The time spent in an army hospital is applicable toward ones total years tour. Thus I was getting by with what amounted to two months free time. The news perked everyone's spirits up to an extremely high level. I couldn't envision us lying around with nothing to do. The Army just doesn't work that way. My observation proved to be correct.

I was assigned to the laundry detail. This was relatively light duty. Above all else it was clean. After the time spent in the mud in Viet Nam that was the most appreciated factor of all. Our assignment was merely to fold the hospital sheets into piles of twenty, load them on a truck, and transport them off the hospital grounds to a civilian cleaning operation. The work afforded me many opportunities to leave the antiseptic environment of Tripler Hospital. Getting accustomed to seeing civilians in various aspects of day to day living, I felt a longing to join them.

It was possible to leave the grounds and visit Honolulu and all of its forbidden pleasures. However getting a pass was a complicated procedure. Thus by associating with individuals who knew various methods of beating the system, it was possible to visit the downtown area nightly and daily if one wished. Thus in time I was spending more time in the various bars of Honolulu than I was in the hospital. Lack of money proved to be the most allusive thing to possess.

While on ship many of us had signed papers allowing us to draw ten dollars out of our total paycheck while in Viet Nam. As everything was to be furnished free there was no need to draw the total salary. Many of us naive individuals saw this as an opportunity to save a few dollars. At the time I did not envision my spending two months in Hawaii, thus it was impossible to anticipate my present need. Plus, in keeping with Army proficiency, my records were lost and I was receiving absolutely no pay while in the hospital. Card games and being fairly good with a cue stick enable me to pick up a few dollars. Letters home also proved to be a means of procurring much needed money. Being friends with certain paratroopers enabled me to borrow money once in a while. They had a reputation for occasionally mugging sailors on the back streets around Pearl Harbor. This was not a daily occurence but when it did prove available I usually considered it a sort of bonanza.

My first trip downtown found me on a strip of Waikiki beach. The water was swilling around my ankles and the sun beating on my shoulders. My eyes were fixed on a point out in the ocean. Suddenly I was aware that I was looking at the spot where the troop ship had been anchored some months before. I remembered that day when I envisioned myself standing exactly where I was. An unexplainable eerie feeling engulfed my body. I was stunned that my premonition had come true to such a remarkable degree. From that day on any time I had a peculiar feeling about some event happening in the future I stopped and pondered it more than the average individual would.

Thus my second month in Hawaii was spent sunning on the beaches or drinking in some nameless bar. The main attraction was watching the tourists through jealous eyes throwing their money away. I wondered how many of them thought or even knew about the war in Viet Nam. Chances are not many of them cared one iota about the situation. Again the injustice of some suffering while others were enjoying the height of luxury in their expensive rooms seemed grossly unjust. On days that it rained and ruined countless vacations I felt perversely happy.

My nights were spent thinking of my fiance, Brenda, back home in Chicago. The last day of my leave, in one of my weaker moments, I had asked her to marry me. Having dated her for many months and never being able to seduce her into bed, I felt confident this method would succeed. Again, my ignorance was apparent. I felt at the time that I was in love but, as in so many aspects of life, what the hell does a twenty year old know? Thinking about her and her glorious breasts made it possible to pass many unpleasant moments in a degree of pleasure.

The one outstanding memory was our last night together in Chicago. We were in her front room, her elderly parents safely in bed a few feet away, but behind closed doors. Soft music was playing in the background making the atmosphere ripe for some sort of sexual action. A few drinks added to the feeling of ecstasy. Embraced in her incredibly soft arms, smelling her sweet perfume, my head grew lighter with each passing second. While my head grew lighter, my loins were growing hot and heavy. Mentally I felt this was to be my big moment. Surely I would succeed and have my first experience with intercourse. One must remember the year was 1965 and the sexual revolution had yet to begin. Being a good Catholic boy I had been led to believe in the doctrine of sexual abstinence. As I have said repeatedly I was very naive. However, she was giving every indication that my dream was to come true. Her kisses grew longer and more passionate. Our tongues searched the inner recesses of each other's mouths in a frantic attempt to find each other. I could feel her body growing warmer with each passing second. As my lips explored her silken neck and licked their way toward her voluptuous breasts, I could hear moans of pleasure coming from her throat. The moans were a signal to continue. With fumbling fingers I managed to undo the buttons which held her breasts prisoners beneath her lacy blouse. Caressing the incredible softness underneath her brassiere was driving me wild. Beneath the material I could feel the protruding nipple. It's hardened beauty drove me faster in my frantic search. I was too excited to stop and try and unhook her bra; that usually proved a precious waste of time. Instead I maneuvered one breast from beneath the confining bra. In seconds it lay before me in all of its resplendent glory. I immediately attacked the nipple with my lips and tongue. The more I sucked and kissed the more erect it became. I was reminded of myself standing at attention, but that thought only produced a smile on my already happy face.

My efforts in caressing her breasts was having the desired results. Her breathing was hot and coming increasingly fast. Her hand had been resting limply on my thigh only a few seconds earlier. Now, however, it was squeezing my erect, throbbing penis in a rapid and continuous manner. Since she was attacking my most prized possession, I decided to go after hers. I slipped my free hand beneath her pants and began to massage her patch of golden hair. Her panties proved to be a most unwelcome obstacle. With a slight bit of body maneuvering I was able to place one finger under the band of lace encircling her gorgeous thighs. Immediately they came in contact with a wet, sticky substance. I was going out of my mind with anticipation as I was sure this was the final signal indicating her body was ready to receive me. And God how I was ready.

With her fingers massaging my throbbing penis in such a rapid manner, I felt as though it was going to reach a climax at any second. I couldn't let myself come in my own pants, not when I was this close. I began to plead with her to go to bed; the more I begged, the more intent were her refusals. I was not prepared for her refusals as I was sure she was as anxious as I was. My finger began massaging her clitoris more rapidly. I felt progress was being made as the hot, sticky fluid was continuing to wet her silky pubic hair. I was at the point of going insane with desire and seriously considered taking her by force. As I was about to make one last plea, she suddenly bolted upright and put her breast in its proper place, which was not my mouth.

"We can't do it," she said in a serious but excited voice. "It will mean so much more when you come back and we are married." Like an ass I believed her puritan logic.

I left unsatisfied but the memory lingered on in my mind and offerred me solace on many occasions. I relived the scene many nights in lonely foxholes in the mountains of Viet Nam. The only difference was that my semen dotted the landscape from Pleiku to Phu Cat.

Thanksgiving Day was soon approaching. It brought misery rather than happiness. While watching the evening news about a week before Thanksgiving, I heard and saw events which left me absolutely speechless and wrecked my psyche for many years to come. My Company had become involved in a direct confrontation with North Vietnamese regulars. The results had been disasterous. The 7th Regiment had been completely annihilated. Only a handful of survivors were left to tell of the horrendous affair. The Company had been tricked into an ambush. The results were devastating. With the leadership we possessed, how could it have been any other way.

The confrontation had been the first major engagement of the war by American forces with regular troops from the North. They were better trained and equipped equally well as were we. The American forces were completely caught unaware. This was to be the first of many annihilations bestowed upon the 7th Regiment. We were indeed stuck with the curse of General Custer.

My immediate reaction to the massacre was one of total shock. My mind was a blank and for hours I could think of nothing. I could only see the faces of my friends, the majority of whom were dead, flashing before my eyes. After this initial blank phase wore off I began thinking of Sergeant Wilson's death. I hadn't really known him but yet his death became important to me. Probably because he was the first dead man I had ever seen. But the deaths of my friends was a different matter. These men I knew intimately. We lived, worked and shared our most personal feelings with each other. A great deal of comradeship had evolved. Only a few weeks earlier we had been together, going through hell together. Now, most of them were dead.

Why had I not been there with them? Was it merely luck that I had contracted malaria and escaped or was there some deeper spiritual reason that I had been spared. The question still remains unanswered in my mind to this very day. I began to think of their families. How would they react to their deaths? A feeling of sickness overcame my entire body. What made the situation so especially tragic was that they were all to be discharged in a matter of weeks. They paid their dues and now they were dead. I couldn't think of a more tragic sense of injustice. Most of the men were young and had their whole lives to live; now their lives were swept away like so many cobwebs. They didn't know what in the hell they were fighting for. Because they didn't have the connections to stay out of the Army they were dead. Other sons of bitches, many less worthy of living, were back in the States not even aware of what in the hell was going on. I took my hate out on the civilian population in general and the young males in particular. I immediately thought of the many tourists in Honolulu enjoying themselves while my friends had died and would continue to die. Thinking of them intensified my hate for them.

I was suddenly aware that in a month or so I was going to go back into that insane atmosphere. Only days earlier I had been happy due to my extended time in Hawaii. The thought of returning was pushed into the dark recesses of my mind. Now they were brought back into a glaring focus. Back into that blazing inferno where the people were hundreds of years behind times. And I was going to be asked to give my life for that! Thinking of returning produced a unique kind of fear inside of me. I had a strange feeling that something dreadful was going to happen to me just as it had happened to so many of my friends. There was no rational basis for such a deduction but nevertheless it was very much in my mind. I thought of faking a mental illness in order to escape going back. But something inside of me told me I would never be able to live with myself afterward. Going AWOL or deserting was not yet in vogue. The thought never entered my mind.

Rather than pushing the deaths of my friends out of my mind I began searching for every bit of information in regards to the actual battle. I watched the news programs from morning to night in search of answers. One battle was soon replacing another. What was new today quickly became stale the next. I felt dejected that the deaths of so many could be passed over so lightly by the media.

I came across a recent issue of Time magazine. To my astonishment the particular battle of Ia Drang Valley was covered in detail. The article gave credit for the fighting spirit of the men in the First Cavalry Division. That much made me feel better. One point in the article hit me very hard. The G.I.'s were on their first search and destroy mission of the war. We were finally taking the offensive. Search and destroy missions were to be the only type of activity we would undertake in the future.

The Ia Drang Valley was only a few miles from the Cambodian border in the Central Highlands. Thus my Division was right in the middle of the Ho Chi Minh trail. The area we occupied in the Highlands would in the coming years be occupied by no less than three full

Divisions. One can get an idea of the amount of enemy activity prevelant in the area. The article stated that the 7th and 5th Regiments suffered 240 dead and 470 wounded in the week of fighting. However, they were merely figures, cold and unfeeling.

Succeeding issues of Time would tell of the horror and heroism lived by the men I had once known. The more of the articles I read the deeper my hate for anything non-military became. My hatred for the North Vietnamese was reaching a level of unhealthy proportions.

One portion of an article told of the experiences of various men from my platoon. Brave Eagle was particularly interesting. He was wounded three times and the sole survivor of his squad. To call for help would have invited the NVA to respond, insuring his death. At one point he was so close to the North Vietnamese regulars that when they decapitated a wounded American soldier, blood squirted on him. Did I know that particular dead G.I.? I wondered.

After spending a week in the bush by himself with no food or water, Brave Eagle was approached by several of the enemy. One raised his rifle to shoot him, however, by raising his mangled hand and shaking his head no, the rifle was lowered, the enemy moved on and his life was spared. Brave Eagle thought the apparent young age, 16 or 17, of the enemy accounted for his survival. On the seventh day of his ordeal a helicopter spotted his frantic waving and dropped him some C rations. The fact that the meal was turkey loaf was supposed to be symbolic of Thanksgiving. I wondered what his reaction was at receiving those damn C rations. Of all the things in the world that could have been dropped one would think they could have dropped something else. A can of fruit cocktail would have been more appropriate, however to Brave Eagle, after a week with no food, it probably looked like steak.

I tried to envision the battle that my friends had died in. By re-enacting it in my mind I felt like I was a part of it. By not being there with them a feeling of guilt had developed in me. Thus, by thinking about it, I felt I was a vital part of it. Later, when I returned to Viet Nam, a talk with Harold Reed, son of the famous news commentator, made me realize how lucky I was not to have been in it. He showed me an issue of the Army Times, the official paper of the U.S. Army. It was their policy to list names of the dead. Without stirring up unwanted memories, suffice to say the list read like a roll call for my Company. I could almost see my name at the head of the list. I didn't particularly have a deep belief in God but, at that precise moment, I thanked Him anyway for not allowing me to be there. I soon developed the simple philosophy that life must be a hodgepodge of moments; some good and others bad. It was beyond my control to try and foretell the future. It was simply out of my control. Thus, one had to live for the good moments before the bad ones struck. I knew so many of the men who had died so damn well that I would have bet my life they could have come through any situation. Now, for some unexplainable reason, they were dead. Other bastards were walking around enjoying life. There was no other explanation except that they had simply caught the worst moment in their life. The tragedy was that it came much too soon.

My remaining days in Hawaii were spent in a fog of depression. I kept to myself and tried to make no new friends. Why bother, they would probably be dead in a few months anyway. After much delay, brought on to a certain degree by sympathetic doctors, I received orders to return to my outfit on December 13. The reality of having to go back was almost too much for me to handle mentally. I did succeed in avoiding flight after flight back to Viet Nam.

After one last phone call home, I decided to go back. I honestly believe my hesitant actions were not indicative of what a man's should be. Talking to my mother probably had something to do with my decision. Hearing her tear-filled voice somehow made me aware that I was acting like a punk of the lowest form. It was nothing she said that acted as a catalyst in my decision. Rather, it was knowing she and my dad had faith in me to do what was expected of me. I couldn't let them down. More importantly, I couldn't let myself down.

A short while later I was in the cargo section of a supply plane, heading for Saigon. I was not the same person now as I had been when I arrived. Physically I was in relatively good condition. My original weight was regained, although I was quite a bit weaker than I was previously. The biggest change was in my mental condition. I was developing into a cynic whose cynicism was to become most blatant. On the one hand I hated the Army and on the other I was glad that I was in it because I was proving myself a man in the way my society said I should.

I was full of a strange hatred for civilians and my hatred was especially vile in regards for the North Vietnamese. I was sure something dreadful was going to happen to me and I was willingly going forward to let it happen. I was going back to what I considered certain hell and nobody gave a shit except my parents. The rest of the world, especially the United States, was going about its daily business completely oblivious to the whole situation. In short, I was one screwed up young man. While in Hawaii I passed my 21st birthday, on November 29th. That was only a few days after the tragedy at Ia Drang Valley. I wondered if I would reach my 22nd birthday.

CHAPTER 6

After a short lay-over at Guam for refueling, we landed at Ton So Nhut airport on the outskirts of Saigon. A bus was waiting at the airport to transport myself and others to camp Alpha. Camp Alpha was the main receiving and discharging station for new and departing soldiers. Upon my arrival it was undergoing its initial phases of construction. The buildings at camp Alpha were comprised mainly of quonset huts. The camp had an air of familiarity about it. It looked like any other Army camp. Nothing but row after row of those sterile looking huts. Inside there was nothing but row after row of the standard bunk beds. Most of the individuals at camp Alpha were awaiting assignment to various Companies in Viet Nam. Thus some men waited only a few days for orders while others waited weeks. I was one of the lucky ones. My records were so screwed it took the Remington Raiders over a week to reassign me to my original outfit. Army competency was still at the same level I had envisioned it to be.

My time at camp Alpha was occupied by filling sand bags by the thousands. Christmas Day was only a few days away and there was absolutely no indication shown by anyone that they cared. Each day was exactly like the previous. I was particularly irritated by this lackadasical attitude, however, there wasn't much one could do under the circumstances. I would have looked quite silly celebrating the coming of Christmas by myself. Under the hot sun the other men would surely have thought I had suffered some sort of sun stroke.

One evening after a very busy day of filling sandbags, I was sitting alone engaged in deep thought. I had taken pictures of some of my friends during our voyage on the Patch. I was wondering if it would be appropriate to send them to their next of kin. It would be the last pictures anyone would have had of them while they were alive. Before I could arrive at an answer I heard my name being called by someone behind me. Stunned, I turned around and immediately recognized an old high school classmate I had not seen in over three years.

"Larry Famelli, you son of a bitch," I exclaimed. "What in the hell are you doing here?" I couldn't believe it was him; the odds of meeting someone from home must have been a million to one.

"The same thing you are," he said, grinning from ear to ear. "Fighting for my country," From the tone of his voice it was obvious he was being facetious.

We began talking about our happy carefree days back in Chicago Heights. Many of our classmates were in the process of being drafted. That is, the ones who couldn't afford to go to college.

After losing so many close friends I was especially elated at meeting Larry. It was good to talk and regain memories of something besides death and destruction. The topic of discussion got around to our duties in the Army. Larry was in the Engineers. His assignment was to be at Cam Rhon Bay, complete with air-conditioned barracks. I was immediately filled with a jealous feeling. I should have been happy at his good fortune, however, my feelings at this point were that anyone who wasn't in the Infantry wasn't worth a fuck. As the hour progressed our discussion grew to a close, we promised to meet in the morning and continue our bullshitting.

Early the next morning immediately after breakfast I heard my name being blared over the loudspeakers which were situated on the top of each individual quonset hut.

"Pfc. Allen, report to the main station for final processing." The words were spoken by some anonymous individual who was merely reading words off of a list. To me they were the most unwelcome sounds imaginable. The unavoidable could be put off no longer. After being shuffled around like some damn displaced person in a new country I was finally assigned a flight up North to An Khe.

During the flight I refused to look out the windows like the other new arrivals were doing. I knew what it was like down there in that hellish place. I sat there like a piece of baggage waiting to be shipped someplace else until I reached my destination.

Immediately after setting down at some ramshackle air field near An Khe we were met by trucks. The drivers were yelling out names of various regiments to which they were going. When I heard 7th Regiment my heart skipped a beat. I didn't know what it was going to be like and I was overwhelmed with that familiar uneasy feeling of apprehension. I felt like getting back on the airplane and going anywhere but back to base camp. There would simply be too many unpleasant memories waiting. However, like an automaton, my arm went up in the air signifying I was one of his boys. I walked slowly toward the truck as if I were marching toward some gallows.

Sitting in the back of the truck it was unavoidable for one not to look at the scenery. I was amazed at what I saw on the trip to base camp. Construction was going on everywhere. That is, military construction. The same mud huts of the people were also very much in evidence. Roads and bridges seemed to be evolving all about me. The closer we neared our base camp the more obvious the construction became. Barbed wire was everywhere. Where the jungle had once stood was empty land. Wooden buildings, housing rear support personnel, dotted the landscape. Replacing the small pup tents I had known now stood larger and oddly shaped large, green tents. My eyes were filled with wonderment at seeing the progress that had taken place in two short months.

The truck rounded a bend and came to a screeching halt. We were at the edge of our Battalion headquarters. I had to cross three Company areas before I came to A Company. I saw no one and assumed the Company was out on a mission. Large squad tents stood neatly in rows replacing my own pup tent. Not knowing where to put my few possessions I walked toward the Company headquarters hoping to find someone to fill me in on what squad I was assigned to.

A stranger was seated behind a metal desk shuffling through some papers. I reported to him and he instantly informed me the Company was indeed out on a search and destroy mission. Since the massacre of a short while ago that is the only type of missions the Company engaged in. The Company clerk informed me the new Captain would be reporting back to the Company area in a few minutes. He would then ask him if I was to join them in the field. Meanwhile he asked me what platoon I wanted to be in. Being asked such a question was surprising. I had automatically been expecting to be reassigned to Cline's platoon. He too had been in Hawaii with malaria. I told him in no uncertain terms I wanted to be in any platoon but Cline's. Grinning he said Lieutenant

Grove would be glad to have me. Since the incident at Ia Drang all of the platoons were below combat strength and I would fit in anywhere.

Lieutenant Grove was an ex-Sergeant who had gone through Officer's Candidate School and earned his commission. He had a reputation for being an extremely straight individual. I said the assignment would be fine and moved out to the supply tent. I was especially anxious to retrieve my film and get the pictures sent home for developing.

Another strange individual met me at the supply tent and got me my duffle bag. Half of my equipment was missing although the precious film was still there. It was covered with a green fungus as were my few remaining clothes. I was shattered by the sight. I had wanted those pictures so very badly. Like the men they represented they too were destroyed. Feeling dejected I returned to the Company clerk and asked where my specific tent was located. He told me, and in addition said the CO had called in and told me to stay in the Company area as they would be returning in a couple of days.

I picked up my few belongings, along with a set of new fatigues (standard type), and walked dejectedly toward my new squad tent.

Unzipping the large tent and peering inside I had an eerie feeling similar to entering a mausoleum. It was dark and musty smelling. The rows of cots had each individuals belongings stacked on top. Throwing the equipment off of the first bunk I stretched out and instantly fell into a sleep. I was awakened in the middle of the night by scratching sounds that seemed to be coming from every part of the tent. Lying there I tried to determine what was making those damn eerie sounds. Being unsuccessful and growing increasingly fearful I was unable to stand the suspense any longer. I struck a match. Upon seeing the light, furry creatures began scurrying for dark holes in which to hide.

"Rats," I said to myself. "Mother fucking rats." Now I've got them to contend with in addition to everything else. Was there no end to these constant unwanted surprises?

Awakening the next morning I looked for the Company clerk in hopes of finding some information in regards to various individuals in the Company. As he was new there was nothing he could tell me. Feeling utterly useless with no one to talk with I began writing letters to everyone I knew back in the States. I couldn't think of Brenda or anyone else in a serious manner. My mind just wasn't ready to function in such personal matters. Her magnificent breasts even held no interest for me at that point. One can imagine my obviously sterile frame of mind.

I was issued food in the form of C rations by the supply Sergeant. In addition to food he handed me some heating tablets. The tablets were as round in diameter as a nickle but much thicker. One could dig a shallow hole in the ground, drop in a tablet and light it, sit a can of C's on top and, in a few minutes, one had hot food. It was a small thing to consider but those tablets turned many a dull meal into something a little more edible.

I spent the next two days holed up in that tent like one of those damn rats. Being alone gave me a feeling of contentment. Perhaps in a way I was reacting in an adverse way to meeting the new men who would be returning shortly.

The men returned from their mission looking as if they had been in the jungle for months rather than weeks. They all looked like they had been beaten and dragged through the mud. Their clothes were ragged, torn and covered with mud. All of them had scratches on their bodies, some much worse than others. Their eyes were bloodshot enhancing their overall haggard appearance. Upon entering the tent and removing the gear from their cots, most of them collapsed into an exhausted sleep.

I spotted Clark and Sergeant Timura. Since they both had been with the squad when I contracted malaria, I had assumed they had been killed with the majority of others. Feeling like I had seen someone who had just risen from the dead, I raced toward them with an unusual feeling of happiness. Seeing some of the old-timers alive I realized I could get information about some of the others. My adrenalin was running rampant with a feeling of elation. The feeling was short-lived.

Fortunately Clark and Timura had both contracted malaria a few days after I had. Rather than being shipped to Hawaii they were sent to Japan. Returning a week sooner than I, they had been unlucky enough to be fit for duty when the Company went into the field on its latest search and destroy mission. Clark further stated that only one man out of the entire Company was still around who had any information about what happened at Ia Drang. The rest were dead, wounded, or discharged. One platoon was still intact but that was because they were attached to another Company during the campaign at Ia Drang.

The lone individual who could give me the much wanted information was one Private First Class Henry Cooper. When I heard his name I immediately knew that, if anyone would survive such an ordeal, it would have been Cooper. He was the type who could make it through anything. But then again I had thought the same thing about Kirkwood and was proven wrong. Cooper was an older black guy from Harlem. He was a straight guy who gave you a break regardless of your color, unlike so many other blacks who held your color against you regardless of what you were really like. Cooper had a reputation for being good with his hands as well as a knife. I had seen him fight his way out of various fights against blacks as well as whites. No one gave him any shit after he became known in the Company and he didn't give anyone else any. He would make it anywhere.

I couldn't believe he was still around as he was to be discharged on December 8th with the majority of the men who had previously been in the Company. Clark must have sensed my surprise because he immediately said that his records were screwed up and he was still around base camp somewhere waiting for them to be straightened out. He said that if I hadn't seen him he was probably in town.

"Wait a couple of hours and go into town with us," said Timura. "The new Captain promised us all a pass. After we get cleaned up we'll be headed that way."

"Wait, shit," I said, overcome with expectation. "I'm leaving now."

Arriving in the dirty town I was amazed at the circus like atmosphere that greeted my eyes. There were small stalls set up in front of every building. Everything imaginable was being sold. My eyes immediately saw the precious and heretofore unattainable jungle boots and jungle fatigues. Whiskey and cartons of American brand cigarettes appeared to the next most popular items. I wondered how so many of these items so vital to the infantryman could not be had at base camp but were so readily attainable only a few miles away. I was getting my first look at the lively black market. In addition to American products many of the stalls were selling various Vietnamese souvenir type items. Other stalls were offering services to the G.I. These consisted mostly of barber shops, cleaners, restaurants, massage and bath parlors. The buildings to which the stalls were attached were mostly private homes which had hurriedly been converted into bars and whore houses. The Vietnamese were running around grabbing at everyone or if they weren't so ambitious, they merely yelled in broken English what they had to offer. Their incessant jabbering would have rivaled the most obnoxious of midwaymen. Added to this chaotic atmosphere was the fact that children of all ages were running up to everyone in sight and explaining in English, more broken than their elders, of the delights they could find for the right price. Dogs, chickens, pigs, ducks and even a few cows were wandering in and out of the various shops. Army jeeps were parked everywhere giving the carnival atmosphere a degree of unrealism. Everyone seemed to be trying to offer the G.I. something for his dollar. And there he was, dumb enough to give it to them.

Stepping over some garbage in the dirt hardened street I entered the nearest bar. It was named the Florida Bar. The majority of the bars were named after various famous American states and cities. Peering in through some hanging beads I could make out through the smoke that the majority of men were white. I knew Cooper wasn't there.

The Chicago Bar as well as the Hollywood Bar produced an all white clientele. Finding Cooper was going to be easier than I had anticipated. I merely had to locate the bar the blacks chose to frequent. The Wild West Bar produced what I had been expecting. Noticing only black faces, I knew Cooper was probably inside.

When I had only looked inside the blacks paid me no attention. However, as I moved inside, I began to receive many curious looks, many of which were not too friendly. Moving steadily toward the center of the smoke filled room I was beginning to feel uneasy. I wasn't particularly wanted. We weren't on base and I was intruding in an area in which I wasn't wanted. I knew it as well as they. I only hoped Cooper was here. As if on cue, I heard my name yelled over the din of the crowd. "Andrews, hey Andrews. Over here."

Glancing to my right I saw the smiling face of Cooper. He was rushing toward me, pushing anyone and everyone out of his way. Reaching outward, he grabbed my hand and began pumping it as if he were a man dying of thirst and trying to squeeze water out of a rock. With each pump his grin grew wider and wider. The genuine feeling of friendship almost brought me to tears. Here was a true friend I would have been glad to see anywhere. After the past events it was especially gratifying to see him alive and well. We didn't speak for what seemed hours; we just stood there wildly shaking hands like two idiots who just learned how.

"I'm glad to see you're alive," I said, breaking the silence.

"It was close, man, very close," he replied, the smile disappearing from his face. "Come on, I'll buy you a beer and fill you in."

Sitting at a table by ourselves Cooper told me of the horrors at IaDrang. He did state that the guys put up one hell of a fight. Furthermore, he thought the majority of them were murdered.

"Murdered!" I responded incredulously. This was the first I heard of murder. I was stunned and filled with disbelief.

Cooper went on to state that a large group of individuals had been found the day following the heat of the battle. The group included many of my closest friends. They had been found bound hand and foot. Many of them had body wounds, indicating they had been shot, taken prisoner, and tied. In addition to body wounds, every one of the men in the group had a bullet hole in the head. Cooper supposed that they had indeed been taken prisoner and held by the North Vietnamese. When the battle started to turn in favor of the Americans, the NVA simply executed them.

I was dumbounded by the news. Thoughts of the murders began to form in my mind. Cooper continued in reliving the terrifying days. After the fight was over he and others had to gather the dead men from the field.

"Bodies and parts of bodies were everywhere," he continued. "Many of the Americans were chopped up, as if human butchers had gone beserk. Heads and arms were simply removed by machetes. To make the situation more unbelievable many of the men had their genitals cut off and shoved into their mouths." He must have seen my look of disbelief as he constantly repeated the phrase "honest to God, honest to God." Having never heard those words come from him, I knew Cooper was telling the truth when I heard them.

One aspect of the NVA that he thought I might be interested in was the fact that many of the NVA carried meat hooks to carry off their wounded. In cleaning up the battleground, they found meat hooks. Various NVA soldiers had holes in their bodies which looked like they could have been induced by the hooks. The Americans theorized that rather than leave their wounded they tried to drag them off the battlefield when they sensed defeat.

In addition, many first-aid packets were found on the NVA which contained needles but no type of medication which could be administered by a needle. The explanation was that a select group of individuals carried drugs to be administered to the majority of men.

"And the way those bastards fought, I believe they were doped up," continued Cooper.

I asked him how he got away and he said he honestly didn't know. He remembered picking up a machine gun, firing it in the direction of the enemy and running like a madman. Things happened so fast and in the mass confusion it was impossible to tell exactly what he did. He recalled falling, exhausted, behind a large ant hill. After a few hours of hiding, an American squad overran his position in pursuit of the NVA. I later learned that Cooper was credited with killing over thirty NVA in close fighting.

I was anxious to hear more of the events of Ia Drang Valley; I was like a small child listening to a favorite uncle telling adventure stories, however, I was denied my wish.

Cooper, for reasons of his own, decided there had been enough talking. Perhaps the recent events were too painful for him to recount. It was decided that we would visit a local whore house, one of many that abounded in the area. We left the all-black bar and headed for the Florida Bar.

We walked silently through the filthy streets. My thoughts were filled with the deaths of my friends. Suddenly a jeep came to a screeching halt directly in front of us. I recognized one of the men as our Company clerk.

"Cooper," he said, "you are wanted back at Company headquarters right away."

Looking at me in a quizical manner, Cooper jumped onto the jeep. The driver turned the jeep around and in seconds they were headed toward base camp. That was the last I was to see of Pfc. Cooper. His paperwork had finally been straightened out and he was immediately shipped back to the States. I wondered how he would react to civilian life after such a horrendous experience. There was no psychological counseling for men discharged, no matter what was in their past.

Standing alone in the middle of the street I was tempted to return to base camp. The thought of venturing into the whore house alone was almost too overwhelming for me to consider undertaking alone. I had always considered sexual intercourse an event to be treasured for its beauty and love between two people. Having never engaged in it, I had no idea what I was missing. Because I was still a greenhorn and inexperienced, I was embarrassed at my lack of knowledge. The longer I refrained from engaging in intercourse, the more I could rationalize my decision by telling myself that I was saving the moment for when I married. The rationalization was noble and sounded wonderful. The nuns would have been proud of me. The truth was that I was scared of the thought. As in fighting, inexperience is the hardest variable to overcome. Once one becomes somewhat proficient or at least exposed to a new activity, they are easier at any subsequent encounters.

I decided that it was time I lost my virginity. I may never get out of this damn place alive, I thought to myself; what in hell was I trying to prove? I couldn't be a chicken shit forever. The day would have to come sooner or later when I would have to face the situation, it may as well be now. Plus the opportunity had never been as available as it was now. Full of confidence I sauntered toward the Florida Bar and felt very much the man for making such a decision.

I stepped through some hanging beads which acted as a door and entered the bar. I immediately seated myself at a table in order to look over the place. It was like any other bar in town. A bar ran along one wall and the rest of the room was filled with tables and chairs. There were no decorations of any kind adorning the walls. An open doorway led to individual rooms in the rear of the building. Looking around I could see that the clientele was comprised of officers as well as enlisted men. I noticed many of the men wore wedding rings. I couldn't help but wonder what was going through their minds. Were they thinking of their wives and children or were they merely fulfilling a biological need with no regrets. I wasn't going to pass judgement on anyone for being there. Nevertheless I was filled with curiosity.

I had been sitting there for a few minutes wondering what my next step should be. I noticed a good looking woman sitting at the bar. I was surprised to see that she was wearing Western style clothes rather than the Vietnamese type. Her hair was also styled in an American Page Boy. She left her barstool and walked toward me. I immediately became very nervous. I reached for a cigarette to calm myself.

In seconds she was sitting beside me. "G.I. want beer?" she asked in an innocent voice. I nodded my head in agreement. She held up two fingers and a short, stoop-shouldered old man appeared with two cold beers. The beer was Vietnamese judging from the picture of the tiger on the bottle. I was suddenly more interested in the beer than I was in the girl beside me. We began sipping our beer, momentarily indifferent to each other. Looking at the woman I was struck by the whiteness of her teeth. In contrast to the purple color of so many other women I had seen, the difference was most striking.

I later learned that the prostitutes were the only ones able to afford good dental care. Thus their teeth were generally very white in addition to being filled with gold. Their income also made available to them the latest in Western style clothing. Thus they made themselves up to be almost as American as the proverbial girl next door. Since the G.I.'s approved of their Americanization and lavished them with gifts from the various PX's, they, in turn, had no qualms about looking as American as they possibly could.

I was about to ask the girl her name. Before I could get the words out, she asked me if I wanted to boom boom. Since the Vietnamese people, at this point in time, had no command of English, a few simple words sufficed for asking someone to go to bed and engage in sexual intercourse. The words "boom boom" became part of the international language before any other. They were followed by "money" and all of the standard English swear words. Thus the average Vietnamese female could swear, beg for money and ask to fuck before she learned how to ask someone his name. It was also the same for the American soldier.

I said yes, I wanted to boom boom and then asked how much money. She smiled and held up two fingers indicating two dollars. At this point we were using American script which was like play money. It was just like the real thing, completely negotiable in every respect. The script could be exchanged for Vietnamese money (piasters) but at no point could it be exchanged for regular American bills.

The price agreed on, we finished our beer in silence, then headed for a room in the back of the bar. Following the young girl I was filled with anxiety and apprehension. A moment that I had hoped to save for a loved one was about to be shared with a total stranger. On one hand I was glad it was happening; on the other I wished it could be under different circumstances. I suddenly thought of Brenda. A smile came over my face and I thought to myself, too bad baby, you could have had it but were just too goddamn stubborn. Thinking of Brenda made some of my apprehension disappear. It was almost as if I was getting some sort of revenge on her. I was still anxious but in addition I was now actually looking forward to the coming event.

In a moment we entered a long hallway with closed doors lining both walls. She picked one and we entered. The only furniture inside was a bed. There were no windows, the only light came from a candle stuck in an empty beer bottle. The walls were made of flattened out metal beer and soft drink cans. A curious dampness seemed to permeate the entire atmosphere. I stood there not knowing what to do. I had decided to let her make all the moves. I would merely follow. Sensing my uneasiness she motioned for me to lie on the bed. Turning, she walked out of the room. I stood there doing absolutely nothing. I was in a strange situation and felt completely helpless. I didn't know whether to take off my clothes or merely unzip my pants. Taking off my heavy boots would have required much lacing and unlacing, thus I decided to leave everything on until the young girl returned. I had no idea where she had gone but hoped she would return quickly.

My wish was soon granted. She entered the door and locked it. She had gone to another room and changed her clothes. Replacing her slacks and blouse was an Oriental kimona. As she walked toward me, lying on the bed, her kimona became undone. It slipped off of her shoulders effortlessly, revealing a ripe, flawless body. Her small but nicely shaped breasts were very firm in appearance. Her nipples were small but their dark color offered an enticing sight to the lighter background. Following her body downward I noticed the gentle flare of her hips. They were small but every inch a womans. Her thighs converged on a small wispy patch of jet black hair. Vietnamese women are not endowed with a great deal of pubic hair. Her body was small but offered many possibilities. She was slowly advancing toward me, all the while a beautiful smile covered her face. She spoke some Vietnamese in a whisper. I didn't know what she was saying and I could have cared less. Her body in all of its naked beauty was suddenly in front of me. Looking at her I was overcome with the most sensual of feelings. Years of wanting a female body was suddenly going to become a reality. My body indicated it was ready. I had wondered if I could get an erection under such conditions. The swelling and pounding inside my pants indicated that it was no problem.

I reached out and put one arm around her waist and drew her down on top of me. She began nibbling on my neck and moving her body against mine in rapid movements. Being this close to intercourse and knowing my dreams were going to be fulfilled, I was filled with an urgency to have her. I fumbled for my zipper on my pants. I was having great difficulty in getting my pants unzipped. I felt her hands move mine out of the way. In seconds she had my pants down around my knees. My cock felt as if it were ready to burst. I felt her hand grasp the pulsating organ and she began stroking it with an up and down rhythmic movement. I felt if she were to continue that I would come in seconds. Not wanting to reach a climax in such ordinary fashion, I rolled her off of me. With my clothes on, heavy boots included, it was no easy job. Soon she was lying directly underneath me. Instantaniously I was in between her thighs. My cock acted like it had a mind of its own as it seemed to be searching out her cunt. It was moving ahead under its own power. It seemed to be a separate entity on its own private journey. I had no control over it. It was my brains for the moment, the rest of my body was merely following its movements.

After a few false lunges, which proved to be fruitless at finding the velvet opening, I felt her warm hands grasp the head of my organ and guide it inward. As she was so small and tight it required much maneuvering on both our parts to get it situated perfectly. Once seated nicely in her soft body, I began a rocking motion which resulted in a marvelous stroking action on both our parts. The sensation of having the tight vaginal walls wrapped tightly around my pulsating organ was marvelous. Each stroke seemed to automatically produce another, only it was more fast and urgent. Much too soon I felt my body explode with a delicious feeling. The feeling shook my entire body from my boots to my head. Spent and exhausted, I lay there in her body trying to catch my breath. I felt my hardness remain, ready for more action. A knock on the door followed by a rapid stream of words in Vietnamese resulted in the young girl bolting upward and rolling me off her body. My time was up. Giving me a smile as she exited the room, I was once again alone. Feeling as if I had uncovered one of the secrets of the universe, I happily pulled my pants up and left the small room. No longer a virgin at 21 years old.

Riding back to base camp on the back of a truck I felt better than I had for a long time. The knowledge of knowing what it was like to engage in intercourse left me feeling wonderful. I was only sorry I had not discovered it years earlier. I had been a fool not to have undertaken the adventure before. Brenda was surely going to be in for one wonderful surprise when I returned home.

Arriving back at base camp I was introduced to my new squad leader, Sergeant Howell, and the rest of the men who had replaced those who had died at Ia Drang. The vast majority of the platoon was comprised of new men. The only faces I recognized were of individuals who had contracted malaria and had been fortunate enough to be spared death. Most of the new men seemed very likeable. I was readily accepted by them and a good rapport developed amongst us. They seemed to take us "old original" individuals and hold us in some sort of special respect. Perhaps it had been because we had been there first and they felt like the new intruders. I enjoyed being thought of as special by these men and went out of my way to play the role. There were many questions about the people, fighting in the jungles, reacting to sergeants and officers that they seemed to think we original members of the Company could answer. Even though we didn't know the answers to many of their questions, we tried to the best of our ability to answer them in a truthful manner. These men had only been in the Army a few months. Most of them had been sent to our Division immediately after completing their infantry training. They were less prepared to fight over here than we had been when we first arrived. The weapons were as new to them as they were to me.

The Army must have recognized the scope of the problem. After Ia Drang Valley, the Division started building ranges for firing the various weapons and equipment we were supposed to be experts at using. Also classes were started in how to look for and dismantle various types of booby traps. Almost every aspect of fighting in the jungles was gone over repeatedly. The training was most urgently needed. We still had to do various details while in base camp. The goddamn Green Line was being pushed back farther and farther. What had once been a wall of jungle was now open land. One could see straight ahead for one hundred yards. A few months earlier one would have had trouble seeing ten yards ahead. Replacing the trees was now strand upon strand of barbed wire. Claymore mines also dotted the area. This clearing away of the jungle was continuing all around the base camp. The transition of what was now evolving before my eyes was most impressive. The fact that much of it had been done with nothing more than entrenching tools made the progress seem all the more remarkable. Some units were now using power saws and bulldozers to clear away much of the jungle obstacles. Instead of burning the piles of dead lumber the trees would be stacked onto heavy nets. Giant helicopters would swoop down on them, attach a hook to the net and fly off to some isolated spot and drop them. It was a clean and above all else a fast and efficient method.

The day before Christmas I found myself on a most interesting detail. I was to sort through various Christmas packages which had been addressed to the men who had been killed at IaDrang. The mail had been slow in delivering the packages to Viet Nam. When they had arrived it had been all at once. Over the last couple of weeks, while the Company had been in the field, a small mountain of packages had been built up. Letters addressed to a dead man were sent back to the sender; packages, on the other hand, were not. They contained items which were divided amongst the men who were now taking their places. As the packages had set out in the hot sun for so many days, many of the perishable items had done just that; perished. It was my job to go through them and discard anything that couldn't be used. Any item that wasn't carefully wrapped was covered with a green mold. Thus, I found myself throwing away homemade cookies and cakes of every description. An unexplainable feeling came over me while I was doing the job. I knew who the packages were addressed to as the original wrapping containing the address remained. Tearing off the wrappers I could see the face of every man's package I opened. I seemed to be interfering in something personal. I again tried to rationalize why they were dead. Again no answers came. I told myself the foodstuff would probably never find its way back to the original sender, thus, by my taking the usable items out, some good was going to come of it. At least that's what I tried to convince myself was happening. Most of the stuff I was saving for our use was such items as instant soup, Kool Aid and other such instant foods.

Christmas Eve came like any other night of the year. Before in my life this was a special day. Now it was like nothing out of the ordinary. Most of the other men felt the same way. Beer was passed out to the men and everyone tried to get drunk. Not out of celebration but rather as a way to try and forget where we were. There was some singing by some of the religious individuals, however, most of the men were left to their private thoughts. My thoughts were concentrated more on the families of the men who died than they were on my own. How would they be spending this night with the deaths of sons and husbands so fresh in their minds?

Christmas Day found us preparing our gear for a search and destroy mission which was to be undertaken in the next couple of days. Everyone was busy cleaning rifles and checking out various types of equipment. The day was being celebrated by millions of people all over the world rejoicing in the birth of our Savior. I was having serious doubts as to the notion of any savior. He certainly seemed to be closing his eyes to our situation. But then again the nagging thought persisted in my mind that

I, as well as the rest of the men around me, were being punished for some wrong doing. If I knew what that wrong was, I certainly would have corrected it if it would have hastened my departure.

The next morning found us loaded up and ready to move out. The inspection, prior to moving out, was run through with much professional undertaking. There seemed to be less harrassment bestowed on us by the newer sergeants. We appreciated it and responded by doing what was expected of us and more if we could. There seemed to be a better working relationship between the men and the sergeants than there had been when I first arrived. Perhaps the fact that many men had been killed forced us to believe that it could happen again at any moment. It was a reality and everyone knew it. Before it had just been an idea. Having happened, it forced everyone to have a much more serious attitude about our role in Viet Nam. We would still have the various details to work on when we were not fighting but our primary role was fighting and we were beginning to engage in it more so than any other outfit in Viet Nam.

The mission found us flying into a small village where some VC had been spotted. Before, if we found no VC, we merely left the village. Now, however, it was a different story. If we found no one but there had been VC activity reported we left a calling card. We simply burned.

In the highlands the villages are small and located deep in the mountainous ranges. As a result the people have to rely on products close at hand to build their villages. The main product they use in building is bamboo, coconut trees and their by-products: bark, coconut shells, etc. After drying out, these by-products are quite flamable. If the houses themselves were not constructed out of this material the surrounding huts were. Thus, a lighted match worked wonders for destroying them in record time. Huts, or hootches as we called them, containing rice or hootches not containing rice were soon put to the torch. The people were supposed to be made aware that we would not stand for any colaborating with the enemy. To do so meant destruction of their property. In many cases it worked; the people actively fought the VC. It is also equally true that many people, because of our burning, sided with them and actively opposed our presence.

On this particular mission our platoon was lucky. We met no active resistance. Other platoons in the Company were not so lucky. Our platoon did have a few men who stepped on various types of landmines. Having not actually seen the events I cannot describe them. I merely heard the individual screams of the men as they lay on the ground filled with holes watching their precious blood flowing like sand in an hourglass. Medical helicopters (medivacs) soon arrived on the scene and flew them to nearby hospitals. This is one area in which having the helicopters was a godsend. They could send a man on his way to expert medical attention in a matter of moments, provided they came in for him. Thus, many men were saved who would probably have died in any other war. At the same time many men were saved who were probably better off dead.

The next week or so was spent flying into village after village looking for VC. The villages all had the same spartan appearance. Simply constructed on the outside but elaborately constructed on the inside. There were false ceilings, false walls, floors under floors and, I suppose, some of the animals were even false. We had to check everything extra cautiously. A pile of cow dung might contain a rifle or some other armament to be used against us. Whenever a tunnel was discovered it had to be checked out. As they were built to accomodate the VC, they were small. Thus, the smallest man in the squad had to crawl inside and check it out. These individuals became known as "tunnel rats." The job sounded relatively easy but when one learned that the holes were often booby trapped with hand grenades as well as poisonous snakes and often the enemy himself, one realized the grave danger these individuals faced. I never saw one of these men balk when asked to descend into one of those dark holes. I often questioned their intellect but never their bravery.

After going through village after village and burning as we went we bedded down for the night whenever it got dark. Often we would be in the thick of the jungle in between villages. The point we stopped at was usually indicated by the coming of night. A small circle would be set up and that was our only protection. Since we were usually in less than platoon size units our strength was minimal. If we had come across the enemy we would certainly have been decimated, thus, I had the feeling that I was merely bait. Bait for a larger unit of the enemy. Since Ia Drang there seemed to be an urgency for catching up with elements of the Peoples Army of Viet Nam called PAVN for short. What better way to make contact than to send out a small band of soldiers.

Lying on the ground at night and listening to sounds of the jungle was probably one of the more frightening aspects of jungle fighting. It is so dark in the jungle at night one can barely see the man next to him. In the total darkness one's imagination runs rampant. If imagining things is not bad enough one is faced with the reality of knowing what is under him. A plastic poncho is the only item we had to ward off the perpetual rain and chill of the night. Thus to ward off the moisture beneath us and the chilling air above us we wrapped ourselves inside the poncho so that we resembled a worm in its cocoon. Wrapped up in this cocoon affair one developed a false sense of security much like a frightened child hiding under the covers in his dark room. One thing that we could not escape was the sounds of the insects scurrying beneath our ponchos. As they moved they would scrape and bump against the plastic which encased us. The sounds were most terrifying, but what was one to do? There was no choice.

At first light we would be off again in search of the enemy. There was no hot breakfast. One was lucky if there was any breakfast. The food we carried was stored inside our spare socks which dangled from our packs. Thus, one reached inside and took the can that was on top. Often it was something like boned chicken or beans and franks, not very appetizing for any meal let alone breakfast. Water was precious so there was no washing or shaving while in the field. That was unless we came across a creek, in which case, we usually took a break to at least wash our hands and faces.

On this particular mission we spent all of our time walking or flying into villages, checking them out, burning hootches, then moving on through the hot jungle and repeating the process. All the while we were carrying our heavy packs and walking up and down mountains covered by the thickest of jungle. It became easier to walk up a mountain than down. Going down, the ground was extremely slippery. One had to rely on grabbing hold of whatever type of branch was handy to keep from falling and rolling downward. More often than not the branches were razor sharp and we merely had lacerated hands. We fell countless times and watched others fall and often go cascading downward for great distances in the most awkward positions. These silly events gave us rare opportunities in which to laugh.

To further complicate matters, some of the men had developed dysentery, a most handicaping situation when walking through the jungle. One has to stop every few minutes and relieve himself of the watery feces. One was supposed to dig a "cat hole" prior to defacating. Usually the procedure was followed, however, when one has to stop six or seven times an hour, it is too much of an effort to expect them to dig a hole. Thus many areas of the jungle were spot fertilized by human feces.

While walking through the jungle we naturally kept off of the main trails to avoid the booby traps and punji sticks. This afforded us the opportunity to view nature first hand, unspoiled by the human hand. Insects, from foot long centipedes to the tiniest termites, became highly visible. Interestingly enough, the insects were the healthiest looking things in all of Viet Nam. Everything in Viet Nam was small. The people, their dogs and cats, chickens and pigs were small in stature. The insects for the most part were extremely large and vicious looking. If they were not big they were nevertheless dangerous, such as the anopheles mosquito. Rats were a problem in and around base camp but not in the jungle. In the jungle they would have had to work for their food. In base camp and the surrounding areas it was readily available to them, thus, they stayed close to the supply of food.

The many scratches and tears in our bodies soon became infected in the humid and germ-laden jungle. Disease and rot seemed to abound everywhere in the jungle. Because there were no facilities to wash, the infections grew worse with each passing day. Soap and water had a magical curing process so we knew that once we washed the affected areas, the infection would subside, thus there was no real fear attached to the infections. However, one's stomach quivered when one looked at the pus-filled scratches which were so abundant on our bodies.

Marching, or rather walking, through the jungle was a slow process. The bitching and complaining was the only thing that kept us going. Everyone was in the same boat so we all felt equal. We even felt on a par with the officers and non-coms. Before, there had been open contempt for many of the officers, there was now praise because they were doing exactly what we were doing. That is except for Lieutenant Cline. He was still volunteering his men for the hardest and most difficult missions, time and time again. My not going back into his platoon was the smartest move I had made to date. The man obviously had some sort of emotional problem. Everyone hated him yet they viewed him with a curious respect.

On this particular mission I became introduced to two other aspects of life in the jungle which were, to me, the most despicable of everything encountered to date. One was encountering the dreaded leech; the other was realizing that the new M-16 rifle was not worth a shit.

The leech, for being as small as it was, instilled more fear in me and the majority of other men than did all the VC in the whole of Viet Nam. If the VC could have known of our fears in regard to this abhorant little creature, he would have inundated us with them at every opportunity.

In appearance, the leech resembles the American inchworm. The leech, in what I call its "looking stage," is about an inch or so in length. This is the stage in which it merely crawls around on the ground or on tree branches and looks for something to attach itself to. When I first saw them that is exactly what they were doing; crawling around. However, their crawl is quite unique. Rather than crawl aimlessly, they move a few feet in one direction, then rear up on their tails and stick their upper body in the air and sway back and forth, not unlike the cobra which I shall talk about later. They seem to be sensing, through some unknown means, a likely victim. The victim can be anything warm-blooded, man or beast. Not finding anything, after swaying for a few seconds, they proceed to crawl for a few more feet and repeat the process over and over again until a victim is located.

When I first saw them, no one paid them any particular attention. Seeing strange insects was nothing to become excited about. However, after having one attach itself to your body and sucking itself full of ones blood, it usually forces one to have second thoughts about them.

In the particular area we were in they appeared to be swarming everywhere. That is another interesting thing about the land leech. It is not found just anywhere. The ground must be of sufficient moisture to sustain them. The water leech on the other hand is found in just about every body of water in the central highlands. This particular area we were in must have been set aside for them as they were everywhere.

Initially, I wasn't too worried about them, as I was completely protected by clothing, or so I thought. The leech, however, has an amazing ability to squeeze into the tightest of areas. As an example I offer the combat boot and its eyelets. The leech will crawl onto the toe of one's boot. After going through its swaying and looking ritual it will head for the opening offered by the eyelet. Even tho one has the shoelace pulled to its tightest, offering the most miniscule of openings, the leech will nevertheless head for the opening. Upon reaching it, it will somehow enter the narrow space. If one is lucky, he will see it exit a few outlets above which it entered. It will proceed upward until one knocks it off. If one is unlucky, it won't be discovered until it has attached its sucking mouth to one's anatomy. Once it has attached its circular mouth it is almost impossible to remove. The only way to remove a leech is to touch a lighted cigarette to its tail. The shock of the heat will cause it to momentarily loosen its grip. It can then be removed, usually with the tip of a bayonette. If one does not see it in its sucking stage the only clue one has to its past presence is a slow blood-seeping wound. The leech will stay attached to ones skin until it has sucked itself full of blood. It will fall off only when it has filled itself with enough blood to cause it to become too heavy to remain attached. A most sickening sight is to see a wound on ones body and realize a leech caused it. One then searches the ground for the dirty fucking thing. What one sees is not what one would expect. Instead of being long, cylindrical in shape and green, it's shape becomes more round and blackish in color. By sucking itself full of blood the entire shape of the leech is changed into something blimp-like and grotesque.

The leech can also crawl over ones body without one feeling it. Thus you do not know it is there unless you are fortunate enough to see it. Later, as I became more experienced, I could sense them moving on my body.

I have often wondered what purpose the hairs ones body perform. One aspect, I am sure, is to warn one of foreign bodies, of which the leech is paramount. After a time I became so paranoid about leeches that I could actually feel one hair on my arm move as it flexed under the weight of a moving leech. To this day I can be sitting in the quiet of late evening and feel a hair on my arm move. Immediately, out of conditioning, I will immediately look, out of panic, toward the hair that moved expecting to see one of the vile creatures moving across my arm. Ones reflexes are truly a marvelous and wonderous thing.

After months of being subjected to leech country we soon developed the "leech stop." After traveling through an area in which the leeches abounded, it became necessary to cease walking, stop, drop your clothes and proceed to check yourself and your comrads for those mother fucking leeches. As long as I live I will never forget those vile looking creatures hanging onto my body sucking themselves full of my precious red blood.

Trying to stomp and ground them into the slimey earth from which they must surely have come is impossible. Grinding them into the ground has the same useless effect as grinding a plastic worm. It is most discouraging to apply all of your weight and vehemently try to squash them to death. After many attempts they merely rear up and begin that goddamn swaying. The only way to kill them is to cut them in half with a bayonet. When they are filled with blood they can be squashed. But one doesn't usually wait until that long to dispose of them. Besides seeing a quarter ounce of your blood spraying over the jungle floor is a most depressing sight.

I was first made aware of my rifle malfunctioning during an exercise known as the mad minute. Periodically, while on a mission in the early morning, we would engage in a mad minute. The mad minute involves everyone shooting their respective weapons for a period of one frightening minute. Seeing a multitude of weapons from M60 machine guns to hand grenade launchers firing incessantly, is a most hair raising experience. That is, if ones weapon fires. My M-16, as did countless others, fired initially. However after a few rounds it malfunctioned. The problem was that the rounds would not eject from the breech. As there were but only a few cleaning rods in which one could dislodge the round one usually spent but a few seconds firing his M-16 during the mad minute. This malfunction would plague us again and again no matter how clean we kept our rifles. If a few grains of sand became lodged within the rifle it would not even fire the first few rounds. Months later a Senate investigation would result in the testing and subsequent modifications made in the M-16. Nevertheless it would not benefit me. Time and time again my rifle would become jammed. Luckily the misfortunes occurred mainly during a mad minute and not during actual combat. Although there were times that it failed me during actual combat.

After weeks of fighting mostly insects which were more frightening than any VC and being subjected to the most inhumane of living conditions, we got the word to "saddle up" and prepare to move back to base camp.

After arriving at the helicopter pad it was our custom to return to our specific area by walking through Company areas of non-combat personnel. Seeing the homey and personal touches they were allowed to add to their living quarters again made me seethe with jealousy. The thing that really pissed me off was the s.o.b.'s were making the same amount of money I was making. They had the nerve to call it combat pay. The closest those fuckers came to combat was in some bar in An Khe. The injustice of it all was especially acute after we returned from a mission. After being subjected to all of the nightmares associated with living in the jungle, then coming back and seeing these guys getting over, made it especially hard to take.

After I had been in base camp for a few days I noticed an unusually large amount of Korean troops in the area. I later learned that a battalion of R.O.K. troops (Republic of Korea) had been assigned to our Division. They had been in Viet Nam for only about a month but they already had a reputation for being vicious. Rumor had it that on their arrival they captured a Viet Cong suspect in a remote village. Rather than turn him over to the proper authorities they took matters into their own hands. In order to announce their arrival to the populace they cut the hands off of this particular individual, tied them around his neck and turned him loose to return to the village. Accompanying the hands dangling from his neck was a sign which simply said that the R.O.K.'s had arrived. I cannot verify the incident but, knowing the viciousness of the Koreans, I can believe it.

Initially, while in Viet Nam, the Koreans were assigned to search and destroy missions, as we were. However, they did their jobs too well. They would enter a village and, if there was any resistance on the part of the villagers, they would retaliate against the whole village. They would kill everybody and everything from women and children down to the dogs and cows. After their tactics became known, the Koreans never took part in any more search and destroy missions by themselves. Members of their units would be attached out to American units but the Korean units were resolved to pulling guard duty at various installations around An Khe.

While in base camp we were expected to get our equipment back into perfect working order. Thus our days were spent cleaning and recleaning various kinds of equipment. That is unless we were on some special detail. Once in a great while during the daylight hours, we would have a few hours off from work to engage in some organized athletics. Usually it amounted to nothing more than organized grab ass. But at least it was better than working on some damn detail. Work on the Green Line had progressed rapidly. Instead of cutting trees we were now laying barbed wire along the areas that had been cleaned out. Thus our days were filled with various kinds of physical labor. The majority of which seemed to be worthless in terms of being constructive. Its main function seemed to be keeping the troops busy. While in base camp we were relatively safe so in that respect it was better than being out and beating the bush.

Our days were filled with work but the nights were ours. Most of the men were kept out of nearby An Khe for obvious reasons. Thus there was nothing to do at night but bullshit with your friends and drink beer. Beer seemed to be readily available for practically no cost and most of the men took advantage of the situation. Later there would be movies and television for the men in base camp but as of this early moment, early in January, there was not even an electric light and wouldn't be one for some time to come. At this point in time candles were also forbidden during darkness, thus, writing letters was not possible. All there was to do was drink.

The officers and non-commissioned officers were separated from the enlisted men. As there was no interaction of ideas and explanations for past experiences, rumors and talks of revenge against certain individuals were rampant. With the alcohol giving the men a false bravado one wonders why there wasn't more killing of each other than there actually was.

We still kept our individual weapons in our own possession while at base camp. This included machine guns, M-16's, hand grenade launchers and personal side arms of every description. The scene would surely have rivaled any frontier town in the 1800's. And most of the people who had them were just as intelligent. Bullets would be fired by individuals seeking to stir up a little action and rounds would also be fired to settle arguments. The idea of having these weapons left in the hands of so many individuals, many of whom were at least mentally unbalanced, was sheer insanity. Months later, after my departure from Viet Nam, weapons were taken out of the hands of the men once they returned to base camp. On many occassions there was more action in base camp against each other than there was in the field against the VC. The rising tensions brought on by drugs and poor race relations was probably an added incentive to change the rules. As is the case in most situations of this nature there were always enough stronger willed individuals around to break up any potential major problems amongst the men. There were many occassions when they did not. During my tour no one was killed but there were many "accidents" and countless close calls.

There was also much construction going on in and around base camp. The most important of which was the battalion mess hall. I was on a detail to level the area so that a concrete floor could be laid. When I and the rest of the men realized we were working on the floor for a kitchen we worked doubly hard. The thought of having hot cooked meals was too much to comprehend. Knowing that it would become a reality as soon as we finished made us work all the harder. In a few weeks what had been baren ground would be a large sprawling wooden mess hall. Watching the structure rise amidst the valley of green tents did much for our morale. Another structure which rivaled the kitchen in popularity was the E.M. Club. It was merely a plain rectangular wooden and tin building. But it was a place where we could sit at tables and drink beer after a day's work. That is, when we were in base camp, which in a day by day count, wasn't too often. Also an infantry Company was on the bottom of the list in priorities. Thus we were supplied with the raw materials but it was mainly our responsibility to build our own clubs. The other non-combat units had much time in which to build and work on their various living quarters.

I remember distinctly one incident in which this particular injustice was shown vividly. On the way back from a shower I was invited to spend some time with a trooper from the helicopter repair units. The fact that this unit was directly across the road from us and in plain sight made it especially hard to accept. I was invited because the individual who invited me obviously felt sorry for me. Their Club would have rivaled any bar in the world for decor. The walls of the Club were panelled with a rich wood. The bar, tables, and chairs were elegantly upholstered. In addition to a wide assortment of beer they also had a huge assortment of hard liquor. Where the various items were attained still remains a mystery to me, but the fact remains that it was there. Seeing another case of the infantrymen being fucked further alienated my feelings for anyone who wasn't in an infantry outfit.

The remainder of the days in base camp were filled with meaningless details. Occassionally we would be lifted out to pull guard duty on some air strip or guard a pass somewhere around the city of An Khe. On these various details I became extremely good friends with a guy named Cecil Bradley. He was a no-nonsense guy from Birmingham, Alabama. He did his assignments in a conscious manner but at the same time was a fun-loving individual. We hit it off extremely well. After losing so many friends I had decided to make no new close friends. I didn't want to go through the agonizing process of having to analyze their deaths, which I knew would be coming. It was just a matter of time. But Bradley was one individual you couldn't help but become attached to, thus we teamed up whenever possible.

There were other unique individuals who made the nightmarish days bearable. In time I found myself surrounded by good friends. I suppose the nature of being in Viet Nam made one want to have friends, if for no other reason than to help and be helped over the countless days of depression.

After days of boring useless details we got the word that we would be moving out on a three week search and destroy mission. The area we were going to was along the coast. The area was South of where the Marines were operating and had heretofore been free of any American intrusion. The operation was going to be a very large one in total numbers of men committed. We would be working side by side with Marines, Koreans, U.S. Paratroopers, South Vietnamese infantry, and, of course, the 1st Cavalry Division. It was to be the biggest allied operation to date. Each operation had a nickname thought up by some Major in a rear echolon area. We generally didn't know exactly where we had been or the name of the operation until we came back and read about it in the official Army newspaper, "The Stars and Stripes."

After the usual day of checking and re-checking equipment we were ready to depart. Tension was unusually high as an operation of this magnitude meant we would see action of the worst kind. True to form, the operation started out with a tragedy.

Rather than fly to the objectives in helicopters we flew in Army airplanes. Because of the numbers of men involved helicopters were out of the question. Thus two platoons of men fully equipped, were loaded onto each plane. Our particular plane was involved in an interesting episode although we were much more fortunate than one other plane.

During the flight there was a deathly silence among the men. Each was left to his own thoughts. I was thinking of the possible dangers which lay ahead. We had been flying for about twenty minutes in almost total silence. Suddenly the silence was broken by an eerie sound. It was a sharp cracking sound immediately followed by a short hissing noise. Similar to gas escaping from a tire when it is punctured. Simultaneously a screaming voice yelling obsenities could be heard. Glancing quickly to my left I was able to see that one of the photographers from a civilian magazine was clutching his knee. His face was contorted with pain and his pants, around his knee, was turning a dark red. A medic immediately raced to where he was sitting. After a brief examination he was led to the rear of the plane where first aid could be applied. It didn't take me long to figure out what had happened.

We had taken sniper fire from someone below. As we were flying at only two or three hundred feet elevation it is conceivable that we made a good target for some industrious VC. His aim was obviously very good or he had been extremely lucky. At any rate he had succeeded in hitting the aircraft. The bullet penetrated the belly of the aircraft and continued upward. Either the bullet or a piece of metal from the floor of the aircraft sailed upward and tore into the knee, ripping it apart. I couldn't help but wonder at the astronomical odds involved in trying to figure out ones chances of being hit in such a situation. The odds were obviously quite high and it didn't seem to make sense why a certain individual should get hit over another. Again my mind began thinking of how one can't really control his own destiny. It seemed to just be a matter of chance if one got hit or not. It was obviously random selection as to who got hit and where. The flight continued for another twenty minutes or so and all the while I, and I'm sure everyone else, kept wondering when the next round was going to come crashing through the floor. Landing was a pleasure but the news that greeted us a short time later was extremely unpleasant.

Another plane carrying the mortar platoon and one other platoon had crashed. All the men were killed. The mortar platoon was carrying fill combat gear. Thus they were loaded to overflowing with large rockets as well as small weapons ammunition. The thought of what happened to the men in the ensuing explosion was too horrible to dwell on.

What made the situation all the more revolting was that the two platoons that had died in the crash were the same two that had been spared death at Ia Drang Valley. I recalled talking to various individuals in the platoon after Ia Drang. Basically they felt they had it made for the rest of their tours. They thought that because they had been in such a large battle their odds of not getting in another was quite good, thus they would live through the remaining months. Again, the thought of not knowing when death could strike began growing in my mind. Not being able to control such a thing was a staggering contemplation. Knowing that it could happen at any given second and without any warning made the thought all the more gruesome.

Shortly my squad was called together to go out on a patrol to reconnoiter the area. Moving out of the staging area we passed some

Korean troops. They were busy breaking down boxes of C rations and distributing them to their fellow troops. I noticed that the markings on the cans and boxes were of a bigger and darker print than were on ours. I had been eating those goddamn rations long enough to know that the darker print indicated that the food was newer and of a better quality. Again I was struck by the injustice bestowed upon us. Granted, it was a small thing, but the small things were slowly building up. The food was obviously being supplied to them by the U.S. Government as were their uniforms and basic equipment. Why in the hell it was of a better quality than the supplies we had made me extremely angry at my Government. The bastards send us over here to die and don't even have the decency or control to see that we get food equal to that which the Koreans were getting.

The next couple of days were turning into repeats of so many past. Walk all day in the scorching hot sun, burn a few hootches, arrest a few civilians, walk through more jungle, and mercifully we would stop for the night. The next day we would walk until we came to another village and the process would be repeated. The only break that came in the routine was when we would board the choppers and fly to a different village. Once we were in the village the process would be repeated. Following this routine of moving into village after village and finding no active resistance was having a negative effect on everyone's mind. Not finding any VC or PAVN, our anxiety was growing with each continuous failure. Contact was needed with the enemy to relieve the built-up tension.

The officers seemed to realize what was happening to the men and took action on two separate occassions to relieve some of their own tension and anxiety.

While walking through some extremely thick jungle our squad came to a clearing and were greeted by Lieutenant Cline and his platoon. The Captain was there engaged in conversation with Cline. They had an old Vietnamese peasant in their custody. Where in the hell he came from in the middle of that forsaken jungle was beyond me at the moment. Glancing around I could see an A-shaped small dwelling which didn't look big enought to accomodate a large dog. In fact the dwelling resembled a "do-it-yourself doghouse." Obviously it was made by the prisoner. He was dressed in what appeared to be a diaper. He was completely naked except for the dirty rag around his genitals. He was either guarding something hidden in the jungle or else he was merely a hermit. No one would ever know.

We took a ten minute break at the clearing. All the while I watched but didn't hear Cline and the Captain talking. Just as we started to move out Cline marched the old man to our rear. We began moving out, headed into the darkness of the jungle. We had only gone a few yards when I heard the loud explosion of a forty-five handgun being fired. I immediately realized Cline had shot the old man. This was later verified by an individual who witnessed the execution. I couldn't figure out why Cline had done it. If he was trying to prove how powerful he was he certainly didn't succeed in my eyes. My disgust for Cline was further magnified.

The second episode took place a day or so later. We found ourselves walking through some open farmland. As we were walking on high ground a large open area below us allowed for a tremendous clear view of the surrounding countryside. A lone individual was spotted moving suspiciously in the open. The officers decided to test their artillery calling ability. When one sees a target that requires more firepower than the average infantry company possesses he can call in artillery fire. However, he must know what he is doing. One mistake would result in his calling the artillery fire in on himself. The easiest method is to call in the rounds at a distance greater than is required. One is usually in a position to see or at least hear where the rounds are actually landing. It is then an easy matter to reduce the range of the rounds until they are zeroed in on the target. A moving target is another story. The individual in this question was doing a lot of moving. But the officers were not to be denied.

Rounds were called in on the individual who was in the open field below us. He immediately took cover in some bushes when he heard the explosion in the distance. Then the rounds began falling closer and closer to where he was hiding. When he realized what was happening he began running to different spots which afforded him some sort of cover. He was doing a good job of escaping the rounds, however, he was making one major mistake. He was spending too much time in one position. Thus, the Captain had time to zero in on him before he could move one last time. I saw him run and disappear into a clump of trees. An artillery round landed in the exact spot he was hiding. When the smoke cleared there was nothing left of the trees, not to mention the individual who had been there. Upon seeing his work end in success, the Captain's face broke out in a smile. In a sick manner I felt glad that he had killed the individual. I suppose it was the revenge feeling that was pent up inside of me that enabled me to feel happiness at what had just taken place.

Later, I thought about the situation and realized that an innocent man could have been killed. His only crime was in trying to protect his life. On the other hand he could have been an important leader in the VC organization. The point is, some care should have been taken to find out exactly what his status was.

The days continued to pass monotonously. They were becoming physically harder to cope with. Another week or so of being in the field and then we would move back to base camp. Duty on the Green Line was like a vacation compared to being in the field, thus, my thoughts were transferred from the rigors of the field to the relative comforts of base camp. An incident was about to occur which would make returning to base camp seem like gaining entrance into Heaven. In a matter of hours we were going to be in combat from which many men would never see the light of another day.

CHAPTER 7

Late one morning we were to be resupplied food, mail, and the supreme joy--fresh water. Due to a logistics problem there was no food or mail, only ammunition and water. Our disappointment was great at receiving no mail. The fact that we did have fresh water made the situation more tolerable. After weeks of drinking anything that was wet, the idea of drinking clean water was like a sublime gift. How sweet are the simple things of life when one is without them for so long.

The water was transported to us in collapsable five gallon white plastic containers. After everyone had filled their canteens with the sweet liquid there was a small amount of it left over. To my horror one of the Sergeants said to throw it away. Throwing it away would have been a sin of the highest magnitude. Rather than commit such a sin I decided to collect what was left from the various containers and deposit it into one. After much scrounging I succeeded in saving about two quarts. I tied the large container on my back with the rest of my equipment. Walking along with the large plastic bottle on my back I had the feeling that I surely must have looked like a deformed camel.

The area we were marching through in search of the elusive VC was predominately coconut groves. Flying in by helicopter I had been particularly impressed with the panoramic view below me. As far as the eye could see was a blanket of dark green slender trees. The trees seemed to stretch forever in the distance. For a moment I forgot I was in a battle zone. At other times the beauty of the land and particularly the cathedral-like silence of the inner jungle often made me forget where I was. The feeling, unfortunately, was generally short-lived.

Now we were walking through the coconut trees and entering a large clearing. It was obvious we were entering a village by the trails and cultivated land which we encountered. My particular platoon came to a banana-shaped lagoon. The area of the lagoon nearest us had been converted into a rice paddy. In order to cover more territory, the platoon split into two parts. One part veered off to my right, which I later learned contained the main village. I and the remainder of the platoon went to the left. We were separated by the water of the shallow lagoon and mud of the rice paddy.

Before we had travelled fifty meters, small arms fire filled the air. I was immediately stunned by the sound. I had anticipated that enemy fire would sound like a cannon. The sounds I heard were the sound of firecrackers. Rather than loud booming sounds, I was hearing soft, almost muffled 'pops'. Advancing cautiously, I was able to determine that the fire was being directed at the other half of the platoon directly across from us. Glancing across the lagoon I could see that coconut trees dominated the area; a perfect environment for snipers.

The firing was becoming more intense the farther we advanced. As time progressed the sounds were also becoming louder and louder until they evolved into what I thought were the sounds of cannons.

As we advanced forward we came to a dead end. To go farther would have meant going directly into the lagoon. By veering to the left we would have gone away from the rest of the platoon. I was beginning to break out in a cold sweat. The anxiety and uncertainty of the moment was causing the sweat to pour out of my glands. Sweating under the hot sun was to be expected. Sweating so profusely under these circumstances was a unique experience. I was trying to understand what was happening to my body when suddenly the unmistakeable sound of incoming enemy fire became terribly real. The sound was that of a scythe being hurled through the air by Hercules himself.

Without having to be told I immediately hit the ground and crawled for a clump of bushes in front of me. We had been spotted by the enemy who was directly across the lagoon. I was waiting for word on what to do from Sergeant Newhouse, who was one of the new replacements in the platoon. His radioman, Gonzales, was nowhere to be seen. I lay on the ground hugging the sweet earth as if it were some long lost lover. The sounds of the enemy bullets tearing through the air caused me to try and sink farther into the ground.

In an instant of clear thinking I reached for my rifle; it was gone. Frantically glancing to my right I saw it lying a few feet away. I must have dropped it when I initially hit the ground. I tried to reach it by stretching my arm as far as it could possibly reach. Not succeeding, I tried to inch my entire body toward the rifle. I stuck out my right hand to push myself up and sideways. As I moved my hand from behind the bush a stream of bullets raked across the ground, scant millimeters from my fingers. In a flash, I was back in my original position behind the bush. Son of a bitch, I thought. What a place to be and without a rifle.

I was suddenly overcome with the nauseous feeling of wondering what it would be like to be shot with one of those incoming rounds. I got my answer from God. At that exact instant a bullet struck a large tree to my immediate right. Glancing up I could see that the bullet had torn a large chunk of the tree away just as if someone had taken a mighty swing at it with an ax. Upon seeing the damage, I tried to sink deeper into the ground. If the bullet could do that to a tree, I knew what it could do to the human body.

Lying there like a frightened baby I was overcome with a strong desire to live. I realized how sweet life could be and didn't want it to end now, especially after I had found how beautiful intercouse had felt. Before I could ponder my situation any longer, the voice of Gonzales yelling for Newhouse broke the tension.

Looking behind me I could see him running toward Sergeant Newhouse who was lying a few yards to my right. He was hunched over and moving like a bat out of hell. Bullets were slicing through the air much like our own mad minutes. Gonzales suddenly screamed and did the most beautiful mid-air flip I have ever seen. Instantly I knew he had been shot. I was mesmerized by the sight and couldn't take my eyes off of him.

For a few minutes, which seemed like an eternity, he made no movement. Suddenly he picked up his head, looked around, and began moving in a slow crawl toward me. As he crawled toward me I could see the bright red blood which was beginning to drench his pants from the waist down. The whole scene was as if it were being filmed in slow motion. His movements seemed overly deliberate and magnified. To my horror he was moving directly toward me. He was going to depend on me to take care of him. The sight of his pleading face and his blood-covered clothes made me wish I were someplace else. I was ashamed of myself for thinking it but I wished he would crawl someplace else. I just didn't think I could handle the responsibility of giving him first aid with bullets whizzing overhead. What if I fucked up and caused him to die? The thought was overwhelming. As he crawled closer and closer I felt myself wishing he would crawl in another direction.

When he was a few feet from me he did just that. The black face of Sergeant Newhouse must have put him back on the right course. He shifted direction and headed for him. He had a message from Lieutenant Grover who was leading the platoon on the other side of the lagoon. The message from Lieutenant Grover was to join the platoon on the other side. They obviously needed the reinforcements. Newhouse yelled something to the effect of "get ready to move out."

Something inside of me told me to immediately move. Without wasting a second I reached out, grabbed my rifle, and was running hellbent to the rear. After racing to the rear for about ten yards I immediately headed for the shallow part of the lagoon. I was aware that no one else was following me across. I was tempted to wait for someone else to follow me but was completely overcome with the feeling of invincibility. I thought to myself that if those chicken shits aren't going to follow me that's their problem. I'm going across!

Just as I was about to enter the paddy section of the lagoon, I was aware of movement behind me. Those fuckers were coming after all. Knowing friends were behind me gave me added incentive. I jumped a couple of feet down into the paddy. I had pictured myself crossing the paddy like Achilles, however, when my foot hit the bottom of the paddy I realized the precarious situation I had gotten myself into. I immediately sank in the stinking mud up to my shins. There were no rounds being fired at me so I painstakingly pulled my leg out of the mud and proceeded gingerly across. I could hear shouting behind me and realized others were behind me who were in the same boat. Cussing filled the air. Instantly I started to laugh. A G.I. will cuss anywhere and over anything. Being stuck up to our asses in mud and possibly being killed at any second called for a laugh. Seeing them in the same situation as I prompted me to move onward toward the far shore.

Just as I was about halfway across I glanced back to see how my comrades were faring. I noticed that the machine gun crew was just entering the paddy. As if on cue the VC opened up with everything they possessed. They had been waiting for the machine gun crew to make their appearance. Machine gunners are usually the first to get zapped. Hearing another enemy round whiz overhead, I flung myself down into the vile mud. Panic stricken I glanced around for cover. A few feet away was a small dike. Moving like a snail I headed toward it. The dike was only six inches or so above the water line in which I was lying, but at that particular moment, it appeared as high as Hoover Dam. When I was safely behind it I was overcome with a false sense of security. My mind became focused on getting to the opposite shore, about twenty yards away.

As I started to crawl toward the shore I was aware of bullets striking the dike, inches from my face. The VC had me in their sights and were not going to let me escape. With each bullet ripping into the dike I sank lower into the slime below me. My face was almost in the water of the rice paddy. I suddenly noticed water bugs skimming across the stinking water, oblivious to what was happening to me. Out of rage I slammed my fist at them and was rewarded with a handful of mud. Rotten mother fuckers, I thought. How dare you be so nonchalant to what is going on. Looking about for some other crawling insect to inflict my wrath upon, I noticed the bloated body of a small dead snake float past. The sight of that dead object brought me back to the present and forced me to move onward. I imagined leeches sucking at my submerged body and tried to move faster. Every inch I crawled I could hear bullets keeping pace. How in the hell could they see me, I wondered. Surely I was below the level of the dike yet they were following me every inch of the way. Suddenly the water bottle I was carrying on my back flashed into my mind. That was it! They were firing at the moving white water bottle on my back.

You stupid mother fucker, I said to myself. Try and plan ahead and look where it gets you. Motivated by my own stupidity, I kept advancing toward the shore. Slowly it was coming closer and closer. Just as I was about to reach out and pull myself up onto the shore, Lieutenant Grover appeared and told me to go back. Go back! What in the hell are you talking about, idiot, I thought to myself. "Go back and help bring the wounded across," said Grover, with a sadness in his voice.

The thought of traversing the slime back was too much to comprehend. I could hear Lieutenant Grover telling me to move farther down the paddy. There was a much larger dike where I could cross out of the enemy's vision. Moving as if the next second was going to be the last, I was soon at the large dike.

The dike was large enough for one to cross in a crouch. In addition, the footing was much firmer. Muddy, to be sure, but not half as slimy as the mud I had just crossed.

Reaching the other side I now had to walk a few yards ahead to where the wounded men were lying. Rather than pull myself up onto the bank and proceed under cover to where the men were, I stood up along the edge of the paddy, walked slowly, and hoped that the VC would shoot me. I had the feeling I wouldn't die but would be slightly wounded and would be evacuated. It was obviously the feeling of hopelessness which was causing my actions. Stupidity was undoubtedly another important reason. The feeling lasted only a second, however. The momentary defiance of death brought my mind back to reality. I pulled myself up on the shore by grabbing hold of some roots of a tree which extended downward to where I was standing. Seconds later I was crouched on the bank surveying the situation. Everywhere I looked there were bodies lying in every conceivable position. Had it been another place and time I would have sworn the men were sleeping. Now, however, they were dead. Most of them had only been in Viet Nam for a few weeks.

I was amazed to see so many bodies when I had been there only a few moments before and no one had been shot with the exception of Gonzales. By moving out to cross the rice paddy they must have offered perfect targets to the VC. Why they had died didn't seem to matter. The ugly truth was, they were dead.

Surveying the area, I caught sight of a guy named Grey. Lying face up and with his eyes closed, he looked exactly like he was enjoying a midday nap. I turned him over, half expecting him to awaken. When I turned him over I could see that the back side of his skull was blown away. I felt like holding him in my arms and singing to him. I wanted to comfort him even though I knew he was beyond comfort.

Looking around I could see Sergeant Rodna assuming some sort of much needed command.

"Pick up the wounded," he was yelling, frantically.

Before I could respond, two unarmed Americans were making their way toward me carrying a wounded man with them. I then realized they were reporters for Time-Life magazines. Since Ia Drang they had accompanied us everywhere we went. They must have had a nose for action.

126

Glancing beyond them I could see two other men had another wounded man. They had him stretched across a plastic poncho. I immediately recognized the wounded man as Niranda. He was new to the platoon as was nearly everyone else. He had the distinction of being the tallest Mexican I had ever seen. He was easily six foot four. His long legs dangling across the poncho made him seem much taller.

He had been shot in the stomach. Rather than falling to the ground immediately upon being hit, he stood upright. By standing the VC got another shot at him and nailed him again. He was bleeding profusely.

His size was a handicap to the men who were trying to help him. The use of the poncho was to facilitate their work. However, when they picked the poncho up and attempted to move him, the VC opened fire on the standing and slow-moving target they offered. The men had no choice but to drop him and try again every few minutes. Time after time they stood and advanced a few feet only to drop Niranda. Each time they dropped Niranda, I was able to hear him yell with pain. I could almost see the blood squirt out of his body every time he was dropped to the ground.

A second later the two reporters were at my side.

"Take this guy across and we'll follow you with some others." Without saying a word I picked the wounded man up and headed across the paddy. All fear of helping anyone was suddenly gone. Getting the man safely across to the other side proved to be an easy chore. I returned to the bank where the wounded lay.

Reaching the bank I could see that most of the wounded had been taken across or were in the process of being helped. Only the dead were lying unattended. Their still bodies reminded me of crushed flowers after a storm. It was decided to leave the dead for later. Rodna told me to carry all the weapons I could carry and get my ass across to Lieutenant Grover. I scooped up all the rifles I could carry and double-timed it across the paddy behind the safety of the large dike. When I reached the other side I was greeted with a sight the likes of which I shall never forget. That sight is etched in my mind forever. Try as I might I cannot erase it.

Lying on the bank directly in front of me was Niranda. He way lying in the poncho in a spread-eagle position. The poncho, due to its upturned sides, was holding all of the blood he was losing. I didn't realize the human body contained so much blood. He was almost swimming in it. Upon seeing me he raised his feeble hand and asked for a drink through his cracked and dried lips. I couldn't help but notice his hands. The bones of his fingers were stretching his skin to the bursting point. His fingers looked like the bones of a skeleton. His skin had turned an anemic looking yellow which only enhanced his skeleton appearance. I was so loaded down with weapons I couldn't give him a drink even though I wanted to so very desperately. The sound of Lieutenant Grover's voice telling me to move up forced me to leave Niranda in his bath of blood.

Moving up the sloping bank I noticed a large trench. It ran off to my left and disappeared into the brush and trees. Jumping into the trench I saw the spider holes the VC religiously built into all of their trenches. The spider hole is merely a hole dug into the back wall of the trench. An American could not fit into it but the smaller VC were as comfortable as the proverbial pea in a pod. The purpose of the hole is to protect them in case of an air attack. The spider hole performs its intended function marvelously.

This particular area we were in was mostly sand. Thus the VC had an easy time in constructing their trenches. They had done an outstanding job. My assignment for the next couple of hours was to stand guard duty in the trench while the platoon geared for some sort of defense.

Standing in the trench I had an excellent view of the lagoon and the far bank where so much death had just occurred. It was now easy for me to see how the VC had been able to pick off so many individuals. They had an absolutely beautiful clear field of fire. In addition their defensive position was well camouflaged by the trees and scrub brush.

Standing there I began thinking of the men who had been killed or wounded. There had been so many on my side of the lagoon who had been hit and God only knew how many had been hit on this side. I began to get a feeling of superiority in my mind. There was no rationale to explain it but nevertheless I began to get the idea that I was better than anyone else. For some reason I had been chosen to make it through when others were being killed. Why, I asked myself, why me? No answers came.

The sound of helicopters approaching in the distance caused me to refocus my thoughts on the present. Looking behind me I could see the faint outlines of the choppers coming into view. As they came closer, large red crosses identified them as medivacs (medical evacuation choppers). Just as they were about to descend, all hell broke loose. Gunfire seemed to come from all of the surrounding trees. The medivacs were caught in mid-air. They tried to land but were forced to withdraw due to the intense firing. The air was filled with the smell of gunpowder and screaming

G.I.'s. The helicopters reminded me of a flock of ducks about to land on a favorite pond and suddenly being driven off by the gunfire of hunters. There is a second of hesitation caused by fright. For that instant they don't know whether to land or depart. The helicopters seemed to be in that same period of indecision. Like the ducks, they too were forced to withdraw.

With their departure, I began to curse them. All these wounded and dying men and those chicken shits leave. What in the hell kind of service is that. While in Hawaii all I had heard was how brave those pilots had been. They had been built up into supermen. Seeing them in action, I discovered just how human they were. Actually it would have been suicide for them to try and land at that precise moment. In my rage, I saw them as mere chicken shits, merely looking for their own asses.

Even though they were leaving, the firing was continuing with an unrelenting intensity. I didn't know exactly where the rest of my platoon was so I didn't know exactly where to fire. I knew they were not in the trees so I began to fire into the surrounding tree tops. In the massive thick branches of each coconut tree five men could hide undetected. Figuring that it made sense to fire into the tree tops I continued to do so until I shot off almost a full magazine of ammunition.

Just as I was about to reach for a fresh magazine the goddamn rifle jammed. Up to that point I had been relatively calm. Suddenly, I was filled with panic. To be without a rifle at a time like this was insane. I opened the breech and became even more panic-stricken. Mud and sand oozed out of the chamber. How it had fired one round was a miracle in itself. I began wiping at the mess with my shirttail. It was futile due to the mud which covered it and every other part of my body. I felt dejected and more scared than at any other moment in my life. Sweat was again pouring uncontrollably out of every pore in my body. I wanted to run away and hide. Standing there, not knowing what to do, I suddenly started to cry. It was a cry of hopelessness much like a little boy lost from his mother.

The sound of a bugle began piercing the air. Thoughts of the enemy attacking raced through my mind. The sound made me freeze from panic. I turned around toward the sound of the bugle, knowing that I would be dead at any moment. I expected to see a sea of yellow faces advancing on me, their only thought to kill me.

Coming out of the nearby bushes came the face of an American. I recognized it immediately. It was a guy named Raker from another

Company. He was a fat individual who had the reputation for being mentally unbalanced. Seeing him now he looked like the most beautiful man on earth. He was indeed blowing on a bugle. He wasn't blowing anything particular; just blowing.

He was followed by men screaming and yelling various obsceneties at the VC. Most of them had no shirts on. Their chests were draped with strand upon strand of machine gun ammo. They were an imposing sight. I suddenly knew how victims of the Huns must have felt in the Middle Ages. I certainly was glad they were on my side.

They passed by my position and seemed to be heading in the area from which most of the previous firing had come. They were met by sporadic firing. The firing wasn't as intense as it had been moments before. Either the VC were being killed or they had disappeared. Unfortunately most of them had done the latter.

A few moments later Sergeant Newhouse ran up to my position and told me to follow him to where the remainder of the platoon had set up a defense. The usual circle of defense had been set up. The wounded had been transported into a large trench to await evacuation. Tragically, evacuation would come too late for many of them. Walking with Newhouse toward my new position I was struck by the large number of fires which were burning in the distance. A fire seemed to be burning everywhere. The oncoming darkness made them seem all the more bright.

Shortly we were joined by Clark. He immediately asked me what I was doing with that bottle hanging down my back. I had again forgotten about it. I merely told him to cut the damn thing off and not to worry about it. When it was lying at my feet I felt an immediate sense of relief.

We joined two other men on the edge of the perimeter. They were standing there bullshitting with each other. Newhouse told us to join them and set up two positions ten meters apart. Just as Clark and I were about to approach them and decide on who would camp where, one of the men, Pfc. Horner, yelled, "Hey, you mother fucker" at what I thought was no one in particular. He immediately began firing his M-16 at something a few feet in front of us.

The sound of his rifle was momentarily deafening. After he shot off a long burst he immediately ran toward the area he had fired into. It was now quite dark and I couldn't see anything that would have caused such a seemingly inappropriate action. A moment later he came back dragging the body of a dead North Vietnamese soldier. He was pulling him by the feet and seemed to be struggling from the ordeal. Clark immediately went to help. Together they dragged the dead body a few feet from where we were now lying.

Horner said he had seen two of the bastards sneaking up on us. He was sure he had wounded the other one but evidently he had disappeared into the darkness. He assured us the one he did get was very dead. The darkness prevented us from immediately determining this by sight.

Since the threat of infiltraters was very real, we decided to go on 100 per cent alert, which meant no one would go to sleep. For the first time in my military career, I found myself agreeing. Rather than put two men together, we decided to go it alone and thus cover more territory. Even though we were but ten yards apart, they were a very long ten yards.

We lay the dead soldier between myself and Clark to give the impression of another defender. I lay down and vowed I wouldn't move a muscle the rest of the night. I nestled the rifle in my arms so that if I had to fire I could do it with a minimum of effort. I knew the goddamn thing probably wouldn't fire but I was going to be ready just in case it did. Early the next morning, if I saw it come, I was going to get a working model from one of the dead or wounded men. I began to pray that I wouldn't have to fire it simply because I knew it probably wouldn't work.

An eerie silence greeted the night. All firing had stopped. An occasional round fired by some frightened individual succeeded in keeping me from falling asleep. The tension from being so afraid was causing my muscles to tighten into painful knots. I felt that to move would be to give away my position to the enemy, thus I endured the pain. My hands were lying in a thicket of thorns. My fear was so great that I made no attempt to move them. Soon the feeling in them disappeared.

A rain began to fall, producing more eerie sounds as the drops bounced off the trees and onto more branches of smaller bushes below them. The thought that the enemy could be an arm's length away kept coming into my mind. The more I thought about it, the more tense I became. I felt sure I would never make it through the night without screaming and thus give away my position. When I could stand the pressure no longer I called out to Clark in a hushed sort of whisper and asked him if he was still awake. The sound of my voice and his response reduced some of the paranoia inside of me. eerily

A flare suddenly went off overhead. The dull glare brought the surroundings eerily into view. As the flare floated slowly downward the light it produced would gradually disappear. The effect was the same as watching shadows approach you as clouds blocked out the sun on a sunny day. Immediately, I would be plunged into another episode of fear induced by the darkness and potential death. I would remain in this state of fear until another flare went off. I judged the flares to be going off about every half hour. I was only living, in any sane sense of the word, when a flare would go off and produce the wonderous light. I had never been afraid of the dark before but this was different and that dead body to my left proved it.

When the next flare went off I looked over at the body and thought I saw it move. The thought of the body moving meant the son of a bitch was alive. I was filled with a new fear. I swore that the body was moving more and more with each new flare. Now I was beginning to hope the flares wouldn't go off. I was starting to see things as well as hear them. In addition, I had to urinate very badly. Thinking about it only made the desire more intense. After an hour or so I had no choice. I had to go or my bladder would burst. I certainly wasn't going to move an inch, so I urinated exactly where I lay. The physical relief was most gratifying, however, I felt disgusted with myself for behaving in such a juvenile manner.

As the night progressed I could again feel the tension in me reaching the breaking point. I suddenly heard a snapping sound in front of me. Thinking it was another VC I immediately squeezed the trigger with numb fingers. To my amazement the rifle fired. The loud explosion made me feel a little more at ease. Then I realized what a stupid mistake I had just made. The flash from the muzzle would surely give me away. Now my fears were more intense than before. It seemed like every time I did something I was getting myself in deeper and deeper trouble. Thus I decided to lie there and do nothing. Hadn't I been lucky up to now? Why should it change, I asked myself. That attitude seemed to ease my tension as much as anything else I tried.

After what seemed an eternity the sun started its slow climb. The oncomming light had the same effect on me as a breath of air on a smothering baby. The light brought the realization that we were safe. We had made it through a terrifying experience. I felt a close bond with the individuals who had suffered through the events with me. Little did I know there were going to be many such events in the days ahead.

The bright sunlight had a soothing effect on me even though it was early in the morning. I knew that the rays of the sun would dry out my clothing and have a healing effect on my dwindling physical condition. I was looking forward to the day beginning.

The first thing we did that day was to inspect the dead body that had lain next to me all night. I was immediately impressed with the results of rigor mortis. I had never seen anyone in such a condition before and the effect was unbelievable. The man's body was like concrete. I nudged his arm with my foot to try and move it. I had the same result as trying to open a locked door with my foot. It just wasn't going to move. He had obviously been dead for a long time. My fears of believing I saw him move throughout the night made me feel very foolish.

One other thing about the body that especially impressed me was his obvious military manner. His uniform was quite new, as were the various pieces of equipment he carried. He had had a haircut recently as his hair was neatly trimmed. He was young, probably in his late teens. Even dead he looked sharp. I had a hard time deducing where he had been shot. All of the blood had been washed off of him during the night. It was only when Clark moved him that I saw a wide strap slide across his chest revealing a number of neat little bullet holes. One thing about the man puzzled me, however, I couldn't understand my puzzlement. Staring at the frozen face I suddenly realized what had caused my curiosity. The man died with a fucking smile on his face.

Sergeant Timura arrived on the scene and diverted our attention from the dead man. He had a rifle for me, taken from one of the wounded men. We were to scout the nearby edge of a clearing. There were reports of machine gun emplacements which had not been knocked out the day before. It was our job to see if the gun emplacements were still in operation. Without a minute for breakfast we moved out. Without any sleep or nourishment, I felt as though I was merely going through physical motions. My mind was not working in any rational manner.

About thirty meters away from where we spent the night we stopped and surveyed the area around us. We were at the edge of a graveyard. The graveyard was approximately fifty yards across. Directly in back of the graveyard was a thick growth of trees and underbrush. The machine gunner was reported in the growth of trees. Our Company couldn't move forward if indeed an enemy machine gunner was in a blocking position. We would know in a few moments if he was still there.

Our squad, consisting of eight men, got "on line". We were simply strung out in a line about ten meters apart. We were to advance forward and search for the enemy. If no contact was made it was to be assumed the gunner had fled. I felt a curious sense of bewilderment, as I couldn't understand why a machine gunner would have been silent while we had been approaching the area. In addition, we had been standing around surveying the area giving him every opportunity to fire, thus, I viewed the operation as useless as I was sure he was obviously gone.

We had gone about five yards into the graveyard when the unmistakeable rapid firing of a machine gun fire filled the air. As the rapid firing filled the air I heard a scream come from the other end of the line we had formed. I immediately flung myself down behind a headstone. The Vietnamese construct their graves into mound-like affairs. The top of the mound is leveled off and usually a large headstone is added. Thus by falling behind a grave, one is afforded ample protection from incoming rounds. The area was completely composed of sand. For an instant I had a vision of being on a beach. The unfamiliar graves looked as though they were sand castles made by children. The vision was gone when my mouth became full of the sand. As my clothes were still wet from the previous night, I was quickly covered with a layer of clinging sand. My rifle was covered with it also. I immediately wondered if it would fire. I would know in seconds.

I peered over the edge of the grave and was immediately greeted with bullets raking across the top of the mound, inches from my face. I quickly sank behind the mound and thought how ironic it would be to be killed in a graveyard. The sounds of an individual screaming to my right forced me to focus my attention on him rather than the enemy.

The high-pitched voice sounded like a trooper named Phillips. The machine gun fire had stopped as everyone was now behind a grave. Someone was calling for a medic to attend to Phillips. Phillips' screams were the only sound that could be heard. He was screaming for his mother. How pitiful, I thought; a young kid, expected to be a man, dying and calling for his mother. By calling for his mother, one realized just how hopeless and insane the whole situation was. His screams continued unabated for what seemed like hours. He was wasting precious energy but he evidently was in shock and was calling for the one person who could comfort him.

His screams continued and I wished someone would knock him out. By screaming for his mother he was making me think of my mother. It was probably more subconscious than conscious but I didn't want any pleasant memories associated with this sickening situation.

As his screams continued I tried to get a better view of him to see just what in the hell was going on. By crawling back behind another grave I got a good view of him lying face down in the sand. His frantic screaming and sobbing was starting to diminish somewhat. The medic had not yet reached him so only the minimal first aid was being administered to him by another trooper. Looking at Phillips I was puzzled by something that was on his back. There was a large amount of red material lying like a small scoop of cotton candy on his backpack. It was completely unfamiliar and the red color made it stand out vividly against the green of his fatigues. It took me much thinking but I finally deduced that the bullet or bullets had penetrated his body and exited through his backpack. While going through his backpack the bullet had pierced a can of shaving cream. The pressurized cream had leaked out of the hole and formed in a pile on his back. His blood had soaked into the cream like water into a paper towel. It was symbolic of the pagan slaughter of a young lamb; its blood, like Phillips', fouling its whiteness. His screams died from an uncontrolled hysteria into barely audible whimpers.

The sound of the machine gun again spitting forth death forced me back to my original position. A small group of G.I.'s had advanced forward behind the protection of the graves. They had reached the edge of the graveyard when the intensity of the machine gun forced them to stop in their forward position; our entire squad was pinned down. Other elements were trying to get into a position on the side of the machine gunner but his excellent field of fire enabled him to control the whole area. Thus, I remained behind the grave for over an hour.

The sun was now shining brightly in the clear sky. It's warmth had an almost soothing effect on my tired body. Lying there letting the warm rays play upon my weary face I was almost lulled into a much needed sleep. That pleasure was to be denied.

Looking up into the sky I suddenly saw an Air Force jet come screaming into view. It made a pass over our position and continued overhead. Seconds later it was back. This time it dropped two large cylinders of napalm onto the enemy's position a short distance in front of us. The pilot had to release the silver cylinders behind us so that the projectory of the napalm would carry it over our heads and onto the enemy. Looking into the sky I was sure that the napalm was going to land on us. The pilot knew his business. The napalm landed slightly off target but well over our heads. Peering over the grave I could see the cylinder explode in the tree-tops, the jellied gasoline immediately spreading like flaming molasses. I thought that the machine gunner would head for the jungle behind him but his gunfire showed his determination. The jet made pass after pass, releasing the napalm. Each time he dropped the load, I said a silent prayer in hopes that the napalm would make it safely over our heads. The sight of seeing those large cylinders tumbling through the air coming closer and closer and magically sailing overhead was most uncomforting. He made at least six passes but could not dislodge the enemy. More unsuccessful attempts with rockets and gattling guns made me wonder what in the hell we were fighting. How anything could withstand all of that firepower was beyond me. Actually, all the enemy had to do was drop into a spider hole when he saw the jet approaching. Unless a direct hit was made, there was to be no dislodging the VC.

With the Air Force being unsuccessful, the job fell to the infantry, as it so often does. The men in the front advanced on their bellies, inch by inch. When we heard the gun firing to the right we would crouch up and fire from our position on the left. Hopefully we could provide enough cover so that the men could get close enough to throw grenades. One of the men in front was shot, as was evidenced by screaming. One of the men in front came crawling back around the mounds of graves. He crawled directly to my position. His head was completely covered with blood. The sight of the blood running off of his face and onto his shirt made me think he was wounded more seriously than he really was. My past uneasiness at helping someone was completely gone. I wiped the man's face and applied a field bandage to the right side of his head. He continued crawling toward the rear where he could receive proper care. I felt much better about myself after having helped the man.

I began to wonder if we were ever going to get that bastard behind the machine gun. Soon sounds of gunfire accompanied by yelling G.I.'s indicated that another element had succeeded in capturing the enemy from behind. Hearing the victorious men, the men in the front of me went forward to help and return the VC to the rear.

What I had anticipated as one man turned out to be two. One of the VC was a teenager; the other was a very old man. Both had been wounded and were bleeding through the bandages that someone had applied to their wounds. They passed a few feet from where I was lying. I was tempted to raise my rifle and kill both of them. It was predominately an emotional and gut reaction; something in my subconscious made me release my finger from the trigger. The look on the faces of the VC was one of absolute terror and panic. I was amazed the old man hadn't died of a heart attack. I later learned that the two had been chained to the machine gun. I cannot verify the validity of such an account but others who were in the actual capture swore to it. It may have accounted for the fact that they refused to leave their position even in the face of certain capture. We would later learn that a favorite tactic of the enemy was to leave a few snipers behind to cover us approaching infantry while the majority of the men fled into the jungle and rugged mountains. Often we would be pinned down for days. When we finally overran the enemy we would find only a few bodies. The psychological effect of being held at bay by a relatively few men had a devastating effect on our psyches.

After the two prisoners had been taken to our Command post, we were ordered to "saddle up" and prepare to move out. The orders fell on disbelieving ears. Being near physical and emotional collapse I didn't really think I could go on any more patrols. However, seeing the other men, equally as exhausted as I was, "saddle up" and prepare to move out, provided the needed impetus. To be sure there was the usual bitching but everyone was soon loaded up and prepared to move out.

The sounds of incoming helicopters caused a delay in our departure. The helicopters were the medivacs. They had finally made it in. Even though they were late, the knowledge that they were taking the dead and wounded out made me glad to see them. I secretly wished I could have been one of the wounded who would soon be on board. For many, the choppers were too late. Niranda and others had died during the night. To be more precise, they had bled to death.

Another squad from our platoon joined us for the sweep around the area. I learned from one of the men that John Spinner had been shot and died during the night. The news of Spinner's death was especially disheartening. We had been in Hawaii recuperating at the same time. During the stay we had become quite close. Spinner had not been trained to be an infantryman. His training was that of truckdriver. In the Army's hurry to fill slots prior to moving out of Ft. Benning, Spinner and others had been assigned to our outfit. During his stay in Hawaii, Spinner had written countless letters to his original Company Commander requesting he do everything in his power to get him reassigned to his rightful place. Spinner had stated recently that he thought progress was being made in his attempt to be reassigned. He wouldn't have to worry about it any more.

The manner in which Spinner died was quite interesting and served to be a learning situation for me. He was shot in the groin and went into extreme shock immediately. He evidently believed he was shot in a more vital place. Psychologically he wasn't prepared for such an event and gave up hope for survival. His wound was serious, but not extremely critical. Others that saw him react, honestly believed that, if he had exhibited a stronger will to live, he probably would have pulled through the ordeal. Hearing this news I made a vow that if I were to become wounded I would try to remain calm and concentrate all of my energies on surviving. I have seen men react in a variety of ways upon being shot. Some would panic and scream for their loved ones. Others would remain calm and even administer first aid to themselves. All too often the men reacted by screaming and going into a panic. I suddenly wondered again what it would be like to be shot and how would I react. I was certain I would not panic.

Soon we were marching under the hot sun and my mind was concentrating on staying awake. I was walking through half closed eyes and my mind seemed to be in a semi-oblivious state. My eyes were soon awakened by sights I shall never forget.

Our march took us in a wide circle around the entire area of the village. The entire distance was only a mile or so but the amount of death and destruction surely made it 'the devil's mile'. The village had very recently been an armed camp. Various factions of North Vietnamese regulars had been instructing the local people how to be good guerrila fighters. There were trenches, bunkers and gun emplacements everywhere one looked. Where buildings once stood intact; there was nothing left but burned out shells. The action of the previous day and night was more intense than I had imagined.

Most of the people had been detained so there were not any civilians immediately noticeable. As we rounded a turn I spotted a group of South Vietnamese questioning a group of young men who, by their shaved heads and flowing orange robes, belonged to some religious group. The soldiers were beating them with rifle butts in no uncertain terms. I had practiced that same horizontal butt stroke a thousand times in training but I never thought I would see it put into action so energetically. Curiously I had a feeling of remorse for the individuals who were being beaten. I didn't know their crime but my feeling for the underdog was showing.

Moving on around the village we came to a large barnyard setting. There were many buildings but there were no animals in sight. A trench that the VC had dug ran the length of the buildings. Walking up to check out the buildings I noticed the dead animals lying about like broken stuffed toys. The animals had become bloated and beset with rigor mortis. Thus, their legs jutted out in every conceivable angle. The skin on their bodies was drawn so tight over their bloated bellies I expected them to burst at any moment. Many of the cows had their large eyes open and seemed to be looking at me. The scene was disgusting and produced a nauseous feeling inside my stomach. Even though the smell of death had yet to begin, an eerie feeling came over my body. The hot sun would soon cause the air to fill with the sweet decaying smell of death. My skin became clammy from seeing so much death. Looking about I could see dead pigs, calves, chickens and other common barnyard animals. Everyone of them was dead and in various states of decomposition. Blood and intestines were laying everywhere. One had to be careful not to step in the various piles of body parts. The more I looked the more grotesque the animals became. The order to leave the area came none too soon.

A wailing sound reminisant of an Indian engaged in some sort of ceremony broke through the death pervaded atmosphere. As we moved closer to the sound I determined it was a woman weeping. I spotted the woman and a man moving directly in front of us. They were headed for the edge of the graveyard. The old woman was carrying a small plastic bag. Inside were the remains of a small baby. As the man dug into the sand the woman continued to weep uncontrollably. As the man dug deeper and deeper her wailing evolved into hysteria. She was pounding the ground with her fists and throwing sand into the air. As we moved past her, a scant ten yards away, she turned her face toward us and began to shout at us. She was obviously cursing at us. It was the first time I had been the recipient of such hate from any South Vietnamese. I should have felt sad but I immediately felt myself thinking of my close friends who had met the same fate as her offspring. I mumbled for the bitch to get fucked as we moved past her.

I saw no other dead bodies and thought that to be quite strange. Later I learned that the enemy dead had been moved to a central location to await their mass burial. They would be mass buried or burned. The PAVN couldn't come back and carry them back home to North Viet Nam, thus they were usually buried where they fell. If they were buried at all.

Continuing on our journey we came to a wide clearing amongst the coconuts and took a short break. Across the clearing I could distinguish a few small houses. Standing near one of the houses was a small man. He began to cross the clearing in our direction. He had something in his arms. Out of conditioned response I immediately reached for my rifle and trained it on the advancing figure.

As he came closer I could see that he was carrying a bunch of coconuts. He stopped a few feet in front of us with a large grin on his face. The tops of the coconuts had been sliced off and he was offering us the coconuts in a friendly gesture. A Vietnamese interpreter came up to him and questioned him. After a brief exchange of words the interpreter explained that the man was presenting us with a gift. He wished it could have been more but it was all that he had to show his gratitude. It was the first time in years he had been free from the control of the VC. I didn't know if he was serious or merely playing the role but the smile on his face seemed to be genuine. In a matter of moments I had been cursed then greeted like a hero. I enjoyed the feeling induced by the latter.

Shortly we had completed the sweep of the village and were back at the graveyard where it was decided to set up camp. No one had any food of any kind, thus dinner was a cup of instant coffee. We had been without food for a couple of days but I was too tired to worry about it. The events of the past days had been too overwhelming to worry about something as insignificant as food. As darkness approached I found myself on guard duty. I was the first one on watch. Seconds after lying down everyone except those on guard duty had fallen into a sleep induced by sheer exhaustion.

A peaceful silence fell over the area. Sounds of artillery shells exploding in the distance made me aware of the surrealistic world I was now a part of. My body was screaming for rest. I decided to close my eyes for a second. I lay my head back on the ground and was instantly asleep. I was awakened by an unfamiliar shrill peeping sound. I opened my eyes and for a second I was completely disorientated. Looking up into the moon illuminated night I could see the tops of burned trees. Looking slowly to my right in the direction of the sound I could make out the outline of a large rat inches from my face. Instinctively I took the helmet from behind my head and flung it in the direction of the furry creature. Gratefully, it disappeared into the night. Rats were becoming a familiar but most unpleasant aspect of life in the jungle. I began to dread and fear them more than the VC.

I was suddenly aware of where I was. It took a minute for the realization to set in that I had fallen asleep on guard duty for the first time. I was scared and didn't know what to do. I decided to awaken Sergeant Timura and tell him it was his turn. I had no idea what time it was and was afraid to guess. When I awakened the Sergeant he immediately checked his watch and informed me I had been on watch for the last five hours I told him I wasn't tired and had decided to pull extra duty. He laughed and told me to go to sleep. The next thing I knew it was daylight and we again were ordered to "saddle up".

We were moving out in search of the enemy who was reported to be nearby. We walked for about a mile and came to the outskirts of another small village. Our platoon was held in reserve while another platoon advanced into the village. When they were about halfway through we started to advance, thinking everything was safe. Just as we reached the edge of the village the enemy within opened fire. Bullets were tearing through the air from both sides. The air was filled with smoke and the smell of fresh gunpowder. I couldn't believe what was happening. Hadn't we been through enough without having to do it all over again?

I immediately flung myself behind the large trunk of a coconut tree. As I rolled behind it bullets thundered into it directly opposite my head. Someone obviously had me in their sights. I hoped the order to move out didn't materialize or I was sure I would be dead. Sounds of Sergeants screaming orders to everyone in sight added to the overall confusion. Individuals began screaming for medics and it seemed like everyone was yelling orders at the same time. Chaos fitted the situation.

Peering cautiously from behind the tree I could see three G.I.'s running past me toward the rear. They had all been shot as was evidenced by the bandages which had been hastily applied to their wounds. In running they had come loose and were blowing in the breeze. One soldier had a bandage draped around his head. As they neared the rear they slowed to a walk. For an instant I was reminded of the picture of the three wounded soldiers marching and playing various instruments during the

War of 1776. The firing continued unabated for another half an hour. I remained behind the tree the entire time. Most of the firing was coming from the front of the village. Suddenly the firing stopped as quickly as it had started. An occasional round fired in the distance kept us on the alert.

The order to move out filtered into my brain. Hesitantly and cautiously I stood up. Peering around the tree I could see the coast was clear of any conspicuous enemy. Other troopers were beginning to move forward. Everyone was in a crouch and moving slowly, checking each tree and shrub large enough to conceal anyone. I marveled at the difference between the professional attitude now displayed and the lackadasical attitude displayed by others a few months ago. Being in combat has a way of forcing one to make the proper adjustments. Experience, at least in combat, was clearly the best teacher.

As we approached the village I noticed many small igloo appearing structures. The shelters were as large as an oversized doghouse. They were made of layer upon layer of banana stalks, bamboo and seemed to be held together by a mud and straw mixture. The entrance was quite small. Once an individual or individuals were inside, a heavy board was placed in front of the opening, sealing off the occupants from the dangers outside. Once inside they often dug a chamber. The shelters were used primarily for protection from bombs and rockets.

From out of nowhere came the order to check out the shelters. Never having "checked out" a bomb shelter I didn't know what to do. Not speaking any Vietnamese further complicated the situation. I thought one would merely tell the occupant, if any, to come out. That was not the method used by the men.

Since this was a VC village, it was assumed by the majority of men that everyone in it was a VC, or at least a VC sympathizer, thus everyone was the enemy. The fact that there had been hostile fire coming from the village resulting in the death and wounding of many further infuriated the men. Thus they were in no mood to take any chances.

Sergeant Howell, another new replacement, was in the process of checking out one of the shelters. His method was quite simple. He merely threw a grenade inside after kicking the entrance clear. In a few seconds there was a muffled explosion and the shelter shook from the impact. Debris flew out of the opening in all directions. No one was inside so he moved on to the next one a few yards away. This method didn't seem to make a lot of sense when one considered that there might be innocent people inside. Talking them out would have made much more sense. In Howell's case it was easy to see why he was clearing it in this particular manner. He came to Viet Nam directly from Alaska with absolutely no training whatsoever in jungle fighting. Yet here he was in a position of leadership displaying actions I thought were completely inappropriate. Like so many others he seemed obsessed with the thought of actually killing someone. Perhaps it was the pressure one undergoes from being in a combat situation that causes him to react in such a way. I would kill if I had to but I wasn't capable of killing for the pleasure of it time and time again.

As Howell threw the grenade in the second shelter the explosion was immediately followed by cries. Instantly I knew someone had been inside. I expected to see someone exit dripping with blood. What I saw caught me by surprise. To be sure the sight was unpleasant, but, because it wasn't as bad as I had anticipated, it didn't seem as serious as it really was.

A middle-aged woman came crawling out. Her clothes were tattered and she was covered with dust. She was crying hysterically and seemed to be in shock. She didn't know where to turn for help so she stood in one spot staring incredulously at her hand which she had cradled in the other. The hand was laying at an odd angle. I approached her to see if I could apply any first aid. I didn't know what to say and felt frustrated at my stupidity. Before I could reach her a medic arrived at her side and began dabbing at the blood which obliterated the wound. Watching him work with the blood-soaked bandage I could see that the woman's hand was attached to her wrist by the barest amount of skin and tendons. The bones had been completely broken and blown away. Blood was pouring out of the opening in her wrist faster than the medic could soak it up. He applied a tourniquet to her upper arm and led her away to be evacuated.

I looked around for Howell to see if he was satisfied seeing what he had accomplished. He was off at the next shelter ready to throw another grenade inside. After the explosion I was relieved to see that no one came out. The grenade method seemed to be the most popular method of clearing them as most of the men were doing it. I wanted to yell for the stupid asses to stop but I couldn't make the words come out. Instead I watched grenade after grenade being tossed into the shelters.

After a short period of time a Vietnamese interpreter appeared with a loudspeaker. He began shouting something in Vietnamese. Obviously he was telling anyone inside to surrender. Looking about I could see some individuals emerging from the shelters that had yet to be cleared. They were immediately rounded up and taken off for questioning. Mercifully the slaughter had been stopped. I couldn't help but think of the woman who had her hand blown off. What if she were merely an innocent villager caught in this insanity. On the other hand she could have been a hard core VC. I hoped she was. Somehow that made the ugliness bearable.

A month or so later the Division developed a policy designed to eliminate or reduce the possibility of civilian casualties. Prior to our entering a village, or a village about to be shelled, a helicopter would circle overhead and a Vietnamese voice would warn them of the impending danger. Hopefully the civilians would evacuate it and only the military would remain to defend it if they so chose to do so. This method also warned the VC and the bulk of them would disappear leaving a few "volunteers" behind to inflict as much damage as possible on us advancing troops. If the village was a known VC stronghold and a large troop concentration was expected, no warning was given. Artillery rounds were usually called in for a short period of time. We would then follow.

That, however, was in the future. For now we were still in the learning stage. Every day we learned new methods of surviving and ways of fighting in the jungle and hamlets.

After the shelters had been cleared our squad had regrouped to receive new orders. We were going to pass through the village and hook up with Cline's platoon a few hundred meters on the other side. As we entered the village I noticed that the "Zippo Squads" were at work. With their Zippo cigarette lighters G.I.'s were burning everything standing. As the roofing was merely dried grass they were immediately engulfed in flames. Burning huts was an everyday practice. The idea being that the VC would be reluctant to return if it was destroyed. The villagers would also be motivated to resist them if such destruction was to be their reward.

In a few short minutes the whole village was in flames. Looking behind me at the destruction it was evident we had been victorious in our short encounter with the enemy. But looking at the flames engulfing the homes of the villagers I knew that we lost our fight to bring the people over to our side.

Moving past the village and passing through a large stand of coconut trees we came to a large clearing. The clearing was about as large as a football field. A large trench was cut into the sandy soil directly in front of the clearing. The VC had anticipated a helicopter landing in the clearing and the trench was where they had hoped to set up an ambush. Now, however, it was decided we would take a break in the trench. Collapsing under the weight of the pack and from physical exhaustion we all fell to the ground like the limpest of rag dolls. Any further fighting seemed to be an impossibility. I hoped we would stay in that trench for weeks.

Lying in the trench the pangs of hunger began to be felt in my stomach. We hadn't eaten anything of any substance for days. I had figured the fighting was over and we would be resupplied with food and other supplies at any time. Someone had discovered potatoes growing a few feet in back of the trench. Once news of the bonanza spread among the men everyone acted as if they had just received a shot of adrenalin. I joined the others in digging into the soft soil barehanded in a frantic search for the potatoes. Raw potatoes are not a particular delicacy but at that particular moment they seemed very succulent. Soon I could eat no more and the hunger pains subsided.

There was general bullshitting going on between the men. Most of us were concerned about how much longer we could take the physical exertion required to go on day after day with no real rest. Our clothes were ragged and muddy as was the rest of our bodies. A shower and shave would have seemed like the height of luxury. That is, next to a glass of clean ice water. I rubbed the stubble of whiskers on my face which was causing an ungodly itching. How I wished for a chance to clean myself up.

The radio laying in the sand a few feet away began to crackle. The RTO (Radio Transmission Operator) began calling for Lieutenant Grover. I instinctively knew something was wrong. Grover came running, grabbed the phone and, after a brief converstion began shouting orders.

"Cline and his men are in trouble at the edge of the clearing. We're going to the rescue."

"Sonofabitch," I mumbled to myself. "Here we go again."

The plan was that Cline would mark his position with smoke grenades. The Air Force would saturate the area with bombs and white phosphorus. White phosphorus is especially effective in the jungle. Once the phosphorus is activated by an exploding shell, it burns until it consumes itself. The only way it can be put out is to deny it oxygen. One can imagine the horrible consequences if one is unlucky enough to have any of it land on your skin. It will literally eat itself into the inner depths of your body.

Once the area had been saturated with various bombs a layer of smoke would be laid down on the clearing by the planes. As the smoke screen was being laid, Cline would emerge from the wooded area and enter the clearing. We would go out, meet them, and bring back the wounded. There was nothing to do but lie down and wait for the planes to arrive. I could hear small arms fire from the area of the woods in which Cline was positioned. I had no idea what was going on but obviously his platoon had stumbled onto something bigger than they had expected. Sitting there in the trench I suddenly had a feeling of pity for the men in Cline's platoon. He had been volunteering them for every mission he could. They must have been in worse condition physically and mentally than I. I was thankful that I had had the foresight to stay out of that madman's platoon.

Moments later the planes arrived from some unknown air field. I buried my head into the sand in anticipation of the falling bombs. A sound I had never heard before came into my ears. It was very loud but short buzzing sounds indicated something electrical had been discharged. Immediately the ground beneath me shook. The entire clearing seemed to be lifted off the ground, then in an instant, reseated itself. After the initial weird sound and earth-shaking convulsions, more conventional type bombs and napalm began falling onto the wooded area. I later learned that the sound I heard was indeed the electrical discharging of a new gattling gun the Air Force was experimenting with. Twenty thousand rounds of bullets are discharged at one time. The process can be repeated over and over again. It is especially effective on troops caught in the open.

After the area was saturated with all the various armaments, the smoke screen was laid down. Peering over the top of the trench I could see that the clearing was covered with a thick smoke. I was waiting for the order to move out but none came. The smoke was starting to clear away. What the hell was going on, I wondered? Suddenly Sergeant Newhouse began to ease himself over the top of the trench. He immediately took off for the woodline as if he was possessed by the devil. Instantly I was behind him, running like a bat out of hell. I thought to myself, if that little bastard is willing to risk his life, so can I. I knew some of the guys in Cline's platoon very well and felt a personal duty to help them. As we ran to the woodline we saw Cline and his men emerging. Most of them were wounded and were making slow progress.

Newhouse reached the two men leading the way out before I did. One was seriously wounded in the legs and he immediately fell to the ground. He was crying and obviously in much pain. Newhouse immediately helped him to his feet and began dragging him back toward safety. Before another second went by another group of wounded men seemed to appear from nowhere and were suddenly at my feet. I could hear men behind me shouting encouragement to the wounded men. I was overwhelmed with a feeling of comradeship. Guys putting their lives on the line for others causes one to have much respect for his fellow fighting friends. Seeing everyone helping each other pumped new life into me. I felt as though I could single-handedly take them all back. Bullets began whistling over my head. Instantly I threw myself to the ground and put my arm around one of the wounded in a protective gesture.

The man I had my arm around was shot through the stomach and I could see where the bullet came out of his back. I felt a deep attachment toward him and told myself I must get him back as soon as the firing stopped. The enemy's rounds were being fired intermittently. I was just about to take a chance and make a break for it with the wounded soldier when a loud voice startled me.

"Off your ass, soldier, and move this man to the rear." I turned around to tell the individual to get fucked and help out instead of giving orders. Before I could utter a word I saw an eagle on the man's shirt collar. It was a full Colonel, and the Brigade Commander, at that! The shock of seeing someone of such high rank in such a predicament caused me to become momentarily paralyzed. A resounding "Move Out!" spurred me into action.

I helped the individual to his feet and with him leaning on me we made it safely to the trench. The Colonel remained in the clearing until all of the men, both dead and wounded, were brought back to safety. The Colonel was new to the Brigade but his actions told what kind of man he was. He enjoyed more respect from the infantrymen than any other officer in our whole Brigade due to his willingness to be part of the action with his men.

In a short period of time we had all the men from Lieutenant Cline's platoon safely out of the wooded area. Most of the men had been killed or wounded. I was especially grieved to learn of the death of one Pfc.

Matsuno. He was one of the original men who came over on the USS Patch. It seemed as if there were only a handful of us originals left. I had a strange feeling that none of us would make the required year in Viet Nam. The jinx of Custer was definitely a reality. It was to get worse.

After we moved the wounded and dead to a spot where they could safely be evacuated, we got orders to take a couple of hours for rest. We would be moving out of this area and be reunited with the Battalion, or rather, what was left of the Battalion. We were to be resupplied and hopefully this time there would be some food. In all, we had about another week to hump in the jungle. Then it would be back to base camp and a chance to recuperate before moving out again.

The choppers came in low over the trees and we immediately loaded our gear and climbed aboard. The choppers lifted upward and we left the death and destruction. In a matter of seconds it was all behind us, however, for many of us it would never be left behind. I was to learn how easy it is to become callous and nonchalant about killing and destroying. You do so much of it and do it quickly. Minutes or hours later you are on a helicopter and away from the scenes of destruction. The process is repeated again and again. As time evolves and the process is repeated enough times, it becomes as natural as brushing ones teeth.

The helicopters were flying quite high. The cool air was very invigorating. It was so different up here than down on the ground. Everything dirty and ugly was down there. I wished we could have flown among the clouds for the next six months. Six months; how in the hell was I going to make it that long. We were seeing more action everytime we went out on a mission. As we moved into an area so did the VC or PAVN. I said a silent prayer asking God to see me safely through my remaining days with a minimum of risk.

The helicopters started to descend like bees returning to their hive. As we descended I could make out other elements of the Battalion preparing to make camp. Walking toward our Company area it looked like everyone was planning on staying for a few days. Tents were starting to rise and clotheslines were being erected. That was usually a sign of relative permanence. Soon we would be washed up, maybe fed, and perhaps there might even be a mail call. I was actually looking forward to these events. From all indications it looked as if we might be left alone to lick our wounds; physically and mentally.

We came to our area, dropped our gear, and began talking about how long we might remain in the area. Everyone was ecstatic. Merely knowing we would not have to go out in the bush for a day or two was enough to make the most cynical of us grateful.

I had just finished a cigarette and was headed for a well to refill my canteens. For the first time in a long while I was actually happy. A day or two rest would do wonders for our bodies and minds.

I hadn't taken ten steps when I heard the sound of "saddle up". I stopped in my tracks as if I had been shot. It couldn't be true, I thought, we just got here. What the hell do they think we are? Returning to my gear I could see that everyone else was equally displeased, even the Sergeants.

"Where in the hell are we going now, Sarge," I asked of Timura, in a tone filled with contempt.

"Don't blame me," he said. "I just take orders too. But to put your mind at ease we are going to relieve the 5th Regiment. They're pinned down and need our help."

"Why us?" I asked. "Aren't there any other fucking soldiers in Viet Nam besides us?"

"Who knows. Just hurry up and get ready before it gets dark. The word is to expect a hot LZ." (Landing Zone with the enemy waiting.)

Son of a bitch, I thought, what else could possibly happen to make matters worse. Landing in a hot LZ is the next best thing to suicide. The VC usually wait until the first wave of choppers land. When the men depart the VC open up with their automatic weapons. The choppers, if not crippled, take off immediately. You are left to fend for yourself. I hoped to God somebody had been wrong in their information about the hot LZ.

By the time we had packed the gear that we had just unpacked and assembled at the helicopters, it was already dark. Fear was suddenly a very real feeling. I had seen how disorganized we were in broad daylight and knew it could only be worse in darkness.

Boarding the choppers I could see that the pilots even looked scared. Fuckers, I thought. You leave and we stay. What are you so damn scared for? Everything is relative.

The trip to our destination was shorter than I had anticipated. The machine gunners on each side of the helicopters signaled our arrival by opening up with their guns. The sudden and loud firing caused my adrenaline to surge into my veins. The choppers barely touched ground and they were off again. To assist us in leaving rapidly the crew chief gave the slower ones a shove. I had expected to be met with bullets but mercifully there were none. Instead of bullets the voice of Timura broke the silence.

"Over here," he whispered loudly. "Over here, goddamn it."

Our squad was assembled with a minimum of delay. We were lead through the darkness to a nearby hill. The 5th Regiment had been attacked earlier in the day by a large Company of North Vietnamese regulars. The 5th had regrouped on the hill and were expecting an attack at any time. Many of the men were still out in the darkness somewhere. This is but another example of the good organization we encountered. A previous password would identify them if they could find their way to the hill. We tried to dig in with a minimum of noise and after much effort I succeeded in digging a small foxhole. Staring into the darkness I could see fires burning. There was small arms fire going on and I could only wonder as to who was in front of me. The impending attack that was supposed to come at any time played upon my mind. Bradley was next to me and it was some help knowing their was a competent individual near.

"Bradley," I whispered, in an attempt to break the eerie silence. "What are we going to do if they come?"

"Just give it everything you have, that's all anyone can do," he answered.

"Shut up, goddamn it," came a voice from my right. "Make them work to find your ass."

The silence was the worst part of the next couple of hours. Being all alone with the threat of death coming at any minute is a terrible mental anguish to endure. I felt like firing my rifle to relieve the tension but knew better.

The firing that had been going on a few hours ago had subsided. Where were those bastards now, I thought. My mind began hearing imaginary footsteps. Every sound coming from out of the night I imagined to be that of an approaching PAVN. I wished something would happen to break the unbearable tension. I was soaked from nervousness. I began to tell myself to remain calm. Whatever was going to happen would happen. I had been lucky so far, why shouldn't it continue?

The minutes passed as if they were hours. The voice of Sergeant Timura broke the silence. He was to my left and a few yards away. The words he spoke to me sounded as if he was screaming them.

"Fix bayonets, and pass the word down the line."

It was the first and I hoped last time I would ever hear them. The order indicated there was a good chance for hand to hand combat. The thought of having to kill or fight someone with my hands was a stomach-turning idea. Shooting someone from a distance is vastly different than fighting him to the death. Suddenly I didn't care if those mother fuckers ever came. I didn't care about this fucking war or anyone in it. I just wanted to go home and forget all of this insanity. The temptation to go to sleep and pretend none of this was happening was great. I forced myself to remain awake. The remaining hours passed as if I was in another world. I was in another zone of consciousness. My mind was nowhere.

For the first time in my life I was totally unaware of my surroundings. Later I wondered how many people simply become consciously unaware of their own being. The feeling could probably be compared to being in a catotonic state.

As the time progressed and no enemy I knew we would make it safely through the night. With daylight not far off I was overcome with a feeling of success. Both physical success at not confronting the enemy and the mental success of making it sanely through a more vicious battle. That of conquering ones own thoughts.

When morning finally arrived the order to prepare for a mad minute was gratefully received. The prospect of firing ones weapon non-stop for a minute was a most efficient tension-releasing device. I aimed at a clump of trees a hundred yards away and imagined I saw a figure in black pajamas. I flipped the switch to automatic and prepared to fire. I slowly squeezed the trigger but nothing happened. I checked the safety and found it on the off position. Everything was in order; why in the hell wasn't it firing? I repeated the process and again nothing happened. The urge to throw the goddamn worthless rifle at the clump of trees was most strong. I pulled out the magazine and discovered that the rounds had some sand on them. The sand was heavy but didn't appear to be enough to cause the rifle to malfunction. These were supposed to be the best rifles in the world, especially adapted for jungle fighting. Yet mine and others were to continue to fail regularly.

Bradley, kneeling next to me, fired two rounds and his rifle also malfunctioned. We looked at each other, shook our heads in disbelief, and watched as a few of the rifles did work. Thankfully, the machine guns and grenade launchers functioned normally. To satisfy my aggrevated feeling I tore the pin out of a hand grenade and threw it as far as I could. Watching it explode satisfied some inner feeling for seeing something blown up and destroyed.

After the semi-successful mad minute our platoon was called into formation. After the usual waiting period of hours we boarded helicopters and returned to the Battalion Headquarters we had left the night before. Another night had elapsed safely but the thought of what could have happened played upon my mind.

Returning to the Battalion Headquarters resulted in a most unexpected but pleasant surprise. A supply of C rations was waiting as were large containers of hot soup. The soup being hot and flavorful, by Army standards, resulted in a big moral uplift. I was to be amazed time and time again to discover how something as simple as a hot cup of soup can make one's outlook surge upward. It all depends on what one is used to. When you don't have much it doesn't take much to please you.

Arriving in base camp we were greeted by more replacements. The first thing that we noticed about them was that they were from the 82nd Airborne Division. They were also wearing Combat Infantry Badges. The badge is awarded only to infantrymen who have spent a certain amount of days in combat. We were amazed to see them strutting around quite pleased with their decorations. Some of us had been in Viet Nam for over six months and had yet to be issued the badges. There was much resentment among us as to why they were able to wear them. The 82nd had been in the Dominican Republic for about two months on what the government called a police action. It didn't seem justifiable that they were wearing combat badges and we were not. Our contempt for them was quite overt. Even though they were our fighting comrades there was much jealousy. To make matters worse they still wore the insignia of the 82nd on their sleeves. One can wear the insignia he has fought in combat with permanently on his uniform. The point was these prima donnas had not been in combat. Looking back the incident seems quite trivial, however, to us at the time it was quite important.

The last action the Company Commander took while still in command of the Company was to order the men to take off the C.I.B.'s until they earned them. They were also ordered to remove their Airborne insignia. This gave us "old timers" much pleasure in seeing them put in their place. There was another Battalion in our Division which was Airborne. They made no combat jumps, but yet they were getting an extra $65 a month more than we were. To complicate matters, this particular Airborne Division, which was supposed to be so very tough, had drawn easy assignments. They were building bridges, roads, and drawing assignments one would usually associate with the engineering units. We, the lowly grunt, were doing most of the dirty work and getting paid less at the same time. To see any Airborne individual suffer any embarrassment was a precious sight indeed.

While in base camp we were still expected to pull occasional guard duty on the Green Line at night. The days were spent on some patrol around the outskirts of An Khe. The object was to stop any infiltration. It also served the purpose of keeping us busy. Nighttime, when not spent on guard duty, was our own. In between card games, in which gambling seemed to satisfy some insatiable hunger, one usually found time to write a letter or two home. It was most difficult to write by the flickering light of a small candle. My admiration for Abraham Lincoln rose immeasurably.

On nights when I had free time I found myself spending much time with the black soldiers. They had the ability to laugh and have a good time. Most of the whites were up tight in their constant worrying. One's depression seemed to deepen by overly associating with the whites. The blacks, on the other hand, seemed to have the personalities to inject some merriment into a deplorable situation. It probably stemmed from their need to compensate for their past and present living situations.

They always managed to find a record player (battery operated) or radio. Music flowed along with the beer, sardines, and cigarettes. Drugs were not yet prevelant. Taking my mind off of the killing and general destruction was most important. The black soldiers filled this need. The one drawback was that many of the blacks, not all, but far too many, had this same lackadasical attitude on the battlefield.

Base camp was beginning to offer many surprises. After our last mission we received jungle fatigues. Their light weight was most comfortable. We also received the much prized jungle boots. The fact that they dried quickly and offered one a fighting chance against jungle rot (a fast spreading and serious fungus) was their most rewarding feature. We were also allowed to sleep a couple of extra hours in the morning.

The first morning this happened I awoke thinking I had overslept and was in for a great deal of trouble. Jumping out of my cot and untangling myself from my mosquito net I discovered that the whole Company was oversleeping! The Army may screw up in a multitude of ways but one thing you can always be sure of and that is that they will always get you up on time. My surprise at the upper echelons letting us sleep for a couple of extra hours was quite real.

The Battalion mess hall had been recently completed. This caused much excitement among the men. The majority of meals consisted of chili over rice, or chicken prepared in a hundred different ways. Yet no matter how the cooks prepared the chicken it always came out raw in the final stage. We had chicken so often we nicknamed it Leroy. Occassionally we had the ultimate in food; fried eggs and bacon. The lines were usually a mile long when these were served. Milk and fresh fruit were items we never received, however, eating anything besides those goddamn C rations was a real treat. The hot food boosted our morale and the mess hall offered a place to sit out of the rain and share a meal with friends.

Every now and then someone on KP would steal cans of fruit, ice cubes or some other delectable item. If one was friends with that individual one could gorge himself on that particular item.

The Vietnamese people soon learned the value of ice as far as we G.I.'s were concerned. As we traveled on patrols around An Khe it seemed as if all the civilians were selling ice in some form or another. When generators were made available to them they went wild in its production. It was not at all unusual to see the villagers pedaling their bicycles down the roads with large chunks of ice tied on the back fender. Often the ice was yellow, green, or brown, depending on the type of water from which it was frozen. It however served the purpose of cooling ones head or chilling a can of beer or soda.

Base camp also opened my eyes to some unpleasant events. I noticed many individuals who had been nursing extremely minor cuts and various wounds for months on end. How they succeeded in staying on the sick rolls for such long periods of time would always remain a mystery for me. If they were hurt seriously, that was another matter, however, many of these men seemed able to partake in any activity except returning to the field. When I saw an individual getting away with such a "sham" it merely served to lower my morale. Because many of these individuals were Sergeants and/ or black, it was easy to understand why one might view them in an unfavorable light.

The rats in base camp were growing in population as fast as the gooks. Our squad tents had deep trenches dug around them to drain off the rain. Halfway down the trenches (to avoid the water level) one could see many rat holes. During the day they were safely out of sight. At night they came out in what seemed like droves. In our attempts to keep the interior of our tents free from bits of food we would rake down the floor nightly. The only marks on the dirt floor were the marks from the rake. The next morning the entire floor, under and around our bunks, was covered with rat tracks. I was awakened many nights by the squeaking of those vile creatures. Often I discovered them on the edge of my cot trying to chew their way through the mosquito netting which was draped over a frame encasing my cot. A shout or thrown object usually succeeded in scaring them away for a while.

Some men devised a simple method of killing them. They would lay awake at night in the blackness of the tent. The canvas sides of the tent were always rolled down at night as a safety measure against targets for mortar rounds. When the rats could be heard moving about the men would turn on powerful flashlights momentarily blinding the furry devils. In their moment of blindness they made an excellent target for a bayonette or sharpened entrenching tool.

Besides the rats, the most obnoxious thing I encountered was a detail which involved the disposal of human waste. I had heard the word "shit detail" used to describe any detail which was unpleasant. Now I was to learn what it meant in literal terms.

The human feces was collected in fifty gallon drums. When one had to relieve himself one went to the appropriate latrine area. There one would find the fifty gallon drums cut in half. Two boards wide enough to accomodate the fattest ass were placed across the top of the drum. There was enough space between the boards to allow for the feces to drop through. As time evolved many of the latrines became quite fancy. Canvas sides were added to allow one some semblence of privacy.

As these latrines were constructed to accomodate each Battalion consisting of about 800 men, the metal drums became full of the human feces quite quickly. Because of the health and sanitation aspect of group living, the feces had to be disposed of quite quickly. Since the Battalion mess hall was less than a hundred yards away from the large latrine, one can see the need for quick disposal. The flies had but a short flight from their lunch at the latrine to your lunch at the mess hall.

I was told to go to the latrine area and report to a Sergeant Reed. He was in charge of the disposal and would instruct me in the proper method of disposal. At the time I was ignorant of what was involved in latrine duty so I went willingly as it meant a reprieve from another useless patrol the rest of the platoon would be going on.

The first thing Sergeant Reed and I did was to drag the filled drums to a spot immediately behind the latrine area. We then replaced the filled drums with empty ones to accommodate the needs of the men in the Battalion. Our next step was in going to the motor pool, which was a short distance away, and filling up a large number of ten gallon containers with helicopter fuel. The fuel was a mixture of gasoline and oil. The oil would keep the flames burning at a slow but constant degree. I was glad to leave the latrine area as the smell had become quite nauseous. It was to become much worse.

When Sergeant Reed determined we had enough fuel we loaded it aboard a mule (flat bed vehicle used for transportation), left the motor pool and returned to the latrine. It was now early morning and it was already quite hot. There was not a cloud in the sky and the day promised to be another scorcher. Working around the fires was going to make it doubly hot.

Sergeant Reed then demonstrated how much of the fuel to add to the drums of feces. Actually one just poured in any amount; as long as it kept burning, it was the right amount. He flipped a lighted match into the mixture and immediately it began burning. The flames were burning on the top of the mixture only. In order to get the fuel dispersed throughout the drum of feces, one had to mix it up. A large stick was used in the mixing. I had the clearest mental picture of a witch leaning over a pot of mysterious brew and mixing it vigorously. I associated myself with the witch and her mixing. I also had a crazy thought of saying some nonsensical words in the hope of putting some evil curse on Sergeant Timura for sending me on this shit detail.

I had at least eight of the goddamn drums to attend to. This involved adding fuel periodically and constantly stirring the shit to keep it burning. The fuel and feces combined produced a constant rotten smell.

A light smoke was also a constant problem. The smoke succeeded in permeating my clothes, hair, and lungs with the shitty smell.

The drums all had a different consistency to them. Some of them were easy to stir while others were quite hard, due to a thicker consistency. However, one was as equally displeasurable as the next. In addition to the feces, the drums had a collection of other materials including urine, paper and the most interesting of all, worms. The worms appeared to be of the maggot family. With the abundance of flies they could have been produced by them. Intestinal worms were beginning to be a problem with many of the men so they could have been passed by the men in the process of defecating. Whatever the means, they were there in large numbers. The feces in the drums actually seemed to be moving from the large numbers of the worms moving about. The flames would cause them to move and wiggle about in some inate struggle to live. The flames would soon consume them with the rest of the garbage. This burning process was to continue until nothing was left of the mixture but black ashes. Because the fuel was so slow burning, the detail was to continue all day. I was doing the job all by myself as Sergeant Reed had left when the first match was lit. Near the end of the day I was covered with sweat and so saturated with the smell of shit, that I thought I was going to vomit from the smell of myself.

When late afternoon finally approached, Sergeant Reed magically appeared. He assisted me in dumping the ashes into a large pit. We covered the ashes with a layer of dirt but did not fill the pit. It was left for the unlucky guy who would burn the new supply of shit in the next day or so.

I left the latrine area with but one thought in mind. That was to take a shower as soon as possible. The showers were still located a mile from our Company area. Thus I would have to hitch a ride to the showering area. Countless jeeps passed me by in my attempt to hitchhike. Considering the smell which was eminating from me I couldn't blame them for not stopping. Just as I was about to give up and start walking a truck stopped and the driver offered me a ride. Needless to say I rode in the back. I have never looked forward nor have I ever needed a shower as much as I did at that particular moment. After repeated latherings and rinsings I succeeded in removing the obnoxious smell from my body. The clothes I wore while burning the shit, were thrown in a garbage can, which seemed a suitable resting place.

The next week or so at base camp found my squad going on many daytime patrols. The patrols took place around the outskirts of An Khe and amounted to nothing. One particular day I was rewarded with a unique sight I shall never forget. Our squad was walking through a heavily wooded area. The tree limbs had grown so thick and become so entwined overhead that they formed a dark green canopy. I was walking at the rear of the squad pulling rear security. It was late afternoon and the silence was total. All of a sudden Sergeant Howell began shooting into the branches directly overhead. He began moving his rifle in a definite pattern as if he was following something or someone.

Suddenly he began shouting in a voice filled with excitement, "There goes the son of a bitch, do you see him, do you see him?" he repeated.

Scanning the treetops wildly I saw nothing. Howell finished firing his magazine and again there was total silence. A thumping sound behind me caused me to turn quickly around, ready to squeeze off any necessary rounds. I turned just in time to see a large grey primate scurry off into the thick underbrush. He or she was holding two of its youngsters, one in each hand. I was reminded of a human mother holding her children's hands and leading them across a busy street. Seconds later they were gone.

"Hold your fire," I shouted. "They're only monkeys." I hoped that no one would follow them and kill them for the hell of it. Luckily no one did.

Guard duty that night found us on the outskirts of An Khe guarding a pass leading into town. Highway One, a major highway, ran directly through the pass. Two peaks on either side of the highway was our home for the next day. We would pull guard duty in this particular location many times in the near future.

The Koreans had had the primary responsibility for this area in the past. As they were currently assigned elsewhere, the duty now fell to us. They had constructed bunkers out of anything they could lay their hands on. Scraps of metal and wood from various sources produced the sides and tops of the shelters. The area appeared to offer a good degree of defensive protection. The terrain consisted of high grass and an occasional clump of trees. This had been cleared back to offer a good field of fire. In front of each position the Koreans had thrown their empty C ration containers. This served as a warning for any who might approach the position under the cover of darkness. They would give themselves away by stepping on the numerous cans.

The idea was sound except for one drawback; the cans were an attraction for many rats. The rats would run over the cans in search of food. The constant sounds of their claws scratching the cans identified them as rats. If a man had been out there walking around he would undoubtedly stop at the first sound and seek a new route. It was unpleasant listening to those sounds in the darkness and knowing they came from some goddamn rats. At the same time it was pleasant to know they were not coming from a Viet Cong who had something more than food on his mind.

The two peaks that guarded the highway were kept in communication via a field telephone. Whoever was on guard duty had to report to the Command Post every hour on the hour. One particular dark and windy night I was on guard duty when firing from an M-60 machine gun thundered from another position to the left of me. I immediately grabbed my rifle in anticipation of a full scale attack. Nothing happened in the way of an attack but yet the firing persisted. The telephone began ringing. I picked it up and was greeted with the voice of the Lieutenant wanting to know what in the hell all the firing was about.

I told him I would check on it but knew I wouldn't leave the security of my bunker. I knew that a new man had been assigned and was obviously on guard duty in the position from where the firing emanated. There was no way I was going to walk over to him in the darkness and tell him to stop. I reported back to the Lieutenant and told him it was just another new recruit shooting at shadows. That seemed to satisfy him as he merely hung up without another word being spoken. The firing stopped only to be resumed about five minutes later. This went on for the entire time this particular individual pulled his turn at guard duty. I could only laugh at his nervousness. I did it with a little compassion because I realized it wasn't so many months ago I was the same nervous green soldier. I was still green in so many ways but in others I was a true veteran.

The daily patrols we went on brought us into close contact with the local population. Most of the people were peasant farmers. Although many of them became instant businessmen with the influx of Army personnel. While we would be camped on the roadside, in between patrols, and in the early evening, we would be hounded by people of all ages trying to sell us various types of merchandise, the most popular of which was chilled soda pop. As neither party spoke the other's language, a good opportunity to become more friendly was missed. Traveling whorehouses also serviced individual needs. Women would ride up to our position on Lambrettas (small gas-powered vehicles resembling golf carts). If a deal to screw was made, the parties simply went behind a tree or under a bridge and consummated the ritual.

While on actual patrol, which consisted mostly of walking up and down the roads searching for booby traps, we came into direct contact with many peasants engaged in various aspects of farming the rice fields and tending their cattle and water buffalo. Small children and women did most of the heavy work. It was quite interesting watching them go about their work in such determination. I will never forget the small children controlling the huge water buffalo in the planting and cultivation of the ever-present rice paddies. The difference in their size was astonishing. Yet the young children with only the use of a long stick were able to make the huge beasts respond to their every command. I would try and compare their lives to a youngster's back in the United States. There was no parallel. Perhaps by our presence, some day, these kids, or certainly their kids, would enjoy some of the benefits the kids back in the States enjoyed.

The people in general seemed to accept our presence. Whenever we passed them in the fields or went through a friendly village, they always had a smile and greeted us with a wave of the hand. The looks on their faces indicated no fear and they seemed to respect us. The villagers often showed their appreciation by offering us water and various kinds of fruit when we went through the villages. We couldn't take the items because often the VC would poison it. Nevertheless, most of the peasants seemed sincere in their efforts to make us feel welcome. This feeling of acceptance was to reach new heights when we worked in the mountains with the Montagards.

After a week or so of patrolling the outskirts of An Khe our Company received orders to prepare to move out for a short mission. The mission was going to take place at Ia Drang Valley.

The mere thought of going to Ia Drang caused me much personal anguish. Ia Drang was where so many of my friends had been killed in November. I was overwhelmed with the feeling that something tragic was going to happen to me there. I had no factual basis for such a belief but nevertheless the thought was ever present and was a tormenting factor in the days to come. I had gone to mass a couple of times prior to leaving in hopes of finding some magical solution to my problem. None was forthcoming.

The ill feeling caused me to become irritable and extremely tense. I was unable to eat or sleep for any length of time. When the time came to depart for Ia Drang I was probably very near a mental collapse. I was so sure something terrible was going to happen I had even tried to get put on permanent KP in base camp to avoid the tragedy I was certain was going to happen. Nothing I tried seemed to help; I was destined to go and that was all there was to it. I made up my mind to be extra cautious and ride it out. What else was I to do? If something was going to happen it was going to happen so fuck it, let it happen.

Flying over the area of Ia Drang I noticed many areas which had been completely burned out from a previous fire fight. New growth was starting to replace the burned out area but it was unmistakeable that a fight had taken place directly under me. I wondered, was this the spot where so many of my friends had been slaughtered? Suddenly a mental picture of many of their faces came into my mind. Seeing their faces and realizing that they were dead caused tears to roll down my face. By some act of God I had been spared their horrible fate. Now I was in the same area with the feeling that now it was to be my turn. I couldn't wait to get the goddamn mission over and move on to someplace else. If I was to be so lucky.

The helicopters landed in a cleared landing zone. We received no incoming rounds and much of the tension inside me was released. We began patrols immediately in and around the Valley. The terrain was comprised of heavy jungle and progress was very slow. One man at the head of the patrol would chop a path in the thick growth. After a few hours we were covered with cuts and scratches from the ever present thorns. The man in the lead could only cut for fifteen minutes or so. We would then rotate, each taking a turn at hacking out a path. The work was extremely strenuous. After a few minutes one was soaked with sweat and breathing was forced and difficult.

When darkness finally arrived we simply bedded down for the night. We kept in contact with the rest of the Company via radio. When we finally lay down to sleep we merely covered ourselves with our ponchos and collapsed into sleep. Guard duty still had to be maintained and every two hours we took turns staying awake. The sounds of various animals and insects moving about was terrifying. Every sound was believed to be that of the enemy. Daylight was a welcome sight because it meant one more day of life. It was also unpleasant because it meant another day of the same miserable patrols and possible contact with the enemy.

The next day our patrol was moving slowly down the side of a mountain. The jungle was extremely thick and progress was extremely slow. We had stopped momentarily for a short break. I was standing looking at the various plants. I was just about to bend over and examine more closely a particularly strange looking plant. My thoughts were completely on that plant.

A sudden movement to my right caused me to straighten up and turn in the direction of the movement. As I turned my movements became frozen. I was completely paralyzed with fear. Less than three feet away stood a Viet Cong with rifle in hand. Instantaneously his rifle exploded with a deafening roar. The acrid smell of gunpowder filled the air. I immediately fell to the ground thinking I was shot. I began searching my body frantically for the wound. I did not feel anything but thought to myself, how could the son of a bitch miss? He was only a few feet away. I must have been shot.

Before another second elapsed one of the Sergeants ran past me in search of the gook. A moment later I could hear his M-16 firing a short distance away. He returned momentarily, his face all smiles with the news that he had finally gotten one of the mother fuckers. Killing a Viet Cong at close range was really a unique event. Normally they pick the location to fight and when they have the advantage. When a fire fight did break out one usually fired into a house, clump of bushes or some other hiding place of the VC. One rarely saw the enemy until after the fight, then he was so full of holes it was impossible to tell who had shot him.

Getting a close hand kill was a special event. There was a rumor that some Battalions were cutting the ears off the dead soldier and getting monetary rewards from the Battalion Commander. We were not engaged in the practice although we did search the enemy's pockets for souvenirs; cigarette lighters with a Red Star insignia was the most popular. This particular gook had nothing whatsoever on his person. This caused the Sergeant some consternation. The word quickly passed that he had wounded another gook. Our squad immediately began searching for him. His trail was easy to follow due to the tremendous amount of blood he was losing. The man who had just died was left where he lay. Some of his own people would undoubtedly find him in the next day or so. I wondered what his body would look like after the jungle insects had had a few days to work on him. The thought was most unpleasant.

Trailing the wounded man through the jungle reminded me of a hunting party searching for a wounded animal. I felt myself hoping we would find him and finish the job. I was beginning to become nothing more than an animal myself. The thought of killing was becoming exciting. Before it had been repulsive. The game of death was becoming fun. I can't explain why but the fact was that I was beoming fascinated with killing was becoming ingrained in me. Maybe it was the revenge factor or simply the idea that I was pitted against another man in the fight for life. The point is, for the first time I was enjoying my job of killing.

Our search for the wounded man brought us to a part of the terrain where water was cascading downward in torrents. In order to get across the rushing water it was necessary for us to help each other. The fact that the wounded man made it across by himself was most remarkable. As I was to discover later the will to live can make a man do almost anything. Once across the cascading water his trail of blood was again picked up. Directly in front of us was a high bank. Roots of trees were exposed and formed a natural ladder to the top. It required much energy to finally reach the top. Again I marveled at the strength of the wounded man we were following.

On top of the bank we found a path the man had chosen to make his escape on. It was our practice to stay off of paths and walk in the jungle parallel to them. In this way we could avoid the countless booby traps the VC planted for our benefit. We figured this path wasn't booby trapped or this particular gook wouldn't have been on it. Then again, it was impossible for the VC to booby trap every inch of every trail in the mountains.

After five minutes of rapid walking the lead man in the patrol spotted him. He was directly ahead, lying on his back on a huge rock. As we approached the body I noticed his chest was heaving rapidly. He was gasping for breath but before the point man got to him he stopped breathing and his head rolled gently to one side. A thin streak of blood began to run out of the corner of his mouth. It was the last function his body would ever perform. Looking at the blood-covered man I wondered why he hadn't given up, received medical attention and been moved out to a P.O.W. camp. He would certainly have been better off than he was now. The VC had probably been indoctrinated to the potential attrocities of the Americans as we had been about the North Vietnamese. The poor son of a bitch was probably scared out of his mind as to what we would do to him if we caught him.

The dead man was searched and moments later we moved out in search for others. The two men that had just been killed were quite elderly. As they were so very old it was deduced that they were probably acting as guards for a training camp or a cache of weapons. After an hour or so of searching, one of the guys found what the two men had died for. An extremely large supply of small weapons and ammunition had been discovered. Immediately we began cutting a large hole in the canopy of the jungle. This would accomodate the lowering of a net by a helicopter. The guns and ammunition could then be put into the net and raised upward. They would be flown back to Battalion Headquarters and eventually turned over to the South Vietnamese Army. Chances are they would then be recaptured by the gooks and used against us or our allies at some later date. They should have destroyed them by whatever means possible. Finally the entire cache, literally tons of ammunition and guns, had been moved.

Sergeant Long approached me a short while later with the rifle the gook had shot at me with a couple of hours earlier. It was the oldest looking rifle I had ever seen. It was very long and cumbersome looking. It had misfired and actually exploded in the face of the gook who had tried to kill me. I was again saved from the clutches of death through luck and my personal feeling of invincibility was strengthened. I was hoping the Sergeant would give me the rifle but he kept it himself. I felt badly but I knew I would get my chance again.

We moved back to our original location and resumed our patrol. We came into a region that was covered with leeches. Immediately my mind became obsessed with the vile creatures. Nothing else mattered except getting out of the area and keeping the damn things off of my body. It was amazing to watch them crawl through the eyelet at the base of my boot and appear a moment later at the top of the boot. We had to stop every fifteen or twenty minutes and strip to our waists and check out each others backs for the clinging blood suckers. As often as I had picked leeches off of myself and others I still had not gotten used to them.

Their repugnance would always remain with me. It was strange how I could accept killing and destroying and actually enjoy it but becoming accustomed to those little worms was something I would never be able to accomplish.

Thankfully we moved out of the leech infested area and into an area where the jungle was beginning to thin out. The trees gave way to elephant grass and small shrubs. Off in the distance we could make out the outline of a Special Forces camp. Actually it was a Montagnard village which had been converted into an armed camp. We were supposed to rendezvous with the rest of the Company at the camp. We were anticipating a few days of rest and the sight of the camp caused the mood of the men to become more relaxed.

As we approached the camp through the tall grass, one of guys in the squad yelled "Jesus Christ, look over here." Not knowing what to expect I walked cautiously over to where he was standing. He was pointing with his rifle at a dead North Vietnamese soldier. He still had on his uniform complete with hand grenades, rifle, and other parphanalia. Judging by his skeletal appearance he must have been laying there for months. His skin was stretched tightly over his bones. There was no flesh whatsoever on his bones. He was simply a skeleton with a covering of skin. Suddenly other men began shouting that they had found other bodies as well. In addition to whole bodies, parts of bodies were also discovered. Legs and arms were strewn about much like beer cans after a picnic. I was amazed at the sight. Each soldier still had his weapons and ammunition with him or lying near his body. There had been no attempt by anyone to collect the weapons. This was completely against any procedure we had been taught. The enemy's weapons are always collected after a fight. I recalled that this base camp had been under heavy attack a few months earlier. Only through bombing by B52's had the attackers been repulsed. These men had obviously been caught in the open by one of the bombs. Some of the men had started to search them in hopes of finding a souvenier or two. We were quickly warned that the bodies may be booby trapped. We left the skeletons where they lay and continued toward the Montagnard camp.

Arriving at the camp we got our first real view of the Montagnard people. They resembled the Vietnamese in that their physical appearance was much the same. Small, dark skinned and dark haired, and the same oriental facial appearance. They appeared the same to me but I'm sure they considered themselves vastly different from the South Vietnamese. Much later I was to learn that there was much animosity between the two groups. Perhaps this accounted for the lack of cooperation between them.

The one overwhelming characteristic of the Montagnards was their primitiveness. Some of the male Montagnards standing and squatting near us were dressed in loin cloths. Many of the young children had peculiar haircuts. Their heads were completely shaved except for a round circle of hair which remained in the very center of the top portion of the skull. On others, some years older, the hair had grown quite long, so that they had the familiar "pony tail" appearance. The haircuts had some social or religious meaning, however, we had never been told one fact of any kind about these strangely fascinating people. We had been told they were ferocious fighters and loyal to the anti-communist movement. Because of their fighting reputation we did have a certain respect for them but, as for understanding anything about their culture, we knew absolutely nothing, thus another chance for some real human understanding was missed.

We stayed at the camp for a few days merely pulling guard duty while the Green Berets took the local male population out on training missions. Later when we localized our operations in the mountains farther north, around the City of Pleiku, we would continue to come into ever-increasing contact with Montagnard people.

Returning to our main base camp we received a couple of surprises. The most important event was that an electric light had been installed in our squad tent. The fact that it worked rather haphazardly didn't dim our feelings of elation. It was now possible to write letters in our free time at night in light other than that produced by a flickering candle. Card games also could be conducted in a batter atmosphere. This was important because gambling was the main recreation the majority of us were engaged in. The longer one stayed in Viet Nam the more reckless one became in his betting. There certainly must have been some correlation between time served in Viet Nam and amount of money one bet but I'm at a loss to explain the phenomenon. Card games were conducted in the middle of patrols wherever we went. It was not unusual to start playing cards after a battle had just been fought and the bodies of the dead were loaded onto helicopters. Cards and the inevitable gambling was obviously serving to be great tension reducers.

We moved out on another mission deep into the mountains of the central highlands. This was to be the future area of our greatest concentration. Rather than patrols of platoon size, we started to go on the smaller, more dangerous squad size patrols. They were much more dangerous because, if the eight or ten-man squads made contact with the enemy so deep in the jungles, it would have been certain disaster for the squad. Contact was generally made when you were at the disadvantage. It was as if we were watched all the time and the enemy chose to strike only when he could inflict maximum damage.

The other surprise was that our Company Commander was being replaced in a day or so. This was another policy of the Army which we lower echelon troops felt was extremely unjust. When an officer completed six months duty in a line Company he was reassigned to a desk job elsewhere to complete his tour of one year. This policy applied to all officers except Lieutenants.

This was extremely unfair from our viewpoint. With the exception of Second Lieutenants, most officers didn't engage in real fighting. They were at the scene of combat but usually directed the action from some relatively safe spot. I'm not speaking of all officers but the example fit the majority.

Why in the hell did we have to stay and do all the dirty work for a full year? To make matters worse, the Captain were just beginning to work with the men as a well-organized unit. He was replaced with someone green who knew less about fighting in the jungle than the dumbest of Privates.

Our Captain, the third one in seven months, was fresh from Germany. Captain Plum, because of his lack of expertise, would go the way of many of his cohorts and last less than two months as a Company Commander. I wondered if the VC or NVA replaced their officers after six months in the field.

There was a growing feeling of resentment among the men in regard to the patrols we were going on. We had the distinct and correct impression that we were merely being used as bait. The situation was made all the more deplorable as we were often led by a Sergeant who couldn't even read a fucking map. The pace of the patrols was relentless. We walked in the hot, humid jungle all day with the heavy backpacks digging into our necks. Walking in itself was no easy task. Often we had to chop our way through the jungle. One was constantly getting tangled in the growth. Cuts and scratches were as common as the high humidity and heat. It was a fact of life we had to accept. In addition one had to be on the constant lookout for the enemy as well as the fucking leeches.

We would walk from the instant the sun rose until it set. The insects, especially the mosquitoes, seemed to be much worse in the dense jungle. In addition to what we were already expected to do, we were now under orders to pull night ambushes. This meant that, instead of getting a few hours of sleep in the traditional manner, we would now get less. A night ambush is self-explanatory. A group of usually six or so men set up a trap near a trail or some other area where the enemy is expected to be coming during the night. The ambushes were a complete farce.

Once the men are in position they are expected to remain absolutely silent. One is expected to stay awake and be in control of his reflexes. Ones mind must be clear to determine the nature of the various sounds and think about how he will react in case of an actual ambush. We were usually so exhausted after a whole day of walking in the oppressive jungle it was physically impossible to remain awake and do what was expected of us. Most of the men fell asleep after a few minutes. The snoring could be heard for what I believed to be miles around. Also many men chose this time to enjoy a meal. Opening cans and eating in the darkness produces many unwanted sounds. It is no wonder that the ambushers were often the ones who were ambushed.

Some Sergeants saw the futility in these missions. In order to get some rest during the day we would simply stop, lay down, and go to sleep with one man on guard. The Sergeant would call on the radio and report to the Lieutenant that we were actually walking and proceeding in the manner in which we had been assigned. How in the hell would he ever know where we were? Later we would meet with the other squads of the platoon and give ficticious reports as to where we had been. The only squad who had actually done what they had been ordered to do was the one with the Lieutenant in charge.

The Army was reaping its just rewards. We were doing a terrible and ineffectual job merely because we were being asked to do the impossible. It would have made a lot more sense to let the ones who would be on night ambush sleep during the day and do their ambushing at night. Everyone would have been happier and the job would have gotten done. The way we were operating was only causing deep resentment among the men.

The patrols deep into the jungles did provide us with unique opportunities to bathe. We would often come across streams of crystal clear water. While one man stood guard the rest of us would plunge into the cold water and scrub the dirt and dried blood from our many scratches and cuts. The clear water was also a welcome relief from the vile tasting drinking water we had become so accustomed to.

Leeches were becoming more of a constant problem in this particular terrain. One day our squad stopped for a leech inspection. After pulling a few off of my legs and some off the guy's back in front of me the order came from Sergeant Timura to move out. I had just tucked my shirt into my pants when I felt something drip onto my thigh. Instinctively I knew what had happened. Instantaneously I pulled my pants down and looked for the telltale spot which would indicate where the leech had been.

To my horror I didn't have to look very far. The leech had chosen the vein on my penis for its area of concentration. Blood was beginning to drip slowly from the spot of penetration. I was almost in a state of shock, too stunned to move. How that son of a bitch got on my penis without my feeling it will always remain a mystery to me. I had developed my sense of feeling to the degree that at times I could actually feel the hairs on my body move against one another. All because I thought the movement was caused by a leech.

The voice of Sergeant Timura telling me to hurry up caused me to refocus my mind on the present. "Hey, Sarge," I yelled, "I've got a fucking leech on my dick." The laughter from the men was so loud it was probably heard in Hanoi. "Real fucking funny," I responded. "Now what in the hell am I supposed to do?"

"Cut it off," someone said. Not appreciating their humor I decided to apply pressure to the bleeding. I applied layers of toilet papers and held them on the spot while pressing down. It didn't work; the toilet paper was merely absorbing the drops of blood. I then got the idea to put a bandage on it. The field dressings were too large and cumbersome to tie directly onto my penis. The bandage is about the size and shape of a female sanitary napkin. On each end is long strips of cloth to facilitate the tying of the bandage onto a large wound. I ripped off one of the ends and tied it around my penis in the hopes that it would stop the bleeding. Sergeant Timura was telling me to hurry up, so that would have to work.

While pulling up my pants I heard something fall onto the leaves. I looked downward and saw a black half-moon shaped object. It was the mother fucking leech filled to the bursting point with my blood. The fact that the blood came from such a personal area made it seem all the more vile. I stamped on the leech with such force the blood squirted out and splashed on the nearby trees. I kept stamping and grinding at the leech with the heel of my boot until there was practically nothing left. Moving out with the squad my hatred for Viet Nam and everything in it increased.

We walked through the jungle the rest of the day finding nothing. Returning to the platoon area I went to the medic to have him check out my penis. When he saw the way I had it wrapped he went into hysterical laughter for at least five minutes. The wrapping had stopped the bleeding and since we were going to be out in the jungle for another week or so there was absolutely nothing that could be done. He did replace the wrapping with a band aid and said that if anything unusual developed to let him know, thus, in addition to my many worries, I had one more to contend with.

The next day while on patrol we literally stumbled across bunkers and foxholes which had only been recently abandoned by the NVA. Luckily they were abandoned or we would have all been dead. The NVA were masters at camouflage and I was looking at a perfect example. Standing 3 feet away it was impossible to see where the enemy had been dug in. It was obviously meant to be an ambush site. A couple of hand grenades thrown inside made them ineffective. It was really a useless gesture as they could make another in a matter of hours but the action did make us feel better, thinking we had destroyed something of theirs.

Hours later we discovered an area right in the middle of the jungle where a battalion sized enemy unit had been concentrated. The way they used the natural setting was incredible. Ovens were actually constructed out of mud and fireplaces were dug and molded into the bank of a nearby large stream. The numerous vines and small saplings had been weaved into cots and chairs. Holes which were entrances into larger dens were everywhere. The whole area had been constructed under the canopy of the jungle. I heard a helicopter overhead and looked up but could see nothing. It was as if a green net had been placed over us. The barest amount of light filtered downward. A whole army could have hidden here and they would never have been detected from the air. By using the jungle the NVA were able to move freely almost at will. By actually seeing how the NVA used the jungle a curious respect developed among us for them and their talents. I wondered what they used to keep the leeches away. We had captured and killed many VC who were wearing nothing but shorts and sandals. How were they able to keep the leeches from their bodies? Perhaps there was some homemade repellent they made out of one of the jungle plants. If there was a repellent in existance I never found it. The leeches were to remain a nightmarish problem.

We left the abandoned enemy encampment and continued our search and destroy mission. Walking near the radio operator it was possible for me to overhear reports of other elements from our Company reporting back and forth. It was essential that contact be maintained in case contact was made with a large force of the enemy. The reports were frustrating in the number of casualities that were being produced. Some element of our Battalion or Company was making some sort of contact with the enemy. It may have been in the form of a lone sniper or someone setting off a booby trap which were becoming progressively numerous with each passing day. Men were maimed and killed with each passing hour. Quite often they didn't even see their enemy. Often we would come across a small village in the mountains. The huts would number only a half dozen or so but they could be counted on to be booby trapped if they were abandoned. The trails and paths leading into and around the small villages were also laden with traps. Some of the traps were merely punji sticks with excrement on them for poisoning purposes or there were anti-personnel mines which, if triggered, could blow a man in half.

It was becoming increasingly frustrating to see and hear men unlucky enough to trip one of the mines. The fact that the enemy had succeeded in hurting us without him actually even being seen was the supreme insult. Because the mines were increasing everywhere we went, it was becoming obvious that the people themselves, rather than actual military personnel, were setting the mines. It became even more frustrating to enter a village and not know who was friend or foe. Because we didn't know who to trust we began distrusting everyone; it seemed the simplest way to avoid confusion. Ironically we were supposed to be preparing or sowing the seeds of a democracy. A major fundamental of which is that one is innocent until proven guilty. The idea was now completely turned around.

Because of the increasing booby traps and the casualties they produced I was able to detect a difference in the attitude of the men regarding the peasant people we encountered. Before, there had been almost a feeling of pity and concern for the people; we genuinely wanted to help them. Now, however, there was a complete turn about in our attitude. Because so many of them were apparently turning against us, they were held in the same esteem as were the NVA. We began to handle the people in a different manner also. Gentleness was replaced with abruptness. In routine encounters with the people any respect vanished. Not all the people were treated badly by all of the soldiers but the shift in attitude from caring and concern to indifference was unmistakeable.

Having been in Viet Nam for a while I could see the change and understand it. The men just coming into our platoon would see our crude actions and probably assume they had always been that way, thus they would immediately pick up the negative feelings without ever having any of the positive. They, in turn, would pass on the disrespect and lackadasical attitude to later replacements. Instead of improving, relations with the people in the field were deteriorating. In and around towns where whores, beer and other desirable products were obtainable, relations were passable. In the field, where the setting was real and natural and where the most good could have been done, relations were the poorest.

We were never in one spot long enough to do a lot of damage psychologically or physically but, by spreading the distrust far and wide and doing it so quickly, we may have been doing more harm than if we had localized the distrust.

Many of the men in my immediate Company were beginning to react adversely to the pressures surrounding them every second of every day. One way to escape the bullshit was to become sick. One could sham (get out of duty) for weeks and not have to do anything. If one was really lucky he left the country for months and if the ultimate was reached he left the country for good with all of his faculties.

Often at night it was necessary for us to dig in as a defensive measure. Often in digging ones foxhole, water would filter into the hole from the sides and bottom. This filthy, muddy water would be consumed by individuals in an attempt to become sick. Malaria pills would be forgotten and puncture wounds from punji sticks were on the increase. Ways and means of getting sick were only limited to ones imagination.

Our journeys into the remote areas of the jungle afforded me more opportunities to view first hand the resourcefulness of the Vietnamese people. One day we were wading across a rather large river. The Vietnamese had abandoned the time honored method of fishing for a more modern method. They simply threw hand grenades into the river. The resulting shock from the explosions stunned or killed the fish and caused them to float to the surface where the "fishermen" simply scooped them up. While in the same river I found myself standing next to a large water wheel. The water level of the river was at least twenty feet below the top of the bank. The purpose of the wheel was to move the water from the river up and onto the bank for irrigation for the nearby farms. Looking at the wheel I was impressed with the fact that there was not one metal nail holding it together. Rather, wooden pegs held the structure together. Large bamboo trees had been cut lengthwise. The concave lengths would fill with water, the current would turn the wheel causing the water-filled troughs to rise to the top of the bank, and on the downward trip of the wheel the troughs would turn over and the water would be emptied into more concave bamboo trunks. The water would follow the path of the ingenious aqueduct until it reached its destination. The water wheel was extremely large and even though it was simply constructed, it was undoubtedly a complicated procedure to construct it so perfectly. Again, the ingenuity and resourcefulness of the people was illustrated.

After another day of relentless struggling through more jungle, nighttime approached. We were in the middle of the jungle and, as procedure dictated, we stopped for the night when it became too dark to move onward. Exhaustion caused sleep to come easily. The deafening sound of a nearby machine gun sputtering its sound of death instantaneously jolted me into consciousness. The sound of the machine gun had awakened everyone and the new Captain was asking what in the hell was going on. After the commotion died down and it was determined we were not under any attack, we learned what had happened.

There had been three new replacements, recent Airborne transferees from the Dominican Republic, on the machine gun. One of the three had decided to take a crap directly in front of his position. He told no one where he was going as the other two were asleep. Finishing his business he returned to his position. Fumbling about in the darkness he was obviously making a lot of noise. The noise caused one of his buddies to wake up. Thinking he was being encroached upon by the enemy he opened fire with the machine gun. It's very hard to miss a target at close range with a machine gun and this particular soldier didn't. His buddy was very dead. His death, had it been at the hands of the enemy, would have been useless enough but this manner of dying made it all the more ridiculous.

As we were in the densest of jungle it would have taken us a whole day to clear a spot to allow a chopper to come in and remove the body. Captain Plum decided there was not enough time as our presence was needed elsewhere. A makeshift litter was constructed out of shirts and two small bamboo saplings. The two greenhorns who were responsible for the soldier's death had to carry the dead body the next two days. Considering they had to carry the corpse in addition to their own equipment, it was no easy job. The stench eminating from the dead body grew increasingly with each passing hour. The enemy could have smelled us coming for miles around. We finally reached a clearing and the body was put on a helicopter, much to the dismay of the crew.

We got the order to eat. Shortly we would be moving out. Company B had radioed that they were in hot pursuit of a large force of North Vietnamese regulars. Our Company was ordered to get in position and they would drive the enemy into our laps. A small delay ensued while the officers consulted their maps and determined exactly where we were supposed to go.

Shortly, the necessary helicopters magically arrived and we were flown to the top of some nameless mountain. The mountain was probably only about five hundred or so feet high but the fact that it was covered almost entirely with jungle made it seem as if it were five thousand feet high. Tall grass grew at the top and we jumped out of the choppers into a sea of the damn stuff. The grass was up to our chests and caused much confusion when we tried to get organized into squads. After much difficulty we resembled a combat squad and moved out down the mountain. It was a torturous job due to the dense terrain. The nearer the bottom we advanced the thicker the jungle became. The mountainside was quite slippery and the resulting cuts on the men were many. Due to the falls, no one reached bottom with the amount of equipment he started with.

When we all had reached the bottom we learned that we had just come down the wrong mountain. The stupid, fucking helicopter pilot had dropped us on the wrong mountain and our stupid, fucking officers had been too dumb to realize it. Now we had to climb up another mountain and down it again! The mere thought of the ordeal was almost enough to cause me to lie down and simply tell them all to get screwed. Walking in the hot humid jungle was becoming harder and harder. My head felt as if it were going to burst at any second. I don't know how my legs were able to take steps as they grew increasingly heavy with each passing moment. The ordeal was mercifully over before anyone passed out from exhaustion.

Reaching our destination at the base of another nameless mountain, we discovered a clear stream. Most of us had drained our canteens hours ago and the sight was most welcome. I and a few other volunteers went to fill the canteens for the rest of the squad. We reached the rocky creek-bed in pleasant anticipation of the cool water we would soon be drinking. Our anticipation also caused us to be careless. We raced for the water at the same time. No sooner had I reached the water's edge than I heard the sound of bullets whizzing overhead. I immediately flung myself backward and lay perfectly still. Bullets began striking the ground, mercifully missing me and the other two men who were somewhere close by. As we were pinned down, there was no way we could return any fire without completely exposing ourselves. Moments later a helicopter gunship (firepower rather than troop transport) appeared and began spraying the area from which we were being fired upon. The helicopter stayed in the same spot, hovering and spewing bullets at the hidden enemy. The sight of the helicopter being there because we were in danger was a most welcome feeling. It was as if someone really cared about what happened to us after all.

After five minutes and hundreds of fired rounds, the helicopter left. We stayed on the ground a few minutes and, when no more rounds were fired at us, we assumed it was safe. We crawled toward the water which looked twice as wonderful now and proceeded to fill the canteens. We accomplished the job and returned to the squad. No more rounds were fired and we didn't know if the sniper had been killed or was merely scared off. The fact that someone had been out there shooting at us indicated there could be many, many more.

The sniper succeeded in adding one more worry to one's already tension-filled mind. We moved out after a brief rest, toward our destination. After hacking our way through more elephant grass and thorny bushes, we stopped near a wide river. Glancing down the river I was impressed with the raw beauty of the area. Over the centuries the river had cut a large valley out of the surrounding mountains. The area was extremely wooded and fresh looking. A strange quiet pervaded the atmosphere. Looking at the clean water and countless trees I was reminded of the wilds in Idaho or some other similar desolate spot. With all the death and destruction around me, it was a welcome relief to take my mind off the present. The tranquil mood was short-lived.

Our squad was ordered to move into the river and onto some large rocks. The position gave us an unobstructed view of the valley which stretched majestically in front of us. If anyone was moving toward us we could easily spot them and induce instant death upon them. I began shifting smaller rocks to provide a better defensive position.

A helicopter descending on our position broke my concentration for an instant. It landed on an outcropping of sand a few yards behind me. The arrival of a helicopter was no big news so I continued working on my position.

The helicopter had brought in some fresh supplies. There was water but no food. In addition there was also new socks for everybody. I couldn't believe it had brought in something so insignificant as socks. We needed food, not damn socks. Nevertheless the socks were handed out and everyone began taking off their boots and dirty wet socks. Our feet hadn't been dry in days. The wrinkled and damp skin provided the evidence. Putting on the warm dry socks was an unexpected pleasure. My cold clammy feet were suddenly being nestled into something warm and wonderous. The feeling was like running one's hand along a woman's thigh. The feeling of contentment and well-being reaches a climax when the hand is finally nestled in the triangular patch of hair.

When putting on a pair of socks can induce that sort of pleasure, one can realize the pitiful state one is in emotionally and physically. The resulting uplift those socks gave my morale was exactly what I needed.

Moments later I heard a nearby field radio crackle into life. The Captain, who was miles from our position, was merely coordinating our location with the Lieutenant. Just as they had finished their business of grid coordinates I heard the Captain say to make sure Allen was on the return flight for Romeo, Romeo, which meant R and R or rest and recuperation. I heard the words but couldn't believe them. I was scheduled for my "in country" R and R in approximately two days. One qualifies for a three-day pass to some safe location in Viet Nam after serving in the country for approximately six months. If one is still alive after nine months he qualifies for a leave out of the country.

The Army usually starts your time on the day you are actually supposed to leave. If you are in the field on say the 1st of the month and your R and R is to start that day, you lose the time it takes you to get back and get ready, thus your R and R is usually a day less than it is supposed to be. Now here I was being sent back two days early. That was unheard of. Because we were in the field I hadn't really been thinking about a vacation. There was just too many other important things to concern myself with. Now my mind was focusing on getting the hell out of where I was before someone realized the mistake.

The word spread like wildfire among the men. Soon I was swamped with items to take back into base camp. Many of the troops had crossbows and arrows which they had taken from Montagnard villages. The crossbows and arrows were really a treasure. It was hard to believe that a 20th Century people were actually using them but they were an important part of their lives and we were stealing them every chance we got. Next to bananas, they were the most coveted prizes in our searches.

Some of the bows were small and crudely made; others were quite elaborate, being hand-polished and carved with unique designs. The arrows were simply made but most interesting. They were made entirely of bamboo. The shaft was quite straight and strong. The tip was also bamboo sharpened to a fine point. The tail end was simply a flat reed woven to produce the necessary stability in flight. The crossbows were quite powerful as I had seen them completely penetrate a can of C rations filled with beef.

I heard the chopper pilot tell me to get my ass in gear so I took all the crossbows that I could and literally jumped on the chopper. The happiness I felt was like a little kid at Christmastime. For the first time in months I had something to concern myself with besides the fucking war.

The flight back from our location in the jungle to base camp is but a blur in my memory due to my ecstatic feeling. The helicopter even dropped me off right next to our Company Headquarters rather than the helipad a quarter of a mile away. Things were really falling into place.

Walking the short distance to my tent I was suddenly aware of all the troops who were in base camp. I didn't know what in the hell they were doing there as the whole Battalion was supposed to be in the field. Yet there were guys all over the place. Most of them were black. Some blacks were still in the field but from the numbers I saw walking around, there couldn't have been too many in the field. There were whites there too but they were clearly in the minority. They all had some kind of sham going and I suppose I was just jealous but it didn't seem fair with us out in the boondocks and all these able-bodied bastards back here. Well, fuck 'em all, I thought. I'm leaving them all behind for a couple of days.

I dropped the bows off at the supply tent in care of the supply Sergeant. He eyed them greedily and when I told him they were all accounted for he looked a little hurt.

"If you want one so bad, go out and get one," I said, quite cynically. When he said nothing, I left for my tent to clean up.

In the process of washing off the red dirt which was caked on my face, I noticed that my complexion had actually cleared up in spite of all the dirt. I tried to rationalize why there was such a general improvement. I knew it certainly wasn't from cleanliness. The only solution had to be in my high protein diet. Whatever the reason, I was glad for the improvement.

Freshly shaven and semi-clean but with fresh fatigues and shined boots, I moved out for the orderly room to pick up my pass. A short while later I was on a bus heading for the airport at An Khe. After the usual hours of waiting I was aboard a cargo plane headed for Vung Tau.

CHAPTER 8

Vung Tau is a resort city near Saigon. It is located on a tip of land which extends into the South China Sea. The inhabitants were generally vacationing wealthy Vietnamese and high ranking American officers. The architecture, in comparison to what I had been used to, was quite beautiful. Replacing simplistic mud huts were exquisite private homes. From the many wrought-iron balconies and fences surrounding the dwellings one could detect the obvious French influence.

The bus, after passing many beautiful homes, dropped us off in front of an old hotel which had been taken over by the U. S. Army. A high brick wall surrounded the hotel and the lone entrance was guarded by two Vietnamese MP's. Once inside the courtyard it was but a short walk into the hotel. After signing in, the sleeping quarters were pointed out to me. Picking up my shaving gear I walked as if in a trance toward the sleeping area. The thought of actually being in a "safe" place was too much to comprehend all at once. The feeling of well being was so overwhelming I felt like yelling my happiness to the world.

The first thing I noticed in the room was the beds. They were simple metal framed beds but each had a glorious mattress encased in immaculate crisp white sheets. After so many days of sleeping on the muddy and insect laden jungle floor the beds looked like a part of heaven which had been offered to me. I threw my shaving gear on the nearest one as if to claim it for my very own. I was just about to lay on what I was sure was cloud-like softness when a voice from behind me broke my concentration.

"Hey buddy, how about a drink?" Turning, I recognized the face as belonging to one of the men who had flown down on the plane from An Khe.

"Yeh, what the hell," I said, "let's go."

The hotel had a bar around the corner from the large sleeping room and in a matter of moments we were enjoying ice cold drinks. It was the first alcohol I had had in months and the soothing effect of the alcohol soon had my head swimming.

The guy I had just met was in the artillary and, judging from his paunch, his job wasn't all that difficult. Again my jealousy at someone being more fortunate than I was apparent. He seemed a likeable guy and in my particular giddy mood I decided to stick with him. Having someone to talk with seemed to fill some void inside of me. My attention focused on the bartender who was busy preparing another drink for us. I realized that his duty was one that he was going to do for one year. Mixing drinks in an R and R resort! How fucking lucky can a guy get. The son of a bitch was drawing combat pay and probably writing home to his friends how much danger he was in. The more I stared at him the more enraged I became. I felt my hand tighten on the glass and the feeling to throw it at him was growing stronger with every passing second.

"Hey man, what's your name?" I asked of my newly found friend. It was more of an attempt to take my mind off of the bartender than really caring about what his name was.

"Jim," was his response.

"Well, Jim, let's get the hell out of here and find us some women."

We left the bar without tipping the bartender and began cruising the streets searching for prostitutes. My impression of Vietnamese women had reached the point where I assumed every woman I saw was an easy lay. After a few unsuccessful passes at some very attractive women, I realized that I was wrong. Every woman was not a prostitute.

Jim and I decided to check into a civilian hotel. As we weren't having much luck picking anyone up on the street, we thought there might be some action in one of the local hotels. Also, we would need a place to take someone we did pick up.

Near the end of the street stood a large blue brick building. It appeared to be clean and well kept, as were the majority of the buildings on the street. Nearby stood a large group of men with their bicycle-rickshaws. I told Jim to get us each a room in the hotel and I would have one of the men locate us a couple of prostitutes.

Jim departed for the hotel and I advanced toward the group of men. The question of what I was going to say was answered without my having to open my mouth. One of the old men about 50 or so, walked toward me and asked me if I wanted a woman for boom boom. I raised two fingers and gestured toward the hotel behind me. His weathered face broke into a wide grin and he mumbled "number one, number one." He hopped on his bike and left hurriedly in search of the prostitutes. I returned to the hotel to wait for his return.

I found Jim inside holding the keys to the rooms. We walked up the stairs to our rooms without saying a word. Joyful anticipation of sexual adventures seemed to be foremost in both our minds.

We were about to discuss which room I would take when the old man appeared at the end of the hall. His presence was so quick that he must have had the women standing by right outside the hotel. He was talking very rapid Vietnamese to the two women. Slowly they left their spot in the hallway and advanced toward us. All the while the man kept repeating the phrase "number one, number one." Whenever someone used the phrase number one, he meant it to be the best of whatever he was describing. In this case the man was wrong.

The two women he had were at least twenty years our senior and they looked every year of it. The women wore dirty clothes and their overall squalid appearance did nothing to heighten my sexual desire. I began shaking my head and telling the man that these women would not do. At the same time I made the familiar world-known gesture indicating we wanted someone with bigger breasts. The man nodded, indicating he knew what we wanted. He left with the two women, yelling at them in Vietnamese as they walked down the hall.

"I don't care if it takes all fucking day," I said to Jim, "I'm not shacking up with any skank."

"I guess you're right," he replied, nodding his agreement. "Two dollars is two dollars. You may as well spend it on someone halfway decent."

The old man must have had more women standing by as he was back just as quickly as before with two other women. They were slightly better than the first group but were far from what I had expected. The women were almost average looking. My disappointment was in expecting something unrealistic. I was expecting an oriental Marilyn Monroe. Anyone who looked less was bound to be a disappointment.

The two women, young and stylishly dressed, stood directly before us and were waiting for our decision. I glanced toward the better looking of the two. Our eyes met and locked onto each other for a second. Instinctively I knew good times were ahead.

I told the old man that the two would do just fine. I gave him a dollar and he went happily on his way. As I turned toward the women, I saw Jim, my newly acquired friend, reach out and grab the good looking woman and disappear into his room.

"Son of a bitch," I said to myself, "isn't that enough to frost your balls?"

I decided to take advantage of the situation rather than go through the process with the old man again. Besides I had already paid him once. "Come on sweetheart," I said jokingly, knowing she couldn't understand a word I was saying. "Let's have some fun."

The room was quite small and sparsely furnished. A large double bed, chair, and small table was the only furniture in the room. The only thing really unique about the room was the French type toilet. It was the style with the water tank overhead and the long pull chain. I had seen them in various movies and it was a strange feeling knowing I was actually going to be able to use one.

The woman started talking in Vietnamese. I didn't know what the hell she was saying and was immediately up tight with the realization that I couldn't understand her. I told her to shut up and take off her clothes. She didn't understand me and I was beginning to wonder why she had come to the room.

Knowing communication through verbal methods was impossible I decided to demonstrate through action. I began to unbutton my shirt, at the same time I motioned for her to do the same thing. By the time I got to my pants she understood completely. Seconds later we were both undressed and lying on the bed. Again I didn't know what to say so I decided to show her by action what I wanted.

I placed her hand on my erect penis which was throbbing from anticipated pleasure. She gently squeezed it and began to move her small hand in an up and down pattern along the length of my throbbing organ.

I began rubbing her smooth stomach, my hands moving steadily downward toward the patch of hair between her legs. Her hand movements were increasing in their intensity upon my penis. I felt as if I would explode, sending a stream of sperm toward the ceiling. Not wanting to reach a climax so prematurely, I removed her hand.

I decided it might be an interesting experience to get a blow job. In addition to the phrase boom boom, which meant intercourse, every Vietnamese female knew the phrase chop chop, which meant some sort of oral sexual act. Rumor had it that they were quite adapt at it.

Feeling quite relaxed in my nakedness I began fondling her dark brown nipples and whispered in her ear "chop chop, honey, then boom boom, ok?" I wasn't prepared for the verbal tongue lashing she gave me as she jumped out of bed. Obviously she wasn't one to engage in such sexual activities and felt obligated to let me know it. In between unknown words of Vietnamese, I could make out her saying "No chop chop, no chop chop." She was emphatic as she kept it up for twenty minutes or so. Finally she calmed down and returned to the bed.

I was lying on my back smoking a cigarette when she came upon me. Only a moment ago she seemed incoherent and uninterested in any kind of sex. Now, only a few minutes later, she was kneeling over me, her sweet cunt only inches from my penis which was still mightily erect. She braced her hands on my knees for support and raised her body above my knees. Slowly she started to move her body downward. Her cunt was searching for my penis. I grabbed my hot trembling organ and steadied it with both hands. I felt her vagina begin to encircle my pulsating dick. This was another first for me and the sensation was exhilarating. My mind was focused on one thing and that was to hold coming to a climax as long as I could. Eventually she was completely down on me. Strange noises, small whispers really, emerged from her throat. She was obviously enjoying what she was doing.

Her movements were becoming faster and faster. In my excited and undersexed state it was an impossibility to contain my feelings any longer. With a lunge which must have sent my penis inches deeper, I exploded from head to foot. I thought that once I came she would cease in her movements. However, my climax seemed to spur her on. She continued her beautiful stroking. Her movements reached one final frenzy, then she was done. She rolled off of me, a hot sweaty mass of satisfied humanity. She may have been satisfied but I was not. I took an edge of the sheet and wiped the semen and sweat from between her thighs. With no preliminary fondling, I entered her. She wasn't as tight as she had been moments before, but her vagina still gripped me tightly. A moment later I ejaculated and withdrew from her wet body. I was pleasantly relaxed and fulfilled, the feeling of contentment was the first I had known in a long, long time.

The heat in the room was becoming quite oppressive. I decided to take a cooling shower. Just as I was lathered with soap and ready to rinse off, the water stopped running. I turned the spigots frantically in all directions in an attempt to start the water flowing. My efforts were fruitless. I could feel the soap starting to dry on my body. I had to do something to get the soap off. I wiped off all that I could and decided to go over to my "buddies" room for a final rinse. Leaving the shower I could see that the woman I had had intercourse with was fast asleep on the bed. I didn't know her name and it seemed a shame because we had just spent some very healthy moments together. Oh well, I thought, hopefully it will happen again and again, no use getting sentimental over it.

Wrapping a towel around my hips I left my room and knocked on the door of Jim's room. I knocked lightly but heard nothing from within the room. Opening the door slightly and peering inside, I could see Jim asleep on the bed. The good-looking girl was lying next to him. When she saw me, she sat upright and motioned for me to come in.

Seeing me enter the room with just a towel wrapped around my body must have given her the wrong idea of why I had come. She was off the bed and in my arms in an instant. Her hand went automatically under the towel, massaging life into my ever-hardening penis. I looked for a place to lie down but the only bed was occupied by the sleeping artillery-man. Merely seeing her caused my excitement to grow by the second. The woman was wearing bikini type panties and nothing else. Her small breasts, with their erect brown nipples, were pressed against my chest. Her legs were wrapped around my right thigh and she was rubbing herself up and down on my leg.

I gently removed her legs from around my thigh and placed my hand between her legs. The warmth generated by her body seemed to draw my middle finger into her body. I began caressing her more rapidly, the procedure being facilitated by her increasing wetness. In my efforts to excite her, I lost my balance and slipped to the floor with her on top of me. I rolled on top of her sweaty body and attempted to insert my hard organ into her velvety softness. Her wispy panties had magically disappeared. My excitement caused my once nimble fingers to fumble unsuccessfully with my pulsating organ.

Quickly I felt her hand encircle mine and guide my penis into her waiting body. I felt her shift beneath me in an effort to accomodate me.

Feeling that she was ready, I began slow rhythmic thrusting movements. Her body began matching mine in its frantic movements. The coordination was perfect. All too soon, I felt the exhilerating sensation flood over my body. Knowing she had not yet reached her climax I drove myself harder, trying to drive my penis into her throat. Seconds later, her body trembled and shuddered, she muttered a few words in Vietnamese and was suddenly very still.

I looked down at her and saw by the glazed look in her large brown eyes that she had indeed been satisfied. I suddenly realized that I hadn't kissed her. Something that felt so good deserved a kiss, I thought to myself. I couldn't bring myself to kiss her on the lips so I placed my lips in the softness of her neck and began nibbling on her yellow flawless skin. My lips traveled downward toward her breasts. Her body began familiar movements beneath me. My knees were aching terribly from being rubbed on the wooden floor. It hurt me to do so but I gently pushed myself off of her and walked into the shower. She soon joined me. Moments later we lathered each other's bodies until I became sexually excited again. I wanted to screw her but, with Jim in the room, I just didn't want to chance waking him up.

I motioned for her to get dressed and meet me in the hall. She understood perfectly, judging by the smile on her face. I returned to my room, dressed, and left a few dollars for the whore on the bed.

I joined the other woman in the hall and we left together. I had no idea where we were going but as she knew her way around, I let her lead.

I learned her name was Tran Thi. I tried to teach her my name but she was unable to say it correctly. We left the main streets and soon found ourselves on the outskirts of town. We were by a large open air market with goods of every description. The black market goods: cigarettes, booze, and clothes seemed to make up most of the merchandise. In addition there was meat, fish and fowl of every kind. All were displayed in the open and all were covered with flies and other insects. The vegetables and other garden products were dirty and unappealing. I couldn't see myself buying, let alone eating the various items. The Vietnamese civilians were not hindered and were busily checking the various products. This is what they were accustomed to and knew no other way of doing things. I tried to make a comparison between this market and an American supermarket in the States, however, no comparison could be made.

As it was growing late, I tried to explain to the woman that I had to be off of the streets by the 10 p.m. curfew. She must have been familiar with military procedure, but she insisted we get something to eat. She guided me to a restaurant. Conversation was spent by my identifying the various items of food such as rice, fish, tomatoes, beef and God only knows what else. I would try to pronounce their names in Vietnamese and she would pronounce them in English. We both laughed at the others ineptness. I grew bored of the game and tried to get across the idea that I wanted to spend the night with her. She understood but was unwilling. Since there was nothing else to discuss, I decided to leave. She walked me back to the Army hotel. I gave her a few dollars and thanked her for the tour. She departed into the night and I never saw her again.

I returned to the bunk I had claimed earlier in the day. To my surprise it was still empty. I climbed in, fully clothed, and fell asleep before my head touched the pillow. I slept into the afternoon of the next day. The sleep seemed to recondition my whole body. Much tension and anxiety seemed to disappear from my body. For the first time in many weeks I felt totally happy.

That evening and the next day was spent drinking and watching the people go about their daily living. There were other G.I.'s to bullshit with but no one to really talk about anything important. I wanted to talk with some of the Vietnamese but the language barrier made it impossible.

On my last day I was sitting at one of the little stands which dot the beach every hundred yards or so. They sell primarily cold beer and pop. Vendors passing along the adjacent street offer other wares. It was mid-morning and already it was hot and oppressively humid. I was on my third beer and minding my own business. A young Vietnamese orphan of about ten years of age had been bugging me for an hour to play cards with him. The only way to stop his incessant talking was to accomodate him.

I took my beer and we walked a few feet to a table under a large palm tree. He knew how to play Black Jack and that became the game. The words in our languages were a problem but the numbers we both understood. Soon a very interesting game was underway. As we played, more and more people joined in. I had become "banker" and was taking on all comers.

After an hour or so of playing and drinking beer, my kidneys felt as if they were about to burst. It would have been extremely rude to quit, so I explained to the kid that I had to go to the bathroom. He understood and I left my money on the table with him in charge. I trusted him and that gesture of faith seemed to please the people watching and those playing the game.

I went into the rear of the little stand and looked for a commode of some sort. There was nothing even remotely resembling a toilet. There were just the four walls constructed of flattened out beer cans. There was nothing to do but urinate on the walls. It turned out that that is exactly what you are supposed to do. A woman later comes along the beach and cleans out the various stands. She simply throws water on the walls. The water and urine flow down the walls, across the floor and out onto the beach, where it disappears into the sand. Amongst the other garbage strewn about, who would ever know the difference?

I returned to the game and everything was in order. Many new people were being drawn to the game by the cheering and merriment. I was playing the game extremely honestly and the people knew it. We were having a wonderful time. People of every description were playing the game. Some merely played a quarter and left; others had been playing as long as I. Soon the crowd had grown to such a large number that I was completely surrounded by them. The larger the crowd grew, the louder they became.

Suddenly in the middle of a hand, they all started jabbering wildly. Some of the people started leaving and I was perplexed as to what was happening. The young boy who had started the whole affair picked up my money and stuffed it into my pockets. Seconds later I heard a shrill whistle and realized the game was about to be raided by the local police.

By the time the uniformed man was standing in front of the table, the majority of the people had dispersed, taking their money with them. Seeing no illegal activity, he smiled and continued on his way. His presence seemed to spoil the once gay mood.

I was wondering what to do next when I heard someone yell, "Hey, G.I." Turning I saw a group of young Vietnamese males. One of them was motioning for me to join them.

I walked over to where they were sitting and joined them. They appeared to be in their early twenties and were drinking beer. They offered me one and immediately a rapport was established. One of them spoke English and he acted as interpreter for the group.

They were all in the South Vietnamese Army with the exception of the one who spoke English. He was affiliated with the military but in a civilian capacity. They were all dressed in civilian clothes and I assumed they were on some sort of leave.

We began talking about a variety of subjects. They were especially interested in what I thought about fighting for them in their country. I merely told them that I and other Americans were proud to help them in their fight against Communism. They were grateful for our presence and couldn't begin to thank us enough. They didn't particularly like having their country torn up but then again, if it stopped, the threat of domination by the North, it was worth it. The conversation soon shifted to other topics. Their view of America was as cloudy as mine was of Viet Nam. They were especially interested in life in the American cities. Chicago held a special fascination for them. They were under the impression it and other cities were controlled by machine-gun democracy under Al Capone types. I tried to convince them it just wasn't so but I don't think I was very successful. It seemed that once their minds were made up on a certain issue it was impossible to change their view. Another topic that interested them was race relations between the blacks and whites. I tried to give them an honest answer in that the blacks were the recipients of much discrimination but that things were getting better, however it would take much time. They seemed to understand and drew a parallel between relations with various minorities in Viet Nam.

The conversation hinged mainly on generalities and never got very technical. It was fascinating talking with them as they understood so little about life in America. They probably felt the same way about me and my lack of understanding of various facets of life in Viet Nam. The main thing that came out of the discussion was that they generally approved and wanted the American presence to continue in Viet Nam. I was only talking to a few individuals but the fact that someone wanted and actually told me they appreciated what I was doing, seemed to make it all worth while.

It was late afternoon and they suggested we go for a swim. They produced a pair of swim trunks for me and we went swimming for a short time. Even in the water the interpreter was asking me various questions about life in America. Politics and the military were rarely discussed. They were just genuinely interested in everything American. I felt good answering their questions and was proud to be able to do so. I felt that more good and understanding between strangers came out of those precious hours than all of the months of burning and killing. It's a shame we couldn't have continued the discussion for a much longer time.

After our swim they insisted I join them for more beer and hard boiled eggs. Evidently beer and eggs were as popular in Vung Tau as they were in some working class bars in America however there was one big difference. I discovered the difference when I bit into one of the eggs; the egg was fertilized and the chicken embryo was quite developed. I almost gagged when I heard the crunching and saw the young embryo. With a minimum of chewing and drinking lots of beer I was able to swallow the egg and partially developed chicken. It was quite a shock at seeing the chicken in the shell however it simply pointed out another difference on our cultures. They would undoubtedly think our hard boiled eggs, void of the embryo, quite strange. Following a few more rounds of beer I announced that I had to go back to the hotel and prepare to return to my unit. They insisted I join them later for dinner. Not wanting to appear ungracious I had no alternative but to accept. We agreed to meet at the same spot at seven o'clock that evening.

Arriving at the beach a little before seven I began to think that perhaps they were some sort of agents for the Viet Cong. The thought was quite sobering and I decided to be careful about anything I said. They arrived at seven, sharp. The whole group was back and this time they had motorcycles. The interpreter told me to hop on the back of his cycle and I did so. I had no idea where we were going and I must have appeared quite frightened as my friend told me not to worry. I could tell by his smile and tone of voice that he was sincere. After a wild ride through the streets we arrived at a restaurant on the far side of town. They had brought me here because the owner was the uncle of one of the other men in the group. He wanted to prepare a genuine Vietnamese meal for me. I can't recall all of the various types of foods but I do recall them all being delicious. One thing that I do remember and that is when we were served a rice and chicken dish everyone, with the exception of myself, ate the complete pieces of chicken, including gristle and bone. The chicken was cut up in small pieces but nevertheless they ate the bones. I must have looked quite the foreigner gingerly picking the meat off the bone. Nothing was said about either ones habits.

Discussion again was concerned with living and working in America. There was so much that they didn't understand about our concrete, neon-lighted drive-in world that, after a while, I knew they would never really understand unless they saw it for themselves. They were starving for any information. I suddenly wished I wasn't here. Trying to describe things I had taken for granted was proving to be quite difficult. It was like trying to describe the sea to a blind man. You can say the words but the true description is within each man's heart. I asked to be taken back to the hotel and they obliged although I could tell they were disappointed. I shook hands with everyone and expressed my gratitude. The few hours I spent with the men were some of the most memorable hours of my entire time spent in Viet Nam.

Arriving at the airport the following morning I was in for another surprise. The airport was full of men like myself who were waiting for a plane to take them North to their respective units. A Sergeant behind a counter in the terminal said that a group of doctors had to go to An Khe due to a recent battle. It was extremely urgent, therefore some individuals were going to have to stay behind. Then the Sergeant asked one of the dumbest questions I have ever heard. "Were there any volunteers?" Every hand went up immediately. The Sergeant looked dumbfounded. He probably thought everyone had a soft job like himself. At any rate, since there were too many volunteers, he had no alternative but to pick the men alphabetically. Since my last name started with an A, I was one of the lucky ones who would remain in Vung Tau an extra day or so.

I checked with the Sergeant about when would be a good time to report for the next flight. The next one was leaving in two days. Two more days; the thought of not having to go back to my unit was wonderful. I suddenly reasoned that maybe I wouldn't even show up for that particular flight. When I did decide to go I could always use the excuse that the planes were full or that a doctor needed my seat. Furthermore, what could they do to me?

I was already in Viet Nam so there wasn't much else they could do. They could take my newly acquired rank of Specialist 4th Class and bust me back to a Private. But who in the hell cared. As fucked up as the Army's paper work was they probably wouldn't even miss me back at the Company. I was only going to stay 3 or 4 days in addition to the two bonus days I had just received. That would have made my time in Vung Tau just about a full week; I figured I deserved it.

I had enough money left from what I brought plus I had won some money in the Blackjack game. Yes, indeed, I had enough money for a good time. I left the air terminal in a cocky frame of mind. I had gotten a break and I meant to make the most of it.

The next four days went very quickly. They were spent whoring around and drinking. I had always wanted to spend a day drinking and fucking everything in sight. I succeeded in doing just that. Looking back now I can see how unimportant they were. The women were merely bodies to satisfy a biological urge. There was no attempt to establish any kind of understanding or rapport with anyone. Just, wham bang, thank you, ma'm. It was a waste of time in one respect but, at the same time, it was something I had to do to satisfy an inner urge and besides, it was a hell of a lot of fun.

On my last night in Vung Tau I had a unique experience, not so much in the sexual aspect, but rather in a spiritual sort of way. I picked a girl up in one of the local bars and paid her the necessary money to spend the night in her room. She spoke fairly good English which, at this point in time, was quite an achievement. She lived in some small village in Central Viet Nam but had relatives in Vung Tau. On their suggestion, she came down to make some money while the opportunity was available.

Judging from the looks of her room I could see that she was doing all right. The room seemed small but only because of all the merchandise she had stored there. There were numerous radios, record players, toasters, and other appliances. The one closet in the room was overflowing with clothes and shoes, all in the current American style. She either knew someone running a PX or else she had many boyfriends who were treating her right.

The one thing that stood out in the room was her bed. It was enormous, or at least, it looked enormous to me. It was easily seven feet across and ten feet long. The sheets on the bed were the whitest I had ever seen. It had been a long time since I had seen sheets on a regular basis so I didn't have that much to compare them to, but at that particular moment, they were as white as the purest snow.

Surrounding the bed on all four sides and falling to the floor was a white mosquito netting so dainty it appeared transparent. A window nearby allowed a soft cooling breeze to caress our soon-to-be naked bodies.

The woman tuned on a radio which, to my surprise, was playing American music. After unbuttoning my shirt she pushed me gently onto the bed and finished undressing me. She slid the mosquito netting together and said she would be back in a moment. She reappeared in a moment dressed in a most revealing negligee. The negligee was two-piece and I suddenly felt myself growing with desire just looking at her. The bikini portion barely covered her triangular patch of pubic hair. I could make out bits of hair curling over and around the panty portion. The top piece resembled a loose-fitting shirt. Instead of buttons there was one small bow tied at the top to keep it together. As she walked the few steps toward me I could see her magnificent breasts sway from side to side. Her nipples pushed against the flimsy material resembling two miniature pup tents. When she was by my side the aroma of flowers heightened my already burning desire. My penis felt as though it was trying to find its own way into her body. I held myself back in order to savor the moment. Lying in the diaphanous setting I felt like a small bird high in the clouds, carefree and adventurous.

As if by instinct my lips found their way to her nipples, erect and sweet. I was amazed at their fullness and hardness compared to the soft mounds they topped. I continued to suck and kiss them like a newborn baby going from one to the other in search of milk. My lips started a downward movement finally resting and searching for her navel. She grabbed my head gently with her hands and brought my lips back to her breast. Releasing my head, her small but strong hands grasped my pulsating penis and inserted it into her warm, wet body. She then began slow rhythmic movements increasing in intensity as she neared her climax. Her body stopped its rapid movements and a moan from deep within her throat signaled her climax. She began repeating the phrase "number one, number one" over and over again. After a few moments of rest she forced me over onto my back and took my penis in her hand and began to stroke it, gently at first and then rapidly for a few seconds. Just as I felt myself ready to explode she slowed her movements to slight rubbing. By continuing this procedure a number of times she had me on the verge of insanity. When I could contain myself no longer I placed my hand on hers and together we stroked my organ until it attained satisfaction. In my aroused state it remained hard. Not wishing to waste such a beautiful erection she placed her body in such a position that she merely squatted down and in one motion my penis was nestled inside her soft cunt. Bending forward her breasts were but a few tantalizing inches from my mouth. My tongue made up the distance and instantly I was savoring them like a child devouring a lollipop. I didn't have to move a muscle as she was doing all of the work. I felt the familiar tingling of my body. I gave my loins a push that made her rise inches upward. Exhausted, she rolled off of me. Our bodies were still united with my organ still hard within her. After a few wonderful moments of rest her body began its now familiar rocking movement. This time I matched them and together we both came instantaniously. My penis was actually starting to become sore. One second I was hoping she was done and the next I was hoping she would continue. Looking at her closed eyes I knew she was done. Lying there on the bed of whiteness I felt like a king. I was completely at ease with the world. I was suddenly conscious of the breeze gently drying my sweaty body. I became chilled and moved my body next to hers. With one arm around her shoulders, grasping onto a breast, and my penis nestled between her buttocks, I let the breeze lull me into a deep and relaxing sleep.

When I awoke the next morning the sun was shining brightly through the window. I was covered with a sheet and for a moment was disorientated. I closed my eyes and concentrated on where I was. When I opened them a second later all the memories of the past night came into my mind. Just thinking about what had transpired caused my penis to harden. I looked wishfully for the woman but she was gone. There was nothing to do but leave.

I decided to stop off at the enlisted mens dining hall and eat a decent breakfast. In all the days that I had been there I had not yet eaten a decent American meal. The thought of eggs, bacon, toast and juice caused me to pick up my pace. Sitting at the table enjoying a cigarette and coffee waiting for my meal, the thought of what I was going back to filled my mind. Leaving this place was going to be hard but I began to feel guilty about my friends back in the jungles. "Hell," I said to myself and then realized that in a couple of months I would be going on R and R out of the country, perhaps to Bankok. It was supposed to make Vung Tau look like a Boy Scout camp. Thinking about the future R and R made me forget about my guilt.

At last my meal arrived. I stared at the eggs and freshly buttered toast and let the aroma drift into my nostrils and fill my brain with their wonderous scent. When I could hold out no longer I picked up a piece of toast and brought it toward my mouth. Just as I was about to bite down on it I noticed a black pubic hair curled around my little finger. I dropped the toast and began wiping my hand violently on my shirt much as if I had just discovered a leech. As ravenous as I was, my appetite was completely gone. As much as I wanted that breakfast I couldn't bring myself to eat. Why that one hair caused my appetite to disappear was a mystery. I felt myself become nauseous and knew I had to leave. Staring at the eggs as if they were a favorite puppy I would never see again, I stood and left.

CHAPTER 9

Arriving back at base camp the silent and quiet surroundings told me that the Company was out in the field. There were relatively few troops in the camp so I judged the Company had not been in the field too long. In a few days the malingerers would begin drifting back and base camp would look like the south side of Chicago on a Saturday night.

After checking in with the Company clerk, who said not one word about my being days late, I was on board a chopper loaded with food supplies headed for my Company deep in the jungles of the highlands.

After landing in a freshly cut landing zone, I was directed by troops in the mortar platoon to my particular platoon. The first members of my Company I came across were Captain Plum and a group of Sergeants. They were sitting around some cases of C rations. One of the Sergeants had a cross bow and the group seemed to be in some sort of shooting contest with the bow. I looked at the group and realized that I knew very few of them, even though they were from my Company. The turnover rate of personnel was tremendous. The longer we stayed in Viet Nam the higher the casualties became. Walking past them, I wondered how long this group would last.

Finally I arrived at the position that my squad occupied. I saw Horner with three other guys, but I didn't see Bradley or the others. I assumed they were out on a patrol. Approaching Horner I could see he was in the middle of a poker game.

"Hey," I yelled. "Where in the hell is everyone?"

"Well, look who decided to come back," answered Horner.

"You should have stayed away," came another voice from amongst the group.

Grinning, I said "I would have but I ran out of money."

"No shit," said Horner. "It's good having you back but things are really fucked up around here."

I asked him what the problem was. Looking into his eyes I could see that they looked far older than they really were. They seemed to be void of any real emotion. He began talking and he sounded older than I had last remembered. Being away from the men for the short week that I was seemed to make them appear much older. It was as if the week was really many years.

He began his tale by stating that Captain Plum was under some sort of investigation. His tone of voice indicated that he was glad the investigation was taking place. My squad had been sent out on a night patrol the very night I left them on the river bank. It had gotten dark before the squad reached its destination. Sergeant Saxton, leading the patrol, had radioed back to Captain Plum requesting permission to stop as it was getting dark and set up an ambush at their present location. Horner had been carrying the radio for Saxton and was able to hear every word. Plum denied them permission and told them to proceed to the original location. After walking in circles for almost an hour in the darkness, Saxton again radioed Plum for permission to stop and again permission was denied.

They decided to move to a more comfortable spot and then radio back that they were at the location even though they had no real idea where in the hell they were. They walked for a few more minutes when suddenly the point man stumbled across a trip flare. Illuminated by the flash of light they were momentarily frozen by surprise as well as fright. Before they could take cover, bullets began tearing into them. Taking cover in the jungle they began firing back into the darkness. The firing on both sides was intense. Bradley had been shot in the stomach and Adaro had been shot in the head. Two others had been shot in the legs and arms; the others had escaped the initial onslaught of bullets without being hit. Believing they were in contact with a larger enemy force, Saxton began screaming into the radio for help from Captain Plum. While he was yelling into the radio the firing ceased. One of the individuals who had been doing the firing heard Sergeant Saxton hollering and recognized the American voice. An instant later everyone realized what had happened.

The squad had walked into an ambush set up by another American Company. Identified by their voices screaming for help, the squad had been saved from further death. The troops that initiated the firing produced a medic to attend to the wounded. For Adaro it was too late; he was dead.

The Army had notified his parents in the next couple of days. Evidently Adaro's father was an individual who had a few connections in high places. Not being satisfied with the Army's explanation of how his son was killed, he decided to start his own investigation. And that was what was happening now. There had been various officers from the Inspector General's office asking questions. Saxton was so pissed off at Plum that he was trying to put the blame for the whole affair on him. The affair was not yet over and no one was sure how it would end. It did mean easy duty for the squad for the next couple of days.

I began thinking of Adaro. He was one of the most liked guys in the Company and it was hard to believe that he was dead. It was a double tragedy that he had to be killed by his fellow soldiers by some fucking mistake. It was easy to understand his dad was going to such lengths to understand what had happened. His dad was so proud of his son that I knew he would stop at nothing until he found out the truth. Adaro, before entering the service, had been an obese spoiled kid. His father had quite a bit of money and there were rumors that he had connections with the Mafia. Adaro had shown me many pictures of himself behind the wheel of his expensive drag racing car. He evidently wanted for nothing in civilian life. He evidently wasn't very happy with his spoiled life and decided to do something about it. A good place seemed to be the Army. His goal was simply to make his dad proud of him and pay him a little genuine attention. In the course of his training Adaro had lost almost a hundred pounds and had changed his personal philosophy as well as his physical appearance. He had become quite religious and I remembered his going to church and receiving Holy Communion every chance he got. He carried a rosary and said it every night. I only hoped it helped him in the end.

I realized that it probably should have been me that was killed instead of Adaro. He had assumed my position of rear security when I left for R and R. The fact that I had left early, something that happens rarely in the Army, only intensified my belief that someone or something was indeed looking out for me.

Our platoon moved from the jungle to the outskirts of a large village. The purpose was to provide security for a nearby artillery unit. There was a large multi-roomed house that Captain Plum took over for his command post. In a matter of hours he had converted it into a whorehouse. It was to be his last function as a Captain in the 7th Cavalry. He was replaced the following day. No one knew where he went although we heard that it was out of Viet Nam and he would never lead troops again.

We stayed at this position for two days. In addition to a new Captain, our squad was also receiving a new Lieutenant. Captain Bradford was the new commander, our fourth in nine months. His first order in taking over the Company was to close the whorehouse and send the girls on their way. The only troops who seemed to mind were the blacks. Being able to screw anything remotely white was really a boost to their egos. Naturally the only women available were Vietnamese and the blacks biological needs were the same as anyone's, however, the fact that the women were not black seemed to give them an added impetus. When the choice was available to them to choose a woman they invariably chose the lightest one. Thus the new Captain was off on the wrong foot with many of the black troops by closing the house. Our new Lieutenant was a West Pointer, named Green. I only hoped he could read a compass.

Our platoon moved again back to the outskirts of our main base camp. Our activities consisted of patrol after patrol in the scorching heat. The purpose seemed to be to familiarize the new Captain and Lieutenant with the men of the Company. The only enemy we encountered was the dreaded leech. One episode was particularly unpleasant.

After fording a filthy, neck deep stream we stopped to check ourselves for leeches. I was in the process of burning one off of my leg with a cigarette. Just as I was about to flick it off with the tip of my bayonet I heard Horner let out a blood curdling scream. It was the first time I had ever seen him shook up. He was standing on the muddy bank with his pants down around his ankles. He had both hands around his penis and was squeezing it with all of his might. With every squeeze came an outpouring of commands for the leech to please come out. The leech had crawled into the opening of his penis and was about halfway in.

"Hey, Horner," I said, trying to inject a little humor into the situation. "Don't pull it off."

"Fuck you," he replied in a scared tone completely foreign to his character. "I've got to get it out."

"Well, I'm sure in the hell not going to help you," I replied, laughing.

Before he could answer he succeeded in squeezing out the vile creature. He began stomping the leech into the ground so hard I marveled that he didn't break his leg in the process. When we had succeeded in removing the leeches from our bodies we returned back to our posts and another night of guard duty.

The next day found us back at base camp. A return to base camp lifted everyone's spirits immensely. It meant we could have a night of uninterrupted sleep. It also offered us a chance to clean our bodies and weapons. It also meant nights of drinking beer and writing letters home. On our return to base camp we rode in trucks. Even though it was a rough ride it was a pleasant departure from the goddam helicopters. The only time we were glad to see the choppers was when they were giving us supporting fire or were coming to pick us up. The trucks brought us through the gates of our base camp. The first troops we saw were the finance clerks playing softball in bermuda shorts. Looking at them enjoying themselves I felt a jealous hate engulf my body. "Rotten mother fuckers" I said to myself.

After a night of drinking beer, going to sleep was easy. I was awakened from my sleep by someone shouting "mortar attack, mortar attack". I immediately grabbed my rifle and headed out of the door of the tent. Men were running everywhere; most seemed to be heading for the Green Line. Lieutenant Green was suddenly on the scene. He led us to a spot near the motor pool. He placed us in a defensive position from where we could watch the action. Explosions in the distance indicated we were indeed receiving mortar rounds. The majority of them were falling away from our area.

Glancing toward Hong Kong mountain I could see that that was where most of the rounds were exploding. From my safe position, it was almost like watching a fireworks display. A helicopter gun ship began shooting rockets at the top of the mountain. This was most strange as the top was occupied by men operating sophisticated radar equipment. I watched in fascination as balls of fire smashed into the mountainside sending showers of flame in every direction. My mind went back to the first week in Viet Nam when I was flown to the top of the mountain that was now under attack. It must be vastly different now, I thought. The VC obviously thought so, too. I later learned that the choppers were firing at groups of infiltraters trying to blow up the equipment on the top of the mountain. I got my information first hand as the next day our platoon was picked to walk to the top of the mountain and search for the infiltraters.

The walk to the top of Hong Kong mountain was extremely exhausting. The incline was so steep that we had to pull ourselves up by grasping onto anything that offered a handhold. The heat was especially bad; its effect was almost suffocating. When we reached the top we were greeted by a group of very frightened men. When they found out we were from the 7th Cavalry their exuberance was overwhelming. Their impression of us was slightly overrated, but it did succeed in making us feel like supermen. I have never seen a group of people so happy to see another.

We were put into position around the top of the mountain until our Lieutenant could get an idea of what had transpired during the night. I was put right in front of a bunker that had been burned out during the night. As I sat there I could visualize what had happened. A few yards in front of me and stretching around the large mountain top was barbed wire. The barbed wire in front of me had been tied down with strips of bamboo. The VC had then slipped across unmolested and proceeded to raise holy hell. The men who had been in the bunker directly behind me surely met a quick and firey death. I later viewed their charred bodies and wondered which one of them had fallen asleep on duty.

Our primary duty was to scout the area, however those that weren't out on patrol were busy clearing out the trees to provide our group with a better field of fire. While taking a cigarette break, Horner kept telling me he heard a moaning noise. Listening intently, I too heard the moaning sound. Walking to the edge of the mountain top we peered over the side but could see nothing. Again we heard the sound directly below us. There were many large boulders and large stone outcroppings which could offer someone shelter. Horner, against my wishes, decided to go down and see who or what was making the noise. Advancing gingerly down the moss covered rocks Horner came to a large crevice in the side of the mountain.

"The sound is coming from in here," he yelled up to me. Before he could say another word two young men came out of the narrow opening. One of the men was shot up badly; the other was unwounded. Horner brought them up to the top.

They had no weapons, only small football-shaped bundles of rice. The rice bundles were their entire food supply. Kicking it apart I could see that bits of meat and dried vegetables were mixed into the rice. I marveled at their ability to exist on such meager rations. No G.I. could ever do it. The way we bitched about our food would have seemed a shocking crime to these men. But then, everything is relative.

We turned the two men over to Lieutenant Green. He, in turn, had them questioned by a Vietnamese interpreter. A short time later Green returned with the news that the prisoners said they were to be picked up tonight by some of their comrades. Considering that they had just blown up half the mountain and killed half a dozen men, we did not take it as an idle threat.

The ensuing night was one of the longest and most nerve-wracking I ever spent. We were positioned outside of the barbed wire with no place to go. We had trip flares set up in front of us as well as Claymore mines. The Claymore is a concave type mine filled with thousands of steel pellets. It sets on a tripod and is discharged electrically. It is usually set in the front of one's position pointing outward. A long cord enables one to get a safe distance from it. When a noise is heard one merely pushes a button and the mine is activated. Following the explosion the steel pellets are sent forward in a fan shaped pattern. The mine is especially effective against a group of people. The only problem with the Claymore is that in the darkness VC often turn them around toward your position.

Sitting in the darkness every sound I heard I imagined to be that of the enemy. My mind went back to the afternoon when I had seen and touched the barbed wire where the VC had tied it back. Actually touching the same spot that the VC had only a few hours before made my skin feel clammy. If they could sneak up last night, they certainly could do it again. Thinking about the possibility made the situation worse. I tried to take my mind off of the present by thinking about home, which, of course, meant my family and Brenda. They were important to me and usually, by thinking about them, I was able to take my mind off of something unpleasant. This time it didn't work. Nothing I tried enabled me to refocus my attention. Every minute my thoughts were somewhere in the darkness before me. Like a small child waiting for Christmas morning, I prayed for the morning to come. Slowly the darkness evolved into light. The tension eased from my body as light of day grew progressively lighter.

To the dismay of the men on the mountain we received orders to move back to base camp. Instead of walking we flew back in helicopters. We were going back to base camp, but it was merely to get resupplied preparatory to moving out on another mission. We were spending more and more time in the field. With each passing day the VC and North Vietnamese were becoming more and more active. Thoughts of the war ending in a year or so were but dreams. More and more American soldiers were being sent over every day. Many of them were taking up permanent positions in the highlands, indicating the importance of the area.

Our mission was again that of search and destroy. Destroy is what we did. As time developed so did our frustrations and hostilities. Each day it seemed as if someone else was getting killed or maimed either from snipers or the ever-increasing booby traps. I actually looked forward to the burning of villages. Combat, while frightening, was never wished for, but, if it happened, the fright lasted only a second. The desire to see and kill the enemy replaced the wish of non-contact.

One particular day we were deep in the jungles of the highlands. Sergeant Timura discovered a trail leading into the dark jungle and our squad decided to follow it. It snaked its way through the thick foliage and stopped to reveal a newly-constructed village. The village consisted of about twelve individual huts. The huts in this instance were marvels in engineering. The base of the huts rested on bamboo stilts approximately three feet in height. The hut itself was constructed entirely of different thicknesses of bamboo. The walls in the various huts were made of thin bamboo sticks, as were the floors and roofs. Everything was, of course, hand cut and assembled. The huts were simple but, at the same time, complex. I could only marvel at the ability of the people who made them. There was no one in sight to indicate who lived there. Even though there was no one there physically, I could sense their presence. It was as if there were a thousand eyes peering through the jungle foliage, watching our every move. A few of the men found cross bows and spears but nothing of a military nature. I kicked over a large clay urn and to my surprise an American ammunition box rolled out. I picked up the box and opened it. Inside was an American military can opener, tooth brush and a couple of bullets. How in the hell those articles found their way to the middle of nowhere was beyond me. I put the bullets in my pocket and threw the rest on the floor.

The rest of the men had started to look for the coveted bananas. Various villagers often put them on top of the huts or inside of a covered urn to speed up their ripening. Finding none, a curious feeling seemed to come over everyone. One man started to break up the various urns and pots which were scattered amongst the huts. Another started to smash in the side of one of the marvelous huts. In a matter of seconds, I was joining everyone else in destroying the village and everything in it. There was no justification for our actions. It was as if we had all been overcome with the thought to destroy at the same time. We seemed to be destroying for some inner reason. I can personally blame the destruction on the months of increasing tension and frustration. With each smash of my rifle butt, I began to feel more relaxed. Looking back I'm thankful there were no people in the small village or they certainly would have been killed.

As suddenly as it had started the destruction stopped. The village, which had been so naturally beautiful only a few moments ago, was now in complete ruin. I felt no remorse for my actions. With nothing else to destroy we were on our way to some other point in the middle of nowhere. As we left the village I looked behind me and saw some of the wreckage going up in smoke.

Being deep in the jungle we came across more and more small isolated villages. Each one seemed to be more crudely constructed than the last. Most of them were but one-room affairs built on stilts. Between the floor and the top of the stilt was a round piece of wood. I didn't know if its function was to keep out crawling insects or evil spirits. They would remain a source of mystery to me.

The people inhabiting them were the Montagnards. Judging from the way they lived and dressed, they were more primitive the deeper we went into the jungles. It was not unusual to come across them attired in nothing but loin cloths. It was like going back in time to the Stone Age. It seemed incredulous that we were risking and often giving our lives for them. Somehow, it didn't seem worth it.

Moving out of the jungle and into the large cities or hamlets meant more contact with the enemy. With increasing frequency we would come across bands of the enemy. They would flee and leave behind a sniper or two to serve as a delaying force. They would pin us down for hours while the others made their escape. When we finally took the village we would be lucky to find one dead body. My hatred for the enemy was taking on monumental proportions, as were the rest of the men. We were lackadasical in the past about many things, especially searching huts and civilians. Now we were much more efficient. If a building even looked suspicious we burned it. Civilians were turned over to the South

Vietnamese soldiers for the slightest provocation. So many of them seemed to be helping the enemy it seemed the safest thing to do.

Young Vietnamese males were prime suspects. When one was detained he was the subject of much harassment. For one to act in a suspicious manner often meant his death. On a hot oppressive day one met such a fate. While advancing through a village, the whole squad saw the young man at the same time. He was sitting in a field of tall grass and picked the wrong moment to stand. The fact that he was wearing black pajamas and decided to run also added to his demise. As if on cue we all fired at him at the same time. It was a perfect execution. He was hit a number of times in various parts of the body. He tried to crawl away but the tremendous loss of blood resulted in his death. Watching him die had absolutely no effect on me at all. For all I knew we could have just murdered someone innocent of any wrongdoing. It didn't matter. He was dead and nothing was going to bring him back. It was easy to rationalize his death as just one less potential enemy. We didn't realize it could have been one dead friend.

Walking through the village I was conscious of the hatred and fear on the faces of the people. They had taken the dead boy, bathed him and placed him on display for all the villagers to see. Judging from the wailing and crying of the people who viewed him he was quite a popular figure.

Walking through the village, I was more intrigued with the strange religious symbols I saw than I was with the people. I had seen the same symbols many times before but they seemed much more numerous in this particular village. There was a crudely painted human eye on the roof of many buildings. There were also swastikas painted on various buildings. Wooden and brass swastikas also adorned the tops of many poles. No one knew exactly what they represented, although we wondered about them as often as we wondered why we never saw any cats. In all the months I spent in Viet Nam I never saw a cat of any kind. Like so many other questions it too would go unanswered.

Our squad passed through the village without incident until we reached a clearing just on the edge of the village. The point man just stepped into the clearing and the air was immediately filled with bullets. We moved back to a safer position and began to dig in. I was standing to take off my shirt when a bullet passed so close to my head I could actually hear it burning its way through the air. I immediately fell to the ground and finished my foxhole from a prone position. It was merely a shallow hole deep enough for my body to be below ground level. It would suffice. The sniper fire continued in its intensity. A couple of squads had gone out in the direction of the firing, but each time they returned carrying a few of their own men who were wounded or dead. As the intensity of the firing was not decreasing, I knew we would again spend another night pinned down. I was only hoping they retreated or at least stood their ground. The thought of them trying to sneak up on our positions during the darkness of night was too frightening to think about.

As the darkness came, the firing from the enemy slowed in its intensity. A round or two would be fired every couple of minutes just to remind us they were still there and had the upper hand. The Captain had radioed for a gun ship and the Air Force complied. They had a special plane we nicknamed "Puff the Magic Dragon". It had a formidable arsenal and didn't hesitate to use it. Also, the plane would constantly drop flares to keep the area illuminated. The night would be black then suddenly the immediate area would be lit up like noontime. Slowly the flare would float to earth bringing the darkness with its descent. It would remain dark for fifteen minutes or so then the process would be repeated over and over until daylight appeared.

On this particular occasion the plane stayed for four or five hours and departed before sunrise. With the plane gone I felt much less secure. The firepower of the Air Force had a positive psychological effect on me. I felt strong with their presence and with their absence, weakness. We had developed an unhealthy dependence on them. The fact that they had helped us out of so many incidents accounted for the powerful attachment. Being alone I felt terribly inadequate.

Sounds of someone or something approaching my position caused me to sit up and concentrate on the area directly in front of me. Staring into the darkness I could see nothing but could hear that the movement was coming closer. I believed the enemy was advancing toward my position. My rifle was in my sweating hands, my brain saying shoot, but my experience told me not to reveal my position until I was sure of what I was shooting at. I was just about to abandon reason and start firing when an opening appeared in the clouds and allowed the moon to cast just enough light to enable me to see what was in front of me.

To my relief it wasn't the enemy but rather two cows. To be more precise, one bull and one cow. The bull was hunched up on the cow and was screwing away, completely oblivious to what was happening. I couldn't contain my laughter. The fact that life goes on despite the war and our presence was vividly being enacted before my eyes.

In the course of the next day we overtook the few remaining soldiers and, true to form, the majority of the enemy had disappeared with the night. There was but one dead body and two prisoners to show for our work. The body count was higher on our side. After more days of walking and searching for the enemy with no contact being made we returned to base camp. Prior to waiting for the helicopters one incident did happen to take our minds off the elusive enemy for a few precious seconds.

We were waiting near some hedges, more for the shade than for any protection. One of the troopers, a big strapping black, stood up and began running as if the devil himself was after him. He ran right past my position and a minute later I could see why he was running. A King Cobra was in pursuit of him. A group of us began chasing the snake with entrenching tools and bayonets. We chased the snake, screaming and hollering obscenities, for about twenty yards or so. Suddenly the snake stopped and stood up on its tail. It was at least six feet tall. At the time it looked twenty feet tall. It spread its magnificent hood and began to sway slowly back and forth. It was obviously preparing its defense and seemed ready to attack at any second. The instant it reared up on its tail we froze momentarily and then made the quickest retreat I ever participated in. As we retreated the snake slithered safely off into the brush. I had seen countless snakes but this was my first, and hopefully the last, encounter with one.

We arrived at base camp but our stay was short. In a matter of days we were running patrols on the outskirts of An Khe. The VC were blowing up bridges and it was our responsibility to stop it. Thus the patrols consisted of walking up and down the various roads searching the people for explosives, as well as searching the bridges themselves. There were simply too many people to do an adequate job of searching. The people acted as if it was one big game and, after a short while, so did we. We would just go through the motions with a lackadasical attitude. Amazingly the bombings stopped. Perhaps our presence acted as a deterent but whatever the reason the bombings did stop.

The close contact with the people did give us a chance to interact with them on more friendly terms. The vendors were more numerous and an occasional afternoon would be spent trying to converse with them. The Vietnamese got a big kick out of watching us shave. The sparse facial hair of the Vietnamese male does not warrant everyday shaving. It must have been very strange in their eyes to watch us go through the ritual. A group of them would gather around when one of us was shaving and they would spend the whole time pointing and laughing. We didn't have a chance to shave as often as we would like so the opportunity was put to good use, despite our embarrassment.

The relative easy duty gave us a chance to take advantage of the traveling whorehouses. Various prostitutes would travel up and down the highways in their Lambrettas. They would stop, exhibit their merchandise and, if they had a buyer, would retreat to a nearby spot where there was but the minimum of privacy. This activity would go on all day but would cease with nightfall.

I and another fellow G.I. decided to break past precedent. We were positioned near a river which formed a natural boundary for a nearby airstrip. It was our squads duty to guard the airstrip against infiltraters. There were foxholes dug all along the river bank. Because of the lack of manpower our individual foxholes were farther apart than is usual. Thus we were assured of no one being close to us. Furthermore the river was ten feet below the bank on which we were camped. Thus some local girls could approach under the cover of darkness without being seen. We talked one of the local female vendors into sending two women back to our position at 8 p.m. They were to come via the river bank and hopefully no one would see them. Our foxhole was the first one they would come to, thus they wouldn't have to pass under anyone else and risk getting shot at. Our platoon was constantly getting replacements so there were always green troops to contend with.

The designated time passed and I assumed the arrangements were not made. I took my mind off of the potential sexual encounter and tried to rationalize the disappointment. A few minutes later I heard noises coming from the river bank. The noise resembled whistling, accompanied by laughter. From the loudness I could determine that the noise was being made by a large group of people. They obviously weren't VC, so who in the hell were they, I asked myself. I decided to investigate. I crawled to the edge of the bank and peered downward. Initially I could see nothing but the moving blackness of the river. Suddenly lights appeared and the laughter and whistling grew louder. I lowered myself to the level of the river and waited for the individuals to come closer. In the back of my mind I knew they were the prostitutes, but why were there so many?

In the next instant I saw movement and lights coming around a bend in the river. In another second they would be before me. As they came around the bend I jumped up and ran to meet them. To my astonishment there were at least 15 women bunched up before me. Most of them were carrying some sort of flashlight or lantern. They appeared to be in their late teens and early 20's.

Judging from the laughter at least three fourths of them were in various degrees of intoxication. The head Mama San began haggeling about money. I was trying to explain that we only wanted two women. I also was trying to get them to be quiet and turn off those damn lights. It was only a matter of time before someone else heard them and came to investigate. Mama San wasn't at all happy but she agreed to send the excess women back to town if we paid double. Finally the final arrangements were made and I returned to the foxhole to explain to Adams what in the hell was going on. He was elated at the news and wanted to go first. I told him to go ahead and he disappeared below the edge of the bank. He reappeared about twenty minutes later, his face all smiles. "Your turn," he said, half out of breath.

I complied and a moment later I was kneeling over a young girl. She was lying on the narrow portion of land between the river and wall of land. She was wearing some sort of robe which was open, revealing her young body. She was either poorly developed or too young to be fully mature. Her breasts were small, even by Vietnamese standards. Her genital area was almost void of any hair. She was obviously very young, probably eighteen years old. I was hesitating entering her. There was something unnatural about having sex with someone so young. Before I could refrain any longer her hands found my erection. Seconds later she had my penis out of my pants and began stroking it. My morality, sense of decency, or something equally dumb, was stopping me from actually entering her. She was getting impatient and began muttering something in Vietnamese. She was obviously telling me to hurry up or something to that effect. While still on my knees I was suddenly conscious of rocks digging into them. I was terribly uncomfortable, both physically and mentally.

I was just about to get up when the young girl took my penis in both of her hands and guided it toward her vagina. I knew I shouldn't be allowing it but I was also conscious of another biological urge which seemed to be telling me to go ahead. With her wanting it so badly I gave in to the stronger of the urges. I was, however, unable to get inside of her. She arched her back and pelvic region and I would strain my loins forward to meet her. No matter how hard we tried I was unable to consumate the ordeal. Another place and another time it would have been possible, however, I was not in the frame of mind to continue. Half disappointed and half glad, I got off of her and simply said "No boom boom". I gave her the money anyway, and she walked off to where Mama San was standing. I watched them walk off around the bend. Relieved that the episode was over I returned to the foxhole determined never to do anything that foolish again.

Base camp was beginning to take on the characteristics of State-side duty. While in base camp we were beginning to be subject to the Mickey Mouse inspections that are so much a part of Army life. In addition, our shoes were going to be expected to be shined at all times, police calls were called numerous times a day, and everything was going to be in its proper place. A little order is needed but the manner in which it is attained is all important. I didn't object to the order, it was the harrassment by which it was carried out. Before leaving on missions we had to stand inspections to make sure the hand grenades were in the right spot and, seemingly, a hundred other irritating little things were checked. The time could have been better spent practicing maneuvers, learning the Vietnamese language, target practice, or anything relevant to staying alive in the jungle. Returning to base camp didn't hold the promise of relaxation and tension reduction it once did. The jungle, with no rules except staying alive, was no longer the enemy it had once been.

CHAPTER 10

Our new mission was going to take us back to Bong Son. That was the same area we had secured in January and February. The Viet Cong had evidently reinfiltrated into the area and regained control. Like so many times we were asked to retake a place we had already taken and turned over to the South Vietnamese. There were going to be many people maimed and killed. In a few weeks we would leave and probably repeat the process over in another couple of months. Somehow it just didn't seem to make a lot of sense.

I had learned a day or so ago that I was scheduled for out of country R and R on May 16th. When I learned that I was going to Bangkok I was ecstatic. Some guys in the platoon had already been there and had brought back pictures of various prostitutes. The women were exceptionally attractive and according to the stories were full of new and exciting tricks. Thus after this mission the immediate future promised to be very bright. Having something exciting to look forward to made me feel a little less apprehensive.

Also, during the last month or so, I really felt that I was able to smell the Viet Cong. Associating the smell with the VC started when we helped the Engineers on top of Hong Kong Mountain. The particular smell was especially prevelant when Horner found the two VC hiding in the rocks. The smell was a mixture of stale urine and caramel. I knew I had smelled the odor before that occasion and remembered it when we had taken other prisoners. After the incident on the mountain I was able to detect the smell more times than not whenever we took other prisoners. I can't account for the reason why that same smell was so prevelant among them but I was convinced that it was there. Perhaps it was an odor caused by living in the jungle.

The mission was going to be a concentrated effort involving the South Vietnamese, the U.S. Marines, Paratroopers and us. Obviously we were going after something big and could look forward to plenty of action. We weren't told the name of the mission which was a shame as the names were quite colorful and seemed to put some esprit de corps in our attitude. We usually found out the name of the mission, where we had been, and the total enemy killed after we had completed the mission. Even then we had to get the information out of the weekly edition of the Stars and Stripes. The Stars and Stripes was our only contact with the outside world for up to date information. Once in a while a replacement would have some information on what was going on in the States but that was relatively rare. Most of the guys we got didn't give a shit or else were sent to our Battalion as punishment for screwing up in another. Other Companies, aware of our reputation for sustaining casualties, would threaten their undesirables with assignment to our Battalion. Quite often they would follow through.

The Stars and Stripes was where I first read about and saw pictures of the long-haired protesters back in the States. I couldn't understand how they could be so comfortable on some college campus and not appreciate what they had. Tearing buildings down and acting like irresponsible children while we were doing all the lousy dirty work to insure their comfort was beyond my comprehension. I wished they could be sent over here to live in the filth, see friends mangled and killed, pick leeches off of their dirty asses, and see that some of the people appreciated what we were trying to do. Perhaps then some of them would change their fucking minds. The more I saw of them in the papers the more irritated I became. It was literally years before I could look at one of them and not wish I was choking the mother fucker and smashing his filthy spoiled head against some rock.

Before arriving at Bong Son our Company was singled out to be diverted to some village and search it for VC. Prior to landing we were told that if we landed and saw any movement at all we were to fire and ask questions later. The landing zone was supposed to be hot, indicating we would meet enemy resistance. Hearing the news made me very tense. Immediately prior to landing I was covered with a cold sweat and was actually hoping there would be someone to shoot at. Our helicopter was descending and the adrenalin was flowing rapidly. My nerves and muscles were aching with anticipation. My mind was completely focused on the enemy outside and I was ready to kill.

The helicopter landed and I was the third one out. I was expecting enemy fire but received none. In that instant I felt a physical letdown. Suddenly movement to my right caught my eye. Swinging my body and rifle toward the movement I felt my finger tighten on the trigger. Through the sweat in my eyes I saw a figure naked from the waist up holding something in his hands. He was bent over near a large bush and seemed small in stature. It had only been seconds since I had departed the helicopter but it seemed much longer. Why I hadn't fired I do not know but something in the back of my mind was telling me no. Advancing toward him I saw the tatoo on his arm representing the Screaming Eagles (101 Airborne Division). He was digging a foxhole with an entrenching tool. I had almost mistaken him for a gook with a rifle. Seething with rage because of my stupidity and the erroneous order to fire on departure I went screaming to Sergeant Timura wanting to know who the stupid fucker was who told him this was supposed to be a hot LZ. True to form, he told me he was just following orders and not to worry about it. There was nothing I could do but stand there like some dumb son of a bitch and ventilate my wrath.

The village we were to "check" was standing about seventy-five yards in front of us across an open field of about fifty yards in width. To get into the village we would have to cross the open field. I was lying on the ground with the rest of the squad right next to the Captain. As he was relatively new I hadn't had much of a chance to see him in action. However, looking and listening to him talk into the radio, I had a feeling of pity for him. He was nonchalantly telling another squad to move across the field and move into the village. He said it as if he were sending them on routine patrol back in the States.

The village across from us had many buildings which were still burning and smoking from recent artillery bombardment. God only knew how many Viet Cong or NVA regulars were lurking in some goddamn hole waiting to kill us. Looking at the men crossing the barren field I wished for God to see them safely across. At that moment I felt a glowing pride for being in the infantry and fighting along side such brave men.

Thankfully the men reached the village with no enemy resistance. The Captain glanced in the direction of my squad and told me to prepare to move out. I was assuming the job of Sergeant with my recent promotion to Specialist 4. I thought of the machine gun in our squad and could almost feel the enemy waiting for us to move out then open fire on our exposed asses. I looked at the sanctimonious Captain and thought, "No, you son of a bitch, you move out and we'll wait behind, safe and sound. Then when the coast is clear, we'll stroll across." However, being a good soldier and knowing my place, I kept my mouth shut and we moved safely across the field. The Captain remained behind until the village was indeed secured.

Safely in the village we began the tedious job of checking the individual homes for weapons and any guerrila-type individuals. The smell of gunpowder, burning flesh and straw filled the air. Seeing the sight of destroyed homes and an occasional mangled dead body I felt as if I was in some sort of hell. There were civilians wandering through the buildings, many with the dazed look of being in shock, which I'm sure many of them were. The wounded civilians who needed medical treatment were loaded onto nearby helicopters as were any civilians suspected of being Viet Cong. I was helping a group of elderly civilians onto a helicopter by lifting them bodily into it. Immediately to my rear was a foreign journalist filming my actions. I felt rather good knowing that someone was filming a worthwhile activity. I could just as easily have been shoving and kicking them aboard. Minutes later the helicopter departed in its usual cloud of dust. Where the villagers were going I didn't know but I did know that at least they would be safe for a while.

I rejoined the rest of my squad who were resting near some giant coconut trees which had been blown down by the artillery fire. I couldn't help but notice how unnatural the trees looked laying on their sides all mangled and ripped apart. It's funny how the trees invoked such feeling when human bodies did not. While walking toward the squad I had to actually step over six or seven civilians lying dead on the scorched earth. The blood had not yet dried on their clothing so they couldn't have died long ago. From the many small wounds on them I knew they had been killed by small arms fire. They were just as mangled as the trees with their missing arms and legs and ripped trunks, however, for some unfortunate reason, they did not appear to look as unnatural as the fallen trees.

It was decided our Battalion would remain in the village over night. We took up positions on the outskirts of the village and dug in for the night. Just prior to dark I had to relieve myself. I finished my duty and was preparing to cover up the cat hole (hole dug for expelling ones feces into) when I noticed that the toilet paper was blood red. I immediately dropped my pants and wiped myself again. The toilet paper was covered with nothing but blood. In a panic I headed for the Battalion medic. He had me strip, bend over and spread my buttocks. He examined my rectum with a flashlight and said I had a bad case of hemorrhoids but unfortunately the medication for such an affliction was moved on ahead to Bong Son. He then suggested that I take a couple of sit-down baths a day. I was carrying two canteens of water and barely enough to wipe the sweat off my face twice a day, let alone take two baths a day. Besides, how in the hell was I going to make time? What really irritated me was that the stupid fucker was serious. I thanked him sarcastically, pulled up my pants and returned to my position. In addition to all of the existing problems I now had something else to worry about. Where in the hell was it all going to end, I thought to myself.

Early the next morning, the Battalion flew out in our armada of helicopters. We landed in the middle of an oasis-like spot and were told to clean up our equipment. We had just unrolled our mountains of equipment and it was in complete disarray when the order to "saddle up" cracked through the air. The general bitching and cussing that followed didn't do justice to the way I felt. It seemed the longer I stayed in Viet Nam, the more fucked up things became.

In moments we had reassembled our gear and had boarded the choppers. Nobody seemed to know where we were going and I didn't particularly care. I just wanted to get the mission over and get my ass to Bangkok. Today was May the sixth; ten more days and I would be on my way to one of the most exotic spots on earth. I felt so exuberant about the upcoming R and R I would have volunteered to burn shit for the next ten days.

After a brief flight we landed on the outskirts of another village. We flew over this particular village prior to landing and the destruction was nearly total. The village was quite large and its largeness made the destruction seem quite immense. I couldn't help but wonder what we would have to face. Was the enemy lurking among the ruins or had they retreated, leaving behind the usual snipers to cover their withdrawal? I was suddenly overcome with the feeling that they were there, waiting for us. The sensation was one that I had often felt before. I knew something tragic was going to happen and mumbled a prayer that my luck would continue.

My squad had been ordered to "dig in" right next to a rice paddy. After a few moments of digging, the soft ground turned into mud. Grayish water was seeping into the foxholes and again I could see individuals drinking the sewer-looking water. The attempt by some to become sick was never-ending. Our squad was extremely undermanned, as was the whole Company. The thought ran through my mind that we might luck out and remain here for a day or so. Just as we finished digging the foxholes, the order to "saddle up" rang into my unbelieving ears. Now what in the hell were we going to be expected to do? I didn't have long to wait to find out.

Our assignment was to provide rear security for the Battalion which was in the process of moving through and searching the large village. It seemed like a safe enough assignment. If there were any enemy in the village they would probably open up on the larger unit as they passed through. We would provide some sort of defensive protection in case the Battalion had to fall back. Our assignment could be dangerous but it was better than being caught in a potential ambush.

As we approached the village I found myself yelling at the few individuals in my squad, telling them to spread out. I remembered my sarcastic reaction to Sergeants telling me that very same thing months ago. I recalled my dislike for them ordering me around. I wondered what the new men thought about me telling them the exact same thing. I knew it was in their interest to keep apart so I kept up my badgering.

A few moments later we pushed our way through a waist-high hedgerow and was inside the village. Instinctively I stopped the squad and surveyed the surroundings. Many of the buildings had been demolished but a large number had somehow escaped the artillery shells and were intact. A smokey haze drifted through the air obscuring our vision. I was reminded of the passover story when death was riding on a similar haze. The silence in the village was also quite ghostly. Normally when entering a village, even one that has been bombed, civilians can be seen in various phases of cleaning up the debris. Now, however, there was no one to be seen. Either the whole village had left or they were holed up in their houses awaiting some assurance that the fighting was over. The absence of animal life added to the unusual silence. Not a chicken or pig could be seen, a most unusual event. We checked the buildings very cautiously but could find no people or weapons.

Finishing our search of the buildings we moved onward. We passed through this section of the village with no contact being made. Directly ahead of us was a large dried up rice paddy. Directly behind that and to our right was a long row of houses. The area we had just passed through seemed to be a small extension of the larger village which lay in front of us and beyond the rice paddy. I assumed the people had moved from the area we had searched and had moved into the larger village. That would have accounted for their being no people there. I had no more time to think about the event as Lieutenant Green came trotting breathlessly toward us. He informed us that the Battalion was moving safely ahead of us and was meeting no resistance, however, they had neglected to search the long row of buildings to our right. He was going to lead two squads, mine and another, in a search of the buildings. It seemed fruitless as the Battalion had just passed within fifty yards of it and met no resistance. However, we had our orders, so I moved the squad out somewhat over-confident that there was going to be no resistance.

As we moved across the open field we passed by a helicopter that had recently been shot down. I had noticed it earlier but paid it no special attention. A downed helicopter was not an unusual sight. Seeing it laying on the ground all crippled and twisted like a squashed insect made me realize that indeed there was enemy in the area. A cautious feeling crept over my body. My mouth became very dry and the rest of my body broke out in uncontrollable sweating. We advanced past the helicopter and it was then that I noticed the charred bodies of the pilot and co-pilot inside. Their entire bodies were burnt to a crisp and only slightly resembled human forms. Seeing them, I had only the slightest remorse. I was sorry they were dead but any real emotion in regard to their death was absent from my thoughts. Only months before I would have reacted differently to such a sight. I was surprised at my coldness. Perhaps I was just being conditioned to death. Visible death had no real meaning for me. I remembered Sergeant Wilson's death and how it had upset me. Now it meant nothing. The war was turning me into an unfeeling, emotionless being. At least I had become a man, but at what price?

We continued past the helicopter and approached the row of buildings. We met the eerie silence but it was only momentary. An old woman came stumbling out of the nearest house. She was holding a small child by the hand. Both seemed to be in some state of shock. They began crying uncontrollably. This sudden outburst of hysteria broke the silence as well as the tension which permeated the air.

The old woman began advancing toward me, her crying increasing in its God-forsaken intensity. I was just about to tell her to get the fuck away when figures began coming out of the buildings and began running past us, toward the area of buildings behind us. Their sudden appearance made me freeze momentarily. Seconds later I realized that most of the individuals were young males. I could see that they were not carrying any weapons, thus I assumed they constituted no real danger. Six or seven of them raced past me and others were running in other directions. I didn't know what to do so I let them continue running. Suddenly Lieutenant Green, who was a few yards in front of me, began shouting "some of them have rifles, kill the fuckers".

The sudden order caught me off guard. I turned toward the fleeing figures and prepared to shoot. However, in the seconds it took me to orientate myself to what was happening, they had disappeared. Green had spotted one hiding behind a small bomb shelter. As he advanced toward him the gook paniced and began running toward a house. He took two steps and Green zapped him with a burst of automatic fire. As the VC stumbled to his death I saw his rifle clatter across the hard ground. Seeing the rifle I knew we were in serious trouble. I quickly turned around looking for the gooks that had disappeared. I knew they were in the buildings locating their hidden weapons. In a matter of moments I knew bullets would begin filling the air. I felt my body tighten and simultaneously my mind was filled with thoughts of the potential snipers. I tried to think about what I was going to do next but in that instant it was impossible to think coherently.

I was standing at the front of my squad trying to decide what to do next. I could see that they were as scared as I and desperately needed someone to tell them what to do. Out of the corner of my eye I saw a male figure duck behind a house. Instantly I told Horner, the second most-experienced in the squad, to go around one side of the house. I ordered Manuel, a citizen of Guam, to go around the other side. Hopefully one of them would see the son of a bitch and kill him.

As they advanced toward the house I looked frantically for Lieutenant Green. I saw him leading the second squad in the same general area as Horner and Manuel were heading. I told the remainder of the squad to follow me and we lagged behind Horner and Manuel as they advanced toward the house. When they reached the house they hesitated for an instant and looked at each other as if they didn't want to go around the house. Horner eventually proceeded and Manuel followed. I and the rest of the squad stayed a few yards behind them and waited. We had just gotten down on our stomachs when I heard the dull twanging sound of a hand grenade launcher being fired.

Instantly I heard Manuel scream a high-pitched "NO!" His panic-sounding scream was followed by Horner yelling "Goddamn it, Goddamn it." By the time I reached Horner he must have repeated the phrase a hundred times. When I finally reached Horner he was standing and pointing toward a small dried-up rice paddy a few yards behind the house. Lying in the paddy was Manuel. He was flat on his back and lying very still. I couldn't determine if he was dead but Horner broke my concentration by saying "Thank God it didn't go off." It was easy to see what had happened. Manuel had come around the corner of the building but Horner had been expecting the gook. When he saw the figure he fired his grenade launcher instinctively. The force of the round knocked Manuel through some bushes and into the paddy. The round, being distance-activated, didn't travel enough distance to explode. I glanced out at Manuel and saw him moving slightly, as if he were regaining consciousness. Relief swept over my body upon seeing he wasn't dead.

"Well, fuck it, Horner," I said, hoping to calm him down. "It's too late to worry about it now. Let's go get him." I was hoping that the round wasn't imbedded in his stomach. The thought of moving him with a live grenade stuck in his stomach was more than I believed I could handle. We were about to push aside the hedge which separated the house from the paddy when another shot rang out. Horner and I hit the dirt but not before I again heard Manuel scream. Jesus Christ, I thought to myself, today isn't your day, Manuel. I lay on the ground pondering our next move. After that last fuck up, I didn't know what to do.

Minutes later, while I and my squad lay on the ground, bullets began whizzing through the air. I could hear the soft "popping" sounds of the enemy's rifles, so close it seemed as if they were coming from my squad. The second squad, led by Green, was running toward a house to our left. They were yelling for us to join them. As the bullets weren't being fired directly at us, we crawled toward them. The second squad, already in position at the house, began returning the fire. The air was filled with the acrid smell of gunpowder and the frightening sounds of what seemed like hundreds of small arms. Nothing is so terrifying as the sound of close, small arms fire. The fact that they are being aimed at oneself only adds to ones terror.

After an exhausting crawl we reached the second squad and Lieutenant Green. The houses were extremely close together with only a few feet separating them. We took up a position in between two mud-walled homes. The firing which had been heavy only moments before tapered off until only a few of the enemy's could be heard. Lieutenant Green took advantage of the lull and was on the radio asking for help. None was forthcoming as the whole Battalion was in a firefight farther ahead. Thus we were stuck in our present position for God only knew how long.

For some reason Lieutenant Green decided to move to another position. We moved from our spot between the houses and advanced into the very rice paddy in which Manuel lay. The paddy was in the shape of a square. Three sides of the square were enclosed by houses. A thick hedge approximately four feet in height separated the houses from the paddy. In addition the paddy in which we lay was a foot below the level of the bushes. Thus we had very good natural cover. The fourth side of the square was vacant and led into a much larger field hundreds of yards across. Green positioned us around two sides of the paddy. The open field was to my immediate right, the hedge was directly in front of me, my squad was spread out on my left and the second squad was spread out on the second side of the square. The third side of the square directly behind me had few houses to offer sanctuaries for the gooks so no one was deployed on its banks. Thus we were spread out in a somewhat defensible position. I lay on the ground still not fully rational. The events of the last hour had happened so fast I wasn't sure of what was really happening. No one else seemed to be sure of what was transpiring and we all seemed to be in a state of shock in a world that was suddenly and completely strange beyond our wildest dreams. I looked behind me and saw Manuel lying in the paddy. The sight of him, motionless, added to the bizarre atmosphere. I was just about to ask Sergeant Timura, lying next to me, what we were going to do when a hand grenade came floating over the hedge and landed a few yards behind me. The explosion acted as an impulse for myself and the rest of the men to come out of our daze. Those that had a clear field of fire began firing their rifles. I and others began throwing grenades across the hedge. Everyone began shouting and screaming orders.

The situation was chaotic. On signal from Lieutenant Green we stopped firing. The grenades kept coming over the hedges as if in a phoney scene from a movie. I could actually watch the grenades sail across the hedge, land in the paddy, and explode. Luckily the grenades the gooks were using were not of sufficient power to cause us any harm. Had they been American-made some of us would have been killed. On occasion a grenade would land close enough for an individual to throw it back. Many of them were landing near Private Reeb, a newly arrived trooper who wasn't even an American citizen. He would pick them up as cooly as John Wayne and heave them back toward the gooks. Each time he did so we would cheer him resoundly. The incident enabled us to laugh and ease the somewhat unbelievable tension.

Reeb had just flung back one of the grenades when he screamed and raised his hands to his face. He was directly across from my position enabling me to watch him spit his teeth out. He had been shot through the face, the bullet tearing through both sides of his previously unmarked skin, taking teeth and part of his jawbone as it exited. He began moaning incoherently. I tried to shut the screaming out of my mind but it was impossible.

The small arms fire began again. I could tell from the sound that they were extremely close. I decided to peer over the hedge and try and determine just exactly where the bastards were. I stood up, peered over the top and couldn't believe my eyes. Directly on the other side of the hedge was a high mound of dirt. Pushing himself backward, trying to get behind the mound, was a fucking Viet Cong. He had a rifle in his hands and was obviously taking up a position from which to snipe. I ducked back down behind the hedge and wondered what to do. He was so close I contemplated clubbing him with my rifle and taking him prisoner, or I could simply shoot the fucker.

Suddenly faces of individuals who had been killed by just such gooks flashed in my mind. I glanced over at Reeb who was lying in the fetal position, holding his face and crying like a baby. Seeing Reeb like that I knew I had my answer. I stood up again and peered over the hedge. The gook was directly in front of me, no more than three feet away. He was wearing a white sport shirt and I thought it quite strange as I was used to seeing them wearing black pajamas. He was trying to get into sniping position and his back was still toward me. I hated to shoot him in the back and I was actually standing there hesitating. The hesitation lasted for a split second. I felt the M-16 spring to life in my hands. In the next instant I saw him lurch forward from the force of the three bullet holes which penetrated his back. The red holes appeared a brilliant red upon his white shirt. The momentum carried him forward and in his last seconds of life he started to crawl forward, away from me. Seeing him doing that really pissed me off. I squeezed the trigger and watched the bullets strike his back like so many red raindrops.

Finally I stopped and knelt back down. The feeling of exhilaration was overwhelming. I couldn't contain my glee and began screaming to the Sergeant next to me, "I got the fucker, I got the fucker." He merely smiled and looked away. Killing the gook made me feel all-powerful. A surge of confidence like I had never felt raced through my body. I had finally gotten one at close range. I decided to change magazines in my rifle. Releasing the magazine from my rifle I noticed there were three bullets left. Since it held twenty rounds, that meant that I shot the gook seventeen times. It didn't seem enough and I wished I could have shot the fucker a hundred more times.

A scream from my left shattered my thoughts and temporary feeling of exhilaration. I looked over and saw that Sergeant Timura had been shot. He was holding his neck with one hand and trying to apply a field bandage with the other. I especially hated to see him shot. He and I, as well as two others, were the only original members of the 7th Regiment who came over on the boat back in August. The majority of the original 189 men in our Company had been killed, plus a large number of their replacements had met a similar fate. Each passing day reduced the number of original members. I suddenly wished to God that He permit me to live my few remaining months of duty.

Seeing that we were slowly being picked off in our present position, Lieutenant Green decided to move everyone, including the wounded and dead, into a nearby house. It was hoped we could hole up there until re-enforcements could come to our aid. We got the wounded and dead transported without further incident. We were all in the house and the scene was one from a horror movie.

Men were sprawled everywhere. Those that were alive were moaning and crying. The most pathetic sight was seeing some of the men, obviously in shock, crying for their mothers. It was absurd to think that their mothers could come to their aid but it was indicative of how, in the final analysis, we are all children.

There were even a couple of men, who, in this desperate hour, were still trying to get out of fighting. I saw a couple of them holding the hands of the wounded and attempting to calm them down. Attempting to make one comfortable in such a miserable moment of time is a very noble thing but, at this particular moment, we could use their talents elsewhere.

Lieutenant Green decided we would set up a line of defense outside of the house. An enemy machine-gunner was preventing re-enforcements from coming to our aid by covering the only approach to our position with murderous accuracy. As there was only a handful of us left, we needed everyone who could pull a trigger to lay down a curtain of bullets in the direction of the gook machine-gunner. I ordered the individuals who were tending to the wounded to fall outside and get their asses on line. Reluctantly, they obeyed.

We left the house and began to set up a position approximately twenty-five yards away. Our target was a small mud-walled shack. Inside was the machine-gunner and his accomplices. Only hours ago there had been twenty or so men in our platoon. Now there were six of us left. The others had been wounded or killed. Again I felt only the slightest remorse for them. I was more concerned with my own life. I wondered if my good luck would continue. I wasn't too sure of the existance of God after seeing so many good men die for what seemed nothing, however, just to be on the safe side, I mumbled a prayer to whoever was listening to spare my life one more time.

Moments later we were positioned in a straight line directly in front of the shack which held the enemy. The shack was about 50 meters in front of us. I was second from the end of the line. To my right and on the end was a black trooper from Chicago. Sam played bass in a small combo which often played in an exclusive go-go joint on Rush Street. He had often invited me to come and watch him when we got out of Viet Nam. Lying next to him on the sandy ground I wondered if we would live to keep our date.

The ground in front of us dropped off to a depth of three feet. In front of us and all the way to the house was nothing but open land. There were a few clumps of bamboo growing nearby. It offered protection to those lucky enough to be near them. For myself I gathered a few boards laying about and stacked them in front of me. By lying tightly to the ground and peering over the boards ever so slightly I could see the house. The boards made me feel secure. I could fire directly into the house and it seemed almost impossible that anyone could shoot me. When my head was above the boards only the smallest of targets was visible. And that was protected by my steel pot. I suddenly thought of our collection of steel pots hanging in the squad tent. The helmets had holes of various diameters caused by bullets and mortar fragments. The steel pot didn't offer total protection but the psychological effect of thinking it did was all-important.

Somebody to my left began firing into the house. I glanced over the boards and could see no movement inside or out. There was an open window in the shack from which the machine-gunner was firing intermittently. I placed my cheek on the top of the stock of my rifle, sighted in on the window, and began firing bullets through the window as fast as the automatic rifle would spit them out. As I continued firing, so did the other men. The shack was being riddled with hundreds of bullets. I could see the hard mud finish breaking and ricocheting off into space. No one in their right mind would have exposed themselves in the open window. Where in the hell was our re-enforcements? The machine gun was posing no threat and still no one was coming to our aid.

We continued the unrelenting fire pausing only to change magazines in our rifles. With every passing second I felt sure I would hear the shouts of my fellow troopers triumphantly coming to our rescue. But it was not to be. We had no choice but to continue our firing and hope the VC didn't take up a new position. A shot had not been fired recently from the house but we knew they were in there.

Just as I was ready to fire off a fresh magazine, my goddamn rifle stopped firing. I didn't have time to stop and determine what the malfunction was. It had happened so many times in the past that I wasn't the least bit surprised. I was mad but not surprised. I yelled for someone to bring me another rifle and a moment later Sergeant Timura threw one toward me. I picked it up and asked God to please let it work. I resumed my firing into the house and was relieved to see that the rifle was functioning properly.

On cue from Lieutenant Green, we stopped firing. The next move was up to the VC. A second later I saw a figure dash from one side of the window to the other. I raised my head up over the boards a few inches hoping to get a shot at him. In the next instant I heard and felt an explosion on my lower back. The sound was like an American grenade exploding. The exploding was accompanied by a tremendously loud cracking sound, similar to the breaking of a large green branch. The cracking sound was caused by one of my ribs being blown off the rib cage and ripping through my back. Simultaneously my body was overcome with an excruciating pain. It felt as if Hercules hit me in the small of the back with a sledge hammer.

The pain was so intense it caused me to become physically sick. I tasted vomit rising in my throat. Instinctively I shouted to Sam that I was hit. He immediately came to my side. Seeing that I was apparently shot in the back, Sam turned and began spraying the treetops. I thought, as did Sam, that I had been shot in the back by someone behind us. In reality I had been shot in the chest from someone in front of us. I did not feel the red hot bullet when it entered my body, only the terrible pain when it exited.

I was lying on the sandy ground, face down, unable to comprehend what was happening to my body. The pain was blocking any attempt to think clearly. I remember Sam telling me I was going to be all right, but his words sounded too cold and they came too automatically to be genuine. I was conscious of him tearing my shirt in the back in order to apply a bandage. I could feel his hands applying pressure and could feel something warm wetting my buttocks. Sam's sudden shouts for the medic shocked me into an attempt to sit up. "Lay still," he commanded, "the Doc will be here in a minute."

I lay my sweating head back down in the sand, suddenly conscious of the fact that I might die. I began to tremble and suddenly I was very frightened. I had seen the face of death on so many others and thought that at last it was my turn. I was suddenly very cold with sweat and the horror of the moment. I didn't want to die like this. I asked God to please not let it happen. My answer was a bolt of pain streaking across my back.

The medic had arrived and was applying another bandage to my lower back. He and Sam then turned me over to unhook my backpack. The medic noticed the blood on the front of my shirt and in a surprised voice said, "Shit man, you were hit in the chest." A second later he was putting a bandage on my chest. His words had fallen on uncomprehending ears as my mind was preoccupied with the fact that I couldn't feel my legs. I had no sense of feeling below my waist. The pain in my back seemed to be blocking all feeling below it. PARALYZED! The words and image of a cripple flashed into my mind. "No God, don't let it be," I mumbled the words over and over.

The roughness by which Sam and the medic were removing my pack caused me to become aware of the present. When they successfully had my pack off they began piling large empty baskets around me. (The baskets were of the type used to transport rice and other grains.) When they finished their ordeal I was completely surrounded by the baskets. I didn't know what in the hell they were doing but as they picked up my gear and returned to the house behind me, I instantly knew. They were going to leave me where I lay. The baskets surrounding me was an attempt to hide me from any VC wandering about. I begged them not to leave me but my pleading was to no avail. Suddenly they were gone.

My first thought was to close my eyes and go to sleep. Hopefully sleep would bring a temporary relief. I closed my eyes and then realized that if I did so I might never open them again. I opened them quickly and vowed not to close them again. The temptation to go to sleep was a constant temptation I had to battle through my ordeal. Knowing I would have to remain awake made me realize that I was in a much bigger battle than I had ever seen before. Tears began to fill my eyes, not so much from the pain as from the thought of being so all alone.

I was conscious of being very uncomfortable and tried to move my legs. Even though I willed them to move they would not respond. Ramifications of being paralyzed began to filter into my mind. Thoughts of my mother seemed to replace them as quickly as they had been formed. I saw her crying and I was overcome with an intense emotional feeling. "Don't worry, mom," I said to myself. "I won't hurt you." The feeling of wanting to lapse into sleep was again becoming very strong. I rationalized that if I talked to myself I would be able to stay awake. I kept telling myself to stay cool and not panic. I had seen so many others go into shock and die. I was determined it was not going to happen to me.

I was again aware of the warm, wetting sensation on my lower back. I wiped my back with my fingertips in an attempt to remove the substance. Out of curiosity I looked at my fingers to see what was causing the wetness. I was horrified to see a slimey mass of yellow and white body tissue tinged with blood. The substance was very sticky and evil looking. Realizing it was coming from my insides almost sent me into further panic. I could feel more warm blood oozing out of my back, flowing down my buttocks and soaking into the ground beneath me. As the blood and inner tissue continued to flow, I became certain I was going to die.

Pictures of events in my past life began to form in my mind. The events danced in my mind as if they were in slow motion. As a defense against dying I was concentrating all of my energies on what had been precious to me in the past. Out of the kaleidoscope of events flashing in my mind I consistently saw myself as a young boy, enjoying the carefree days of youth. My mother's face and various events in which she played a dominant role kept reoccuring. I kept seeing her crying and the sight was unbearable to me. I would live, I told myself, so that my mother wouldn't cry.

For what period of time I kept seeing my past life relive itself I do not know. I do know that I saw my mother's face more than any other image. I am so convinced that not wanting to hurt her gave me the inner strength to continue my struggle for life. Occasionally my mind would be blank. In those brief periods of time my mind would be focused on watching the ants that crawled near my face. I thought that they were very lucky being oblivious to what was happening around them.

It was starting to turn to dusk. I had been shot at about three o'clock in the afternoon. I assumed it was about four hours later and was amazed at how fast the time had passed. Suddenly I heard footsteps and thought I smelled the terrifying odor of urine and caramel. I was convinced the VC were but a few feet away. I tried to remain calm but thoughts of what happened to my friends at Ia Drang Valley raced through my mind. I wasn't about to be butchered by any fucking gooks. Gathering my strength I began shouting to Sam and Lieutenant Green in the house behind me. "Come and get me, you sons of bitches, please come and get me." To my dismay no one came.

It didn't seem fair that I should be lying here slowly bleeding to death (the blood was continuing to flow slowly down my buttocks). Hadn't I risked my life on numerous occasions to rescue a wounded trooper? Now it's my turn and nobody cares. Out of desperation I again pleaded for them to come and get me.

Someone shouted "Can you crawl back?" Crawl back!, I thought to myself, I can't even move my legs and the fucker wants to know if I can crawl. "Fuck, no!" I screamed, tears of desperation choking my words.

"Hang on," came the reply. "We'll be out to get you."

The words had no meaning for me. I lay my head down in the sand, crying softly. I felt so far away from everyone that mattered to me. I remembered the other men I had seen dying and remembered how they had cried for their mothers. Suddenly I understood why. I stopped crying and again concentrated on my mother. Focusing on her made me regain some semblance of reason. I told myself to remain calm and forced myself to do so.

Suddenly I heard someone say "ok buddy, it's all right now, we're here to get you." Through unbelieving eyes I saw Sam and another strange G.I. He was a medic and was obviously from another unit that had broken through to us. A smile of gratitude came over my face upon seeing help. I was suddenly aware of an intense thirst and begged the men for a drink. The medic wet his fingers from his canteen and brushed them slowly across my lips. "That's all you get," he replied and proceeded to rebandage my wounds. I remember him cussing the other medic for not treating a fucking chest wound properly. His competent hands caused me to relax. He and Sam carried me back to the house where the rest of the men were located.

When we reached the huts I could see many other wounded and dead G.I.'s lying about. The sight of seeing so many of them with their heads covered by plastic ponchos caused me to mumble a prayer of thanks for being alive. A Sergeant called for a group of volunteers to carry me to an evacuation area. They placed me, wounded side down, on a large board and proceeded to cart me off.

As we passed one of the huts I noticed a small group of Viet Cong prisoners huddled in a group. Looking at them, alive and unwounded, I wished for a rifle to kill them. The hate that was in me was like a venom which was to remain for years. They probably didn't have much choice in what they were doing and were undoubtedly following orders, the same as I. Looking back, it's hard to believe that the insanity could have been stopped at any moment. All it would have taken was a few words from certain leaders. Perhaps if they had been in our position for a few weeks the outcome would have been different.

Being perched precariously on the board the men had to use the utmost caution in transporting me. As well as being dark, the ground was sandy and irregular. After much cussing and complaining, they finally reached the evacuation point. I was set down among the dead and wounded. It had started to rain adding to the general confusion.

My thirst, the worst I can remember, caused me to call out for water. The longer I lay without any water the more intense the desire for water became. My mouth was so dry my cheeks felt as though they were two giant balls of cotton, pressing in on each other. A medic walked by and told anyone within hearing distance not to give me any. I cussed the medic but to no avail. In my frantic effort to get water I tried to arrange the folds in the poncho covering me so that the rainwater would flow into my mouth. I was too weak to make a sustained effort and after a few futile attempts, I gave up.

My continuing pleading finally succeeded in catching the attention of a soldier lying nearby. He handed me a canteen. I suspect his generosity was more to shut me up than an effort to comfort me. I guzzled the contents like the desert soaking up the rain. A minute or so after drinking, I vomited all over myself. My insides, tearing and burning, felt much the same way they did during the typhoon on the trip over many, many months ago.

Lying in my mess I felt like a drunk on skid row. I was feeling very sorry for myself and cussed everybody in the Army for allowing it to happen to me. The continuing gunfire caused me further anxiety. I knew the medivacs would be reluctant to make a landing with all of the sniper fire. My mind raced back in time to February. I saw Niranda lying in his blood and remembered how he had bled to death because he couldn't be evacuated. Interestingly enough, he and so many others, had died not too far from where I was now lying. Wouldn't it be ironic, I thought, if I were to die in the same location and in a similar fashion? The thought of dying again caused me to think of my family and especially my mother. Thinking of them I again began talking to myself, telling myself I could make it.

The crackling voices coming over a nearby radio confirmed my past reservations about being evacuated. The fucking medivacs were not going to make a landing due to the heavy enemy fire. Hearing the unfortunate words caused my spirits to drop drastically. I began to think the 7th Cavalry was truly the jinxed outfit everyone said it was. I cursed Custer for bestowing the legacy of a loser upon me. In an attempt to release additional frustrations, I cursed the rotten pilots and the helicopters they rode.

Just as I was running out of people to cuss, I heard the radio again come to life. My disbelieving but grateful ears heard the news that the pilot of a gunship was going to attempt to land. He would take out two of the more seriously wounded if he landed successfully. I hoped I would be one of the two.

A Lieutenant, who seemed to be in charge of the wounded, tapped me on the head. I felt as if I had been touched by the hand of God. The Lieutenant ordered some men to prepare to move me and another G.I. to the incoming chopper on the double. Upon hearing the increasing drone of the incoming helicopter, my eyes searched the darkness for some sign of the chopper's landing lights. I saw nothing but the increasing noise of it's engine indicated he was close to our position. Suddenly I felt myself picked up by strong arms and I was being carried on the run to the chopper which had landed in a nearby clearing. The men carrying me hoisted me up and into the chopper. I felt myself being stuffed against the feet of the machine-gunner. The feeling of safety was a beautiful overwhelming sensation. Seconds later we were airborne.

As we ascended I watched the men disappear into the darkness below me. Sounds of gunfire echoed in my ears. I felt a smile come across my face as I realized the war was over for me. I said a prayer for the men below me and hoped they would be as fortunate as I.

Printed in the United States
By Bookmasters